Superbrands

YOUR GUIDE TO SOME OF BRITAIN'S STRONGEST BRANDS 2006/07

ARGENTINA AUSTRALIA AUSTRIA BULGARIA BRAZIL CANADA CHINA CROATIA CZECH REPUBLIC DENMARK ECUADOR EGYPT ESTONIA FINLAND FRANCE GERMANY GREECE HONG KONG HUNGARY ICELAND INDIA INDONESIA IRELAND ITALY JAPAN KUWAIT LATVIA LEBANON LITHUANIA MALAYSIA MEXICO MOROCCO THE NETHERLANDS NORWAY PAKISTAN PHILIPPINES POLAND PORTUGAL ROMANIA RUSSIA SAUDI ARABIA SERBIA SINGAPORE SLOVAKIA SLOVENIA SOUTH AFRICA SOUTH KOREA SPAIN SRI LANKA SWEDEN SWITZERLAND TAIWAN THAILAND TURKEY UNITED ARAB EMIRATES UNITED KINGDOM UNITED STATES OF AMERICA

www.superbrands.org/uk

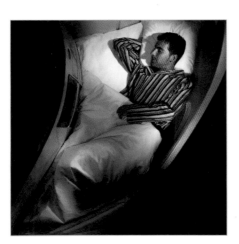  

Managing Editor
Angela Cooper

Editor and Author
Jennifer Small

Author
Karen Dugdale

Design Co-Ordinators
Laura Hill
Christy Lyons

Designers
Chris Harris
Adrian Morris

Brand Liaison Directors
Claire Pollock
Liz Silvester

Marketing and PR Executives
Katy Bienek
Hannah Paul
Rachel Springate

Other publications from Superbrands in the UK:
Business Superbrands Volume IV ISBN: 0-9547510-6-X
CoolBrands Volume IV ISBN: 0-9550824-1-2
Sport BrandLeaders Volume I ISBN: 0-9547510-4-3
eSuperbrands Volume II ISBN: 1-905652-00-3
Kids Superbrands Volume I ISBN: 1-905652-01-1

For more information, or to order these books,
email brands@superbrands.org or call 01825 873133.

For Superbrands international publications
email brands@superbrands.org or call 020 7379 8884.

© 2006 Superbrands Ltd

Published by Superbrands Ltd
19 Garrick Street
London
WC2E 9AX

www.superbrands.org/uk

Printed in Italy

ISBN: 1-905652-02-X

Endorsements

John Noble
Director
British Brands
Group

Paul Gostick
Chairman
The Chartered Institute
of Marketing (CIM)

Hamish Pringle
Director General
Institute of Practitioners
in Advertising (IPA)

The brands featured in these pages richly deserve their Superbrands status. They are known and understood not just by their devotees but much further afield, thanks to the reputation they have earned for delivering superior value.

They cover many categories, demonstrating not only the power but also the versatility of branding. Significantly too, the majority have been with us for a long, long time, demonstrating clearly that branding after all is about investing for the longer term and delivering consistently for consumers.

The British Brands Group is delighted to support this collection of Superbrands as a record of single-minded focus on consumers, continuous innovation and inspiring communication. The result for consumers is true performance and a sure understanding that these brands will deliver for them. We as an organisation will continue to push for a climate in the UK in which such brands may continue to flourish and new brands fostered, bringing us choice, diversity and ever-better performance.

As always competition in the marketplace is fierce and an organisation's brand plays a central role in creating a positive image and in influencing customer choice. Powerful brands are very clear about what they are and should convey a unique promise of value and quality. They must connect and engage with the customer, evoking strong emotional responses. A well thought-out brand provides a clear competitive edge and helps to create a powerful long-term relationship with the consumer, assuring delivery of what the brand owner promises time after time.

The Chartered Institute of Marketing promotes best marketing practice and continually promotes the positive commercial value that professional marketing can bring to an organisation's bottom line. A strong brand contributes to this and The Institute is pleased to recognise Superbrands as one of the champions in highlighting and promoting the importance of a powerful brand.

The brands highlighted in this issue of Superbrands 2006/07 clearly command recognition and respect, and it is good to see them recognised for their achievements in a highly competitive market.

Superbrands remains the A to Z of great brands built by marketing agencies and their commercial communications. The publication now comes with added radar, the new 'Brands to Watch' section, which gives us an early warning of the rising stars in the firmament and another group of successes to learn from. Let us never forget that the creative industry is the hive that builds such valuable intangible assets, and marketing, procurement and advertising professionals are the worker bees with big brand ideas, their Queen.

About Superbrands

This publication forms part of a pioneering and exciting programme that was founded with the aim of paying tribute to the UK's strongest brands.

A dedicated Superbrands Council (listed below) has been formulated, consisting of eminent individuals, well qualified to judge which are the nation's strongest brands. Each brand featured in this book has qualified based on the opinion of this council and the Consumer Election.

Through identifying these brands, and providing their case histories, the organisation hopes that people will gain a greater appreciation of the discipline of branding and a greater admiration for the brands themselves.

The Superbrands Council

Drayton Bird
Chairman
Drayton Bird Associates

Mark Cridge
Chief Executive
glue London

Tim Duffy
Chief Executive
M&C Saatchi

Vanessa Eke
Managing Director UK and Ireland
Nielsen Media Research

Stephen Factor
Managing Director
TNS's Global Consumer Practice

Winston Fletcher
Chairman
Advertising Standards
Board of Finance

Cheryl Giovannoni
Managing Director
Landor Associates, London

David Haigh
Chief Executive
Brand Finance

Jacqui Hill
Market Development Director-
Personal Care
Unilever

Graham Hiscott
Consumer Editor
Daily Express

Michael Peters OBE
Founder & Chairman
The Identica Partnership

Chris Powell
Co-Founder
BMP

Richard Reed
Co-Founder
innocent drinks

Anna Ronay
Editor
the marketer

Tim Sutton
Chairman
Weber Shandwick, Europe

Nicola Watts
Global Portfolio Strategy
& Research Director
Cadbury Schweppes plc

Mark Waugh
Deputy Managing Director
ZenithOptimedia

Donna Price
Chair Person
Superbrands Council

Find a market with built in growth (foreign travel for instance).
Then find a must-be-dealt-with-now problem (the runs for example).
If you can find the solution and make it your own, you will be rich.

Chris Powell on Imodium™

Often, people don't say,
"Have you got health cover?"
They say, "Have you got BUPA?".
That speaks for itself.

Drayton Bird on BUPA

Unremitting focus on
kindness to the skin –
another example that
keeping at it pays.
Who else would you
trust as much?

**Drayton Bird
on Fairy**

A healthy environmental and social stance
stops the chain from being tarred with the
same brush as other US retail/service
empire-builders.

David Haigh on Starbucks

The only plaster brand in the
market with any longevity.

David Haigh on Elastoplast®

A vital, but often forgotten,
part of the value of branding
is to give you time to get it
right when your product has
been trumped by rivals.
Lesser brands than M&S
would have become
irrecoverable, the strength
of the brand kept it going
long enough to get the
product right.

Chris Powell on Marks & Spencer

An uncompromising brand
that has used its heritage to
successfully leverage itself
into new product segments.

David Haigh on Fairy

Still the master brand. Despite all the ups and
downs of technological change in this market
Sony is still the brand most people aspire to.

Chris Powell on Sony

The brand has managed to make the tricky leap to
selling grooming products to men and become a
unisex brand standing for quality product and
innovation.

David Haigh on NIVEA

The retro revival and the support of celebrities like David Beckham, has encouraged brands like Brylcreem to shine once again and be recognised as a modern day Superbrand.

David Haigh on Brylcreem

The brand's consistent emphasis on fine design never falters. People are happy to pay more as a result.

Drayton Bird on BANG & OLUFSEN

Superbrands Council members comment on some of the Superbrands

You don't pay much of a premium for this premium brand. You know it will work – and you know it will look good too.

Drayton Bird on Sony

Contenders come and go, but if you say cereals, most people think Kellogg's.

Drayton Bird on Kellogg's Corn Flakes

The power of listening, then acting. Tesco has consistently learnt from its customers and put what it learnt into gaining competitive advantage.

Chris Powell on Tesco

Another remarkable turnaround – led by huge residual brand strength and made possible by focus on real value.

Drayton Bird on Marks & Spencer

I fly a lot with them – and they really have a character unlike any other airline. But they're also true innovators.

Drayton Bird on Virgin Atlantic

Contents

Foreword
Angela Cooper
Managing Editor

Superbrands

In this, the eighth edition of Superbrands, you will find the case studies of brands that are really embracing the challenge of 'delighting' 21st century customers and gain an insight into just how tough a mantel this is.

It is no secret that we live in a world of contradictions. We expect to be understood to an ever-increasing degree, but don't like to feel that we are being watched. We want to be environmentally friendly and health conscious, but we also want to travel in style and enjoy our food. In addition, we always want to get the best deal we possibly can.

Today's strong brands are those that find the balance between producing excellent products and services which last longer, work faster and are the 'best ever' whilst acting responsibly in the way in which they act towards people and places, both internally and externally. All carried out on an ever more public stage.

I would like to take this opportunity to thank the members of the Superbrands Council, who have voted on which brands they believe to be worthy of Superbrand status. The Council is comprised of eminent individuals and opinion leaders who are all well qualified to judge which are the nation's strongest brands. You can find details of who these individuals are on page 14.

The Council was tasked with identifying the strongest based on their personal perceptions of the brands' strength and quality in the market. When scoring, they keep the following definition in mind; "A Superbrand has established the finest reputation in its field and offers consumers emotional and tangible advantages over other brands, which (consciously or sub-consciously) consumers want and recognise." We have found that the aggregate perceptions of experienced market professionals is as valuable a guide to brand excellence and

enables the brands to be judged against their peers across a diverse range of sectors.

However, for the first time in the selection process, the Superbrands organisation has also taken into account the consumers' viewpoint via an online election managed by YouGov plc. Further details of this can be found on page 18.

We hope that the following best practice examples from some of Britain's strongest brands will help to further understanding of branding and the work and investment needed to be one of the UK's finest.

The Superbrands
Selection Process

An initial population list of consumer brands is compiled by independent researchers, using a range of sources.

A shortlist of approximately 1,200 brands is created by Superbrands' internal experts from the population list.

The shortlist is sent to the council for their rating. Council members are not permitted to score any brand that they are associated with or that they are in direct competition to.

The 650 top ranked brands according to the council's scores are put forward to a consumer election, managed by YouGov plc.

The top 500 scoring brands from the election are awarded Superbrand status and invited to participate in our programme.

Superbrands Council 2006

Drayton Bird
Chairman
Drayton Bird Associates

Three years ago Drayton was named by
The Chartered Institute of Marketing as one
of the 50 living individuals who have shaped
modern marketing. Other names mentioned
were Kotler, Levitt and Peters.

He has written three widely admired
marketing books, over 1,000 articles for
various magazines, spoken or trained in 40
countries on the subject and was on the
worldwide board of the Ogilvy Group.

He has worked with some of the world's
most recognised firms, including Procter &
Gamble, Unilever, Visa, American Express, BT,
Toyota, Mercedes, Volkswagen, McKinsey,
Microsoft®, IBM and many others.

Drayton is the chairman of five firms
involved in various aspects of marketing, from
direct marketing to event management. He
writes copy, trains, runs seminars and is
consulted by a wide range of firms in a
number of countries.

Mark Cridge
Chief Executive
glue London

Mark has worked in interactive since 1994
when he left the world of architecture realising
that it just wasn't his cup of tea. Previously a
senior creative at Modem Media, he left in 1999
to establish glue London to inject some much
needed creativity into the UK's digital
advertising scene.

In the past few years Mark has been cited
by Campaign magazine as a 'Face to Watch',
and has since gone on to feature in the FT
Creative Business 50, picked up the inaugural
Digital Achiever of the Year gong at last year's
Campaign Digital Awards and was voted by
his peers as the number one online pioneer.

glue has grown quickly to almost 100
staff who are hard at work with an enviable
client list including; Virgin, Coca-Cola, Procter &
Gamble, T-Mobile, BSkyB, Nokia, the COI and
Masterfoods. They are the IPA's Best of the
Best Digital Agency, voted Campaign's
'Best Online Creative Agency', New Media
Age's Most Respected Agency for the last two
years and most recently claimed a place in
The Sunday Times' poll of 100 Top Small
Companies to work for.

Tim Duffy
Chief Executive
M&C Saatchi

Tim graduated from King's College,
Cambridge and in 1986 joined Saatchi and
Saatchi, as a Strategic Planner. There he
worked on major projects for clients including
IBM, British Airways, Procter & Gamble and
the launch of the National Lottery.

In 1995 he was one of the Founders of
M&C Saatchi, helping it become a top 10
agency in five years. It now has 20 offices in
15 countries worldwide. In the UK, the agency
works for a wide variety of clients including
Fosters, Transport for London, ITV, Lucozade,
Ribena, Halfords, the COI, Royal Bank of
Scotland, Australia Tourism, Curry's and
PC World.

He was appointed Managing Director in
1997 and Chief Executive of the London
Agency in 2004.

Vanessa Eke
Managing Director
Nielsen Media Research

Vanessa was invited to join Nielsen Media Research, the world's leading provider of advertising measurement and information services, as Commercial Director for the UK and AdEx International in 2002. Based on her achievements Vanessa was promoted to Managing Director in 2003.

Underpinned by her early career at KPMG and further senior management positions she brings a good deal of insight and expertise relating to the media sector and 'Superbrands' at home and abroad.

A former director of the Financial Times magazine group, Vanessa has a lively interest in the financial as well as the consumer impact of brand strength.

Known for her energetic approach, client focus and lively debate, she is a regular speaker at conferences and seminars spanning several markets.

Stephen Factor
Managing Director
TNS's Global Consumer Practice

Stephen is Managing Director of TNS's Global Consumer Practice, part of the world's largest marketing research business. A graduate of the City University Business School, he spent the early part of his career working with new product evaluation tools for leading manufacturers in the FMCG sector. From 1986 to 1990, he was based in Paris and then Milan, as Development Director of the European Burke group. Returning to London, Stephen was appointed Chief Executive of Infratest Burke's UK business. Following acquisition, he took the same role for NFO and subsequently TNS. With the consolidation of the market research industry, he has found himself becoming an expert in the acquisition and integration of marketing services organisations. At the beginning of 2006, Stephen took over global responsibility for TNS's FMCG business, supporting the world's leading brand owners in 70 countries around the world.

Winston Fletcher
Chairman
Advertising Standards Boards of Finance

Winston is chairman of the Advertising Standards Boards of Finance, the Royal Institution, the Knightsbridge Association, and Barnardo's in London and the South East. He is also Vice President of the History of Advertising Trust and on the Advisory Council of the Barbican.

His career appointments include being founder chairman of Fletcher Shelton Delaney, Chairman and CEO Ted Bates UK Group; Chairman and CEO, Delaney Fletcher Bozell.

Winston is the only person to have been Chairman of the Advertising Association and President of the IPA, as well as a council member of the ASA; and Founder Chairman of the World Advertising Research Center.

He has also published 12 books and over 3,000 articles. Winston is a visiting professor at Westminster University Business School and lectures at the London Business School and City University.

Cheryl Giovannoni
Managing Director
Landor Associates, London

Cheryl joined Landor Associates in October 2005 as Managing Director of the London office, one of the flagship offices within the global network. Landor's clients include BP, Proctor & Gamble, Pepsico, Diageo, Nokia, Telefónica and Jet Airways. Brand led business transformation programmes include brand strategy, corporate identity, brand experience, naming, innovation, packaging and brand engagement.

South African born, Cheryl moved to London in 1993 to further her advertising career with Ogilvy, where she worked on Unilever, Mattel Toys, SmithKline Beecham and BUPA, before moving to Lowe Howard-Spink, now Lowe Lintas, to run the Global Braun account.

In 2001 Cheryl joined Brand Design agency Coley Porter Bell as Chief Executive Officer, where she worked with GlaxoSmithKline, Nestlé, GE, Kimberly-Clark and Unilever. During this time, she was also a member of the Ogilvy Group Board.

Landor was a Business Superbrand in 2001 and is currently Marketing's Design Agency of the Year for 2005.

David Haigh BA, ACA, FCIM, MAE
Chief Executive
Brand Finance

David qualified as a Chartered Accountant with PricewaterhouseCoopers LLP in London. He worked in international financial management before moving into the marketing services sector, firstly as Financial Director of The Creative Business and then as Financial Director of WCRS & Partners.

He left to set up a financial marketing consultancy, which was later acquired by Publicis, the pan European marketing services group, where he worked as a Director for five years. David moved to Interbrand as Director of Brand Valuation in its London based global brand valuation practice, leaving in 1996 to launch Brand Finance.

David is a fellow of the UK Chartered Institute of Marketing. He is the author of 'Brand Valuation' (FT - Retail and Consumer Publishing, 1998), 'Brand Valuation - a review of current practice' (IPA, 1996), 'Strategic Control of Marketing Finance' (FT/Pitman Publishing 1994) and 'Marca Valor do Intangível' (Editora Atlas, August 2003).

Jacqui Hill
Market Development Director – Personal Care
Unilever

After graduating from the University of London, Jacqui joined Unilever as a commercial trainee, quickly moving through the ranks to marketing manager for Bachelors Soup. Jacqui turned the declining market into growth, returning six percentage points onto the company share. Key factors were the 'Hug Mug' TV campaign and introduction of granules.

In 1995 Jacqui was promoted to marketing controller and business group leader for the entire Batchelors portfolio, where she re-wrote the business and brand strategy. This resulted in a string of advertising awards for the SuperNoodles TV campaign, the launch of Cup-a-Soup Extra being voted the best new launch by The Grocer, and an increase in brand profit by 70%.

Jacqui took up her current position in 2000, liaising with brands such as Dove, Sunsilk, Sure, Lynx, Impulse and Vaseline. In the last three years the Business has grown by nearly 20% and there has been significant activity behind extending the Lynx and Dove brands and launching Sunsilk.

Richard Reed
Co-Founder
innocent drinks

After graduating from Cambridge University and working in advertising for four years, Richard and two college friends, decided to set up a fresh fruit smoothie company. Following six months of developing recipes and the success of their first stall at a music festival they resigned from their jobs to focus on their new venture.

Seven years on the company employs 105 people, has a turnover of £75 million, and sells over one million smoothies a week. The innocent range has expanded to include special smoothies for children, one litre cartons for families, juicy waters for a more refreshing natural drink and thickies for a yoghurt and fruit blend. The drinks regularly win industry awards, including Best Soft Drink in the UK at the Q Awards for four years running. innocent regards itself as a profitable company which acts responsibly, striving for sustainability across all areas of the business. They also donate 10% of profits to the innocent foundation, which funds projects in countries where they purchase their fruit.

Anna Ronay
Editor
the marketer

Anna is editor of 'the marketer', the monthly member magazine of The Chartered Institute of Marketing (CIM). She launched the title in April 2004 and has collected a series of industry awards, most recently for Most Effective Membership Magazine at the Association of Publishing Agencies Awards in November 2005. Before working on the marketer, Anna edited Marketing Business magazine and Critical Marketing, a quarterly journal for senior marketers. She has also edited titles for financial services provider Alliance & Leicester and law firm Davies Lavery. Prior to this she worked for Lafferty Group, writing and reporting on the global financial services industry.

Tim Sutton
Chairman
Weber Shandwick, Europe

Tim is one of the European PR industry's most respected practitioners. He is also European Chairman of the Constituency Management Group of the Interpublic Group of Companies, including its businesses in the areas of public relations, events management and corporate & brand identity.

Educated at Magdalen College Oxford, he is a renowned corporate PR professional having directed corporate programmes and campaigns for some of Europe's top companies and industries. He has a particularly strong track record in reputation strategy, public issues campaigning and brand development, which has won him significant industry recognition. His long term programme for bmi british midland remains the only European PR campaign to have won both of the industry's top awards: the PR Week Grand Prix and the IPR Sword of Excellence.

Tim has been heavily involved in advising numerous other companies on communications strategy; and is also a recognised authority on crisis management, brand strategy and employee communications.

Graham Hiscott
Consumer Editor
Daily Express

Graham has been a qualified journalist for 11 years, five of those specialising in consumer affairs. His career started with a degree in journalism at the University of Central Lancashire in Preston. After graduating he landed a job as a reporter on the Cambridge Evening News. Eighteen months later Graham left to become a reporter at a press agency in Birmingham called News Team International. His career continued to progress 18 months later with a move to the Press Association as a regional reporter covering the East Midlands. It was here Graham developed his interest as a consumer affairs correspondent, which led to another move to the Press Association's HQ in London.

Graham was runner-up at the London Press Club Awards 2005 and 2006, for the Consumer Affairs Journalist of the Year. Among the reasons for his nomination was breaking the Dasani bottled water story and a series of stories on soaring energy bills.

Michael Peters OBE
Founder & Chairman
The Identica Partnership

Michael Peters' name is synonymous with British design, having been at the forefront of the industry for more than 30 years.

In 1970 he established Michael Peters and Partners, which revolutionised the role of packaging design in the marketing of consumer products. In 1983, the company was led onto the London Stock Exchange, and by 1989 it had an annual turnover in excess of £45 million. Clients included the BBC, British Airways, the Conservative Party, Redland, ITV, United Distillers and Unilever.

In 1990 Michael was awarded the OBE for his services to design and marketing. Two years later, he founded The Identica Partnership. The London based company is now one of the leading international brand and corporate identity consultancies, specialising in the creation, development, management and design of brands around the globe. Clients include Diageo, Universal Studios, National Power, NatWest, Vodafone, Co-op, Nike, Wembley Stadium, Bank Leumi, Aeroflot and Roust Inc.

Chris Powell
Co-Founder
BMP

Chris was a Co-Founder of the advertising agency BMP that went on to build the strongest creative and planning reputation in the world and became the second largest UK agency, working on such well loved brands such as Cadbury's, Smash, John Smith's Bitter and Walkers crisps.

He now chairs the National Endowment for Science Technology and the Arts (Nesta) that fosters innovation and business start ups, the Institute of Public Policy Research (IPPR), the UK's largest Think Tank and is Vice Chair of the Public Diplomacy Board. He is a member of the Board of United Business Media and the corporate advisory Board of PricewaterhouseCoopers LLP.

Nicola Watts
Global Portfolio Strategy & Research Director
Cadbury Schweppes plc

Nicola Watts is Global Portfolio Strategy & Research Director at Cadbury Schweppes plc.

Responsible for leading the market research function globally and creating the frameworks that turn data and insights into action, Nicola also sits on the Cadbury Schweppes Commercial Leadership Team. Cadbury Schweppes operates in over 200 countries and is the world's leading confectionery company and holds the number three position globally in beverages.

Previously head of strategy development, Nicola has also held senior marketing and strategy positions in the Canadian, Russian and UK businesses. She was educated at London School of Economics where she gained her MSc (Econ) Statistics and previously at Queen Elizabeth College, London University.

Mark Waugh
Deputy Managing Director
ZenithOptimedia

When Mark joined the UK media planning fraternity from Oxford University, media was seen as an exceptional, trading-based discipline that followed the strategic lead offered by the advertising agency. In the intervening 16 years Mark has been a key player in driving the strategic importance of media planning in the industry and at the age of 28 became the youngest ever Managing Partner of Optimedia. He grew his expertise beyond the traditional 'Big Five' advertising media into events, ad-funded programming, sponsorship, product placement, field marketing, and now digital. Mark joined market leader ZenithOptimedia as Deputy Managing Director in 2003.

In his career he has amassed experience across almost every market category, from motors to luxury goods and financial services to FMCG. This, coupled with ZenithOptimedia's 100 clients, including blue chip companies such as British Airways, L'Oréal, Toyota and Masterfoods, who spend over £700 million in the UK, allows Mark a unique scaled perspective on the behaviour of Britain's brands. Furthermore, Advertising Age named ZenithOptimedia Global Agency of the Year in 2005.

Donna Price
Chair Person
Superbrands Council

In her role as Commercial Director and Head of Superbrands UK Donna was responsible for the marketing, PR, editorial and the sales process for all of the UK programmes. She also chaired three other Superbrands Councils including, CoolBrands, eSuperbrands and Kids Superbrands.

Previously, Donna spent three years at The Mirror Group where she was responsible for the launch of both M magazine and M Celebs. Both of these launches represented a significant strategic move to take The Mirror slightly more upmarket.

Prior to this Donna worked at Emap for nine years, where she worked on some of the UK's premiere magazine brands including Elle, FHM, Sky, Mixmag and Kerrang!

Her experience spans a mixture of advertising, marketing and publishing. Donna has now left the Superbrands organisation and has set up her own consultancy.

The YouGov Consumer Election

By Panos Manolopoulos
Managing Director

YouGov

About YouGov

YouGov is a full service online research agency, collecting high-quality in-depth data for marketing research and opinion polling. It operates a diverse panel of over 130,000 UK residents with similar operations in America and the Middle East.

Based on its record over the last eight public opinion election events, YouGov is the UK's most accurate public opinion pollster and dominates Britain's media polling today through the publication of its work in the media. Based on its work in the consumer research and opinion polling sector, the agency has one of the fastest growth rates in the industry.

YouGov is a pioneer of online research and e-consultation and uses its strong market research skill set and industry expertise to support its clients. The agency's full service work extends across industry sectors including consumer, financial, healthcare, media, new media and technology. A range of different research types and data collection methods are used in survey designs tailored to individual client requirements.

YouGov offer innovative and tailored market research solutions, quality of service and insight that allow its clients to make effective decisions about their business.

It offers a wide range of market research services designed around putting its clients' needs first. Based on traditional market research skills, YouGov demonstrates industry leading expertise in opinion polling and online research methods and techniques.

YouGov services include omnibus, syndicated, continuous and tracking research and bespoke research solutions. The agency also specialises in creating and managing specialist audience and client-branded proprietary panels. Examples include senior level professionals from the private and public sectors, health professionals, local authority residents, utility customers and global news consumers.

The scope of its research solutions include Consumer Research, Daily Omnibus, Opinion Polling, Usage & Attitude Studies, Advertising Research, Brand Research, B2B, Children/Youth and Family Research,

Concept Testing, Customer Satisfaction, Employee Research, Multi-country Studies, New Product Development Testing, Packaging/Design, Product Testing, Segmentation Research, Syndicated Research and Tracking Studies.

Detailed demographic, marketing and other lifestyle profiling information is collected for panel members. This enables YouGov to select a national sample representative of the elector or adult universe. YouGov also selects samples for marketing research from the panel based on individual survey selection quota and profiling requirements.

Respondents are then emailed an invitation to complete a survey online. Alternative data collection techniques are also used where appropriate. Raw data for national opinion surveys can be weighted post-field to ensure it is still representative of the target sample. During the panel registration process, YouGov collects a vast amount of information on each panellist and can therefore design almost any sample. This registration information is regularly checked and updated. For quantitative research, YouGov generally provides larger samples and delivers data at a greater speed than other research methods.

Response rates of at least 40% are normally achieved within 24 hours and 60% within 72 hours. Little difference has been detected between early and later responses, once the data has been weighted to demographic and attitudinal variables, including past vote and newspaper readership.

YouGov is a member of the Market Research Society and of the British Polling Council. YouGov is also registered with the Information Commissioner.

YouGov and Superbrands

For the Superbrands 2006/07 Consumer Election, over 2,000 consumers were contacted online, drawn from the YouGov panel of 130,000 registered respondents. These were split into two separate (but matched and nationally representative) samples of over 1,000 consumers. One sample evaluating all Superbrands together and the other grouping them by sector. Consumers were asked to evaluate brands based on various criteria that give an overall measure of brand strength.

Moving forward, the Consumer Election process is being rolled-out across the Superbrands European country network. Consumer samples are generated online following a series of promotions and campaigns that are designed to drive respondents to the in-language questionnaire and survey website. Brand lists covering all relevant brands across all sectors, are specific to each country market and are developed by a council of marketing professionals in each country before being presented to consumers for their vote.

As consumers have begun to take a more active interest in the brands they consume in recent years, they are inherently qualified to aid in the judging process. This allows brand owners a direct insight into consumer perspectives about their brands. Some further analysis of the data can also help brand owners to gain a better understanding of some of the key demographics that might drive perceptions of their brands in their market, and how these perceptions compare with other brands in their competitive landscape.

Since its launch in 1932, Anadin has become, and remains, an iconic British brand, well loved and trusted by the nation. Seen as 'experts in pain', Anadin delivers substantial consumer confidence. Its product range is regarded as an effective and trustworthy method of pain relief. 'For people who just get on with it', Anadin products are designed for better relief of consumer's pain, so that they can get on with their lives.

Offerings and Values

Anadin understands that most people have hectic and enjoyable lifestyles, and don't want to be interrupted by pain. That's why it has built on years of expertise to create a range of effective and trusted products, designed to let people get on with their lives.

Anadin is the only brand in the UK whose product range covers the three principal analgesics: paracetamol, ibuprofen and aspirin. The brand also offers an extensive choice of products and formats to meet consumer's pain relief needs.

The most popular Anadin product is Anadin Extra. Its triple action formula contains aspirin, paracetamol and caffeine and is designed to provide fast, effective relief from all types of pain, from headaches to muscle aches. For even faster pain relief, Anadin Extra Soluble tablets dissolve in water.

Anadin Ultra hits tough pain such as chronic back, joint or muscle ache, hard. Its capsules contain the most concentrated form of liquid ibuprofen available.

Anadin Ibuprofen is a sugarcoated tablet designed to target the site of pain.

Anadin Paracetamol is gentle on the stomach and suitable for all the family, including children over six years. This is particularly effective for fevers associated with colds and flu.

The range also includes Anadin Original, with dual action (aspirin and caffeine) tablets coated and shaped for easy swallowing.

Innovation and Promotions

Anadin has been at the forefront of the pain relief market since its launch in 1932. A history of innovative product launches has maintained its position as a leading pain killer brand and today Anadin has the number one selling over the counter (OTC) pack with Anadin Extra 16s (Source: IRI October 2005) and is the second biggest branded analgesic in the UK, with sales worth £44.5 million (Source: IRI December 2005).

2005 saw the launch of a new campaign for Anadin Extra, consisting of TV and radio advertising and an integrated press campaign.

An emotional stance was taken to target consumers and reinforce Anadin as the brand 'For people who just get on with it'.

The Anadin Extra advert features a woman who, while juggling her children, husband and mother, suddenly gets an attack of pain and stops to take an Anadin Extra so she can get on with her life.

The Triple Action Formula is also highlighted and emphasis is put on the different ingredients and what they do (aspirin targets the point of pain, paracetamol blocks the pain messages to the brain, while caffeine accelerates pain relief).

An £8 million media spend to drive awareness and volume of purchases is planned throughout 2006, with consumers being exposed to Anadin advertising all year. Meanwhile, all Anadin packaging has been re-designed and will be re-launched in August 2006. The new packaging is designed to deliver a clear message about what each Anadin sub-brand can offer the consumer, while still carrying the trademark yellow and the Anadin logo.

In line with the re-launch of the Anadin products in new packaging, the Anadin website (www.anadin.co.uk) has also been revamped to reflect the brand's new look and the design of the new packaging. The new website will play the role of a 'pain expert' for the consumer, answering pain-related questions, and strengthening the core brand message: 'For people who just get on with it'. It will also educate users about the Anadin range, suitability and healthy lifestyles.

Anadin is also helping the trade by supporting pharmacists and pharmacy counter assistants, by educating them on analgesics and pain, with the aid of an educational campaign called 'Ask Anadin'. 'Ask Anadin' is aimed at answering all their pain related questions, so in turn they can advise their customers.

Market Context

Today's busy lifestyles, coupled with an explosion in consumer information about health, are driving factors behind the rise in self-medication and the consequent growth of OTC medicines.

In December 2005, the total analgesics market was worth £345.4 million and UK shoppers consumed over 15 million pills a day to treat their pain (Source: IRI December 2005).

Analgesics remain the most effective remedy for pain. A wide range of analgesics is available OTC, differentiated not only by their active ingredients but also by their formats.

Achievements and Future Prospects

Anadin is Britain's most trusted pain killer brand, explaining why Anadin Extra 16s is the UK's bestselling OTC pack in terms of volume and value (Source: IRI October 2005).

Things you didn't know

In 1995, Tamzin Outhwaite appeared as a teacher in one of Anadin's TV adverts.

Anadin was formulated by an American dentist in 1918.

More than 25 million Anadin packs were sold last year. If stacked on top of each other, they would reach over five and a half times the height of Mount Everest.

In 2007, Anadin will celebrate its 75th birthday.

Over the years, the brand has led industry innovation and incorporated all the major 'general sales list' ingredients (paracetamol, ibuprofen and aspirin) into its portfolio, enabling it to offer a range of targeted and effective solutions to combat pain. The brand has a solid base of core, loyal users with increasing frequency and weight of purchase. In 2005 the Anadin brand achieved £44.5 million in value sales and sold 25,300,868 packs (Source: IRI December 2005).

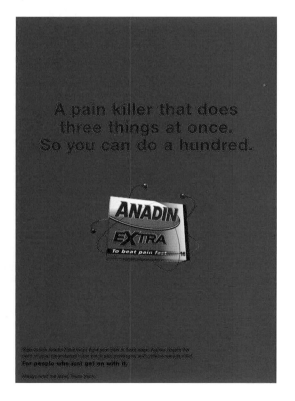

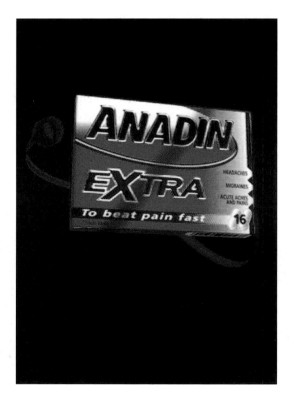

1918
Anacin launches in the US.

1932
Anacin launches as Anadin in the UK.

1962
Anadin becomes the UK proprietary analgesic brand leader.

1981
Anadin Soluble analgesic tablets are launched.

1983
Anadin Extra launches.

1984
Anadin blister packs launch.

1987
The Anadin brand is re-designed.

1992
Anadin Extra Soluble tablets launch.

1997
Anadin Ibuprofen tablets are launched.

1999
Anadin Ultra launches.

2001
The Anadin website goes live.

2006
Anadin packaging is re-designed.

www.ask.com

A leading online search engine, Ask.com is the culmination of years of innovation, combining world-class core search technology with one-of-a-kind tools to make searching better. Ask.com believes its users deserve a search engine with tools that get them to what they want quickly and easily, not just links on a page. Ask.com is the fourth largest search engine in the UK market and commands a 6% share of all user queries (Source: Hitwise).

Offerings and Values

Ask.com began life as Ask Jeeves with the aim of humanising the online search engine experience. In the mid 1990s when search was very much in its infancy and the majority of users found the internet both new and daunting, Ask Jeeves differentiated itself from other search providers by positioning itself with a simple, clear and easy to use proposition – enabling people to search using natural language and providing direct answers to many questions.

The iconic butler character, named 'Jeeves', personified the concept of 'a helping hand online'. However, in today's era of the blogosphere, web mashups and social networking sites, even the most basic internet user is proficient at surfing the web and "Help me find it" has evolved into "Help me get it faster".

In a high profile and competitive marketplace the acquisition of Ask Jeeves by IAC/InterActiveCorp enabled it to put significant investment behind its offering, to help make the site and brand improvements needed to satisfy the needs of today's user.

After campaign evaluations, strategy tweaks and focus group research, changes were planned to build the company's position. On February 28th 2006 Ask.com re-launched its offering with a new name, logo and site design, together with improved functionality and search tools, retiring Jeeves from the site.

Innovations and Promotions

The new Ask.com offers differentiated search technology, instinctive search tools and a sleek design to help people get what they need faster.

The new Ask.com features include: a new Homepage with a sleek design, the page is cleaner and more straightforward; the Ask.com 'Toolbox' – customisable shortcuts to the searches users do the most; a web-based Desktop Search where users now have the ability to access their files and emails through their web browser in addition to a standalone application; Shaded Sponsored Listings, which mean that Ask.com now has fewest ads of any major search destination on the first screen of

Get to exactly what you want with Related Search.
Narrow your search. Or expand it. It's the quickest way to get what you're after.

results and with Smart Answers, Ask.com is also the only search engine to place editorial results above advertisements.

The new site and search tools at Ask.com build on the innovative technologies the company has launched in recent years, including: ExpertRank, which is Ask.com's proprietary algorithmic search technology that ranks results based on popularity within topic communities on the web, rather than simply by link popularity; the Binoculars preview tool, which allows searchers to preview websites by simply mousing over the binoculars icon within their search results, and MyStuff, a personalised search service for saving, sharing, and organising search results.

A clear communication of change was needed to signal these developments and create a brand that appeals to the modern internet audience. First, a viral marketing and PR campaign was developed to publicise Jeeves' retirement. Next, focusing

on the re-launch, the marketing campaign created an opportunity for the brand to shed the baggage of its past and to move into the future, highlighting the updated product and its end user benefits. To promote the new Ask.com brand, the team developed a strong and integrated through-the-line campaign with online, television, PR and brand promotions in order to create the sufficient amount of noise around the change. The 'Ask.com and Get' campaign was launched in early March 2006.

Market Context

As the seventh largest global web property (Source: ComScore Media Metrix, December 2005), Ask.com is a division of IAC Search & Media and delivers world-class information retrieval products through a diverse portfolio of websites, portals and downloadable applications including: Ask.com, AskForKids.com, Bloglines.com, Evite.com, Excite.com, FunWebProducts.com,

iWon.com and MyWay.com. IAC Search & Media generates revenue from advertisers seeking to reach the company's broad-based online audience. Its headquarters are in Oakland, California, with offices throughout the US, as well as in Europe and Asia.

Achievements and Future Prospects

Ask.com's television campaign, 'Ask.com and Get' was named Campaign magazine's 'Pick of the week' shortly after it aired in March 2006.

Looking forward at the longer-term, Ask.com's objectives are to continue to build awareness of the new site and brand and educate target audiences about its improved core technology. Ask.com recently announced its next major marketing and awareness initiative which is its position as official partner of the England cricket team. By informing users of the range of easy-to-use Ask.com tools and how they can simplify and speed up the search process, Ask.com aims to break users out of their 'sleep searching' habits, and try a new everyday search experience.

Ask.com believes it has now positioned itself as a brand intent upon punching above its weight, stealing a march on its competitors and growing its market share by offering a truly viable alternative to competing search engines.

1997
Ask Jeeves, Inc is founded in Berkeley, California.

1998
Ask Jeeves reaches 300,000 searches per day and signs its first syndication deal with Alta Vista.

1999
Ask Jeeves International launches with a joint venture to establish Ask.co.uk. The site officially launches in February of the following year.

2001
Teoma Technologies is acquired and the aglorimithmic search is integrated into Ask.com, resulting in an immediate 25% increase in user satisfaction. Ask.com is now recognised as one of only four world-class search technologies.

2004
Ask Jeeves becomes the first major search engine to offer a personal search system with the launch of MyJeeves.

2005
Bloglines.com, the most popular free online service for searching, subscribing, publishing and sharing RSS feeds, blogs and rich web content is acquired.

2006
Ask.com is launched globally and Ask Jeeves, Inc becomes Ask.com, a division of IAC Search & Media.

BANG & OLUFSEN

www.bang-olufsen.com

Bang & Olufsen products are designed to be not only aesthetically pleasing but also essentially functional and easy to use. The expectations raised by a strikingly individual appearance must be completely fulfilled in terms of high quality sound and picture whenever the system is switched on. Therefore, achieving excellence in providing the consumer with the highest pleasure in ownership and use rests on 'high quality' as the common denominator of all activities and competence areas.

Offerings and Values

Glass doors that gently glide open as the user's hand approaches, elegant, compact yet powerful loudspeakers and TVs that turn to face you when you switch them on: such inventive movements have become one of the hallmarks of Bang & Olufsen.

However, to Bang & Olufsen, technology is not an end in itself. It is the value added for the customer that is the object of applying technology. Application of technology within the Bang & Olufsen product range will always be based upon the experience that it can accomplish for the user. If a technology has this

perspective, it belongs to the core competences of Bang & Olufsen.

The Bang & Olufsen user experience relates to different core competences, with the most important being: Quality, Picture, Sound, Operation, Design, Integration, Elegant mechanical movements, and Materials; with the underlying basic technologies being electronics, acoustics, mechanics and software.

Bang & Olufsen's core competences are in a process of constant evolution because of a continuous flow of applied research projects. These core competences are designed to make Bang & Olufsen different,

and strong enough to survive and prosper as a small company among giants.

Innovations and Promotions

When it comes to innovation, Bang & Olufsen aims at the utmost efficiency. The Bang & Olufsen product development team consists of highly skilled and experienced engineers with qualifications in electronics, acoustics, software and mechanical engineering. This ensures quality, speed and advanced as well as unique solutions in their work.

Furthermore, development tools or facilities are of vital importance for a professional result. So Bang & Olufsen has invested in a

number of unique test facilities that assist in every stage of product development.

One such facility is the Listening Panel, which consists of Bang & Olufsen employees with an extraordinary sense of hearing. All prospective members must undergo extensive hearing tests prior to acceptance. Around 18 months of training is necessary before they can make consistently accurate acoustic evaluations as reliably as a voltmeter. Only a few loudspeaker manufacturers in the world use this type of subjective testing to such an extensive degree.

When it comes to remote control operation and integration, Bang & Olufsen has been a major pioneer. Today, it is the only manufacturer who can offer its customers one remote control that can operate not only TV, DVD and audio systems but which can even be used to adjust the light setting in the room. Furthermore, Bang & Olufsen's BeoLink® makes it possible for the consumer to enjoy their Bang & Olufsen system throughout the home.

Market Context

Bang & Olufsen operates in a niche, high premium end of the highly commoditised consumer electronics market. However, although Bang & Olufsen designs and manufactures products such as audio systems and televisions, its competitors are not traditional consumer electronics brands. Instead, Bang & Olufsen is competing for share of the consumers' wallet against other high-ticket purchases such as premium furniture, a car, holiday or kitchen.

Achievements and Future Prospects

Thanks to its ability to stand out from the crowd, Bang & Olufsen has succeeded in growing into the international company it is today. Research and development, most of

the production, the administrative, marketing and management headquarters still remain in Struer, Denmark, where the company was founded.

Its products are sold through 11 National Sales Companies, all of them 100% owned by Bang & Olufsen, and through a number of independent agents throughout the world. Consumer sales take place through an extensive Bang & Olufsen dealer network of approximately 2,089 dealers located in more than 48 different countries.

Bang & Olufsen employs around 2,700 people with the majority working in Struer, a relatively small town of approximately 11,000 inhabitants in which Bang & Olufsen plays a predominant role.

1925
Two young Danish engineers, Peter Bang and Svend Olufsen, set up their own company with the idea of building a radio which runs on the mains.

1931
The first advertising slogan, together with the first logo – the Bang & Olufsen trademark – is registered.

1945
Bang & Olufsen's refusal to co-operate with the German occupation force during World War II, leads to its building being blown up just before the end of the war.

1950s
Bang & Olufsen participate in the major Danish TV boom.

1960s
Bang & Olufsen are among the first to develop stereo and high fidelity. The advertising slogan: 'Bang & Olufsen for people who put taste and quality before price' is launched.

1970s
Bang & Olufsen builds up an international distribution network with agents or subsidiaries in most western European countries.

1989
Following tough competition and price wars, Peter Bang and Svend Olufsen are obliged to sell 25% of their shares in Bang & Olufsen to Philips.

1993
After heavy losses, it is necessary to reorganise the company completely. This plan, called 'Breakpoint '93', re-establishes Bang & Olufsen as a healthy new company.

 **BARCLAYS**

www.barclays.com

Established over 300 years ago, Barclays is now present in over 60 countries worldwide and employs more than 113,000 permanent employees. It moves, lends, invests and protects money for more than 25 million customers and clients worldwide and manages more than US$1 trillion of the world's money. Barclays' ambition is to be one of the top five global banks, through its diverse portfolio of products and services.

Offerings and Values

Barclays is a major global financial service provider engaged in retail and commercial banking, credit cards, investment banking, wealth management and investment management services. It is one of the largest financial service companies in the world by market capitalisation.

In the UK alone, Barclays has over 2,000 branches and provides current accounts to 11.1 million customers and 183,000 business banking customers.

Barclays delivers banking solutions to retail and business banking customers in the UK through a variety of channels comprising the branch network, cash machines, telephone banking, online banking and relationship managers.

Specialist expertise from other businesses in the Group is available through Barclays Capital, a leading global investment bank and Barclays Global Investors, the world's largest asset manager.

The Wealth Management arm of Barclays serves affluent, high net worth and corporate clients, providing private banking, offshore banking, stockbroking, asset management as well as financial planning services.

Barclays also owns Barclaycard, the leading credit card business, which has 11.2 million UK customers and 4.3 million international customers.

Barclays aims to grow its international stature through its International Retail and Commercial Banking division, which caters for both personal and corporate business across Europe, the Caribbean, Africa and the Middle East.

In 2005 Barclays was concerned that traditional perceptions of large financial services organisations did not justly reflect what the bank stood for as a brand both internally and externally.

Following research, the bank developed a new brand positioning that aimed to reflect

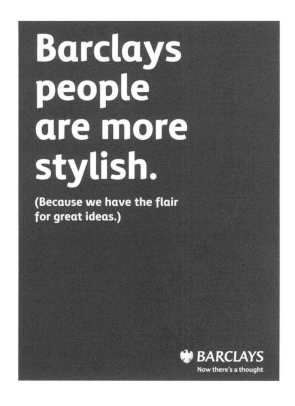

Barclays people are more stylish.

(Because we have the flair for great ideas.)

BARCLAYS
Now there's a thought

the inventiveness of its people and define its personality as being warm, approachable, witty and confident.

Innovations and Promotions

Barclays' reinvigorated brand is led by the 'Now there's a thought' advertising campaign, which aims to encapsulate the creativity of Barclays staff.

The new brand launch led to a complete revamp of Barclays communication, using a tone of voice based on the brand personality as well as a simple, yet engaging, visual identity.

It also led to a £7 million branch revamp and a comprehensive internal marketing programme to ensure the new positioning was understood and truly brought to life.

A total of 1,000 'Brand Agents' were introduced across Barclays UK banking staff in September 2005 to drive the internalisation of the 'Inventive Spirit' campaign. Armed with a 'brand agent kit', their brief was to become brand advocates at work by ensuring their colleagues understood and were starting to live Barclays' new brand positioning. With the

help of brand agents, the organisation is responding and staff are now sharing their ideas, whether big or small. For instance, the creation of new birthday cards that staff can send to their customers when they feel appropriate.

In order to further embed the brand, Barclays created three 'Service Pillars' which drive the whole business: 'We share our ideas', 'We make our customers feel special' and 'We keep our promises'.

Posters in and around the tube station of Canary Wharf, where Barclays' new headquarters is located, were also designed to engage staff through claims about what makes Barclays people special. The campaign idea extended into the Barclays building and branches, using a range of internal communication channels such as posters, coffee cups, postcards and signage.

Barclays also ran a number of large internal events around the country during which the campaign was highlighted, receiving an electronic vote of 97% in support of it from the 12,000 staff who attended.

Market Context

Barclays continues to be among the leaders across the UK banking market. The 'Big Five' UK retail banks have the largest share of all key products and competitive advantage due to extensive branch networks, but are having to respond to changes driven by smaller direct players, and retailers.

Achievements and Future Prospects

2005 was a record year for Barclays: profit before tax rose by 15% to £5.3 billion, while dividends increased by 11%.

Barclays also strengthened its international business when it acquired a majority stake in ABSA Group, one of South Africa's largest and strongest financial services organisations. This added more than seven million customers to the Barclays Group. At present, 40% of Barclays' profits come from outside of the UK. The bank's ambition is to raise this percentage to 50%.

Beyond these commercial achievements, Barclays is firmly committed to corporate responsibility. In 2005, Barclays' financial inclusion work was recognised by the Corporate Citizenship Company. Another highlight of 2005 was that Barclays ranked in the top 20 environmentally managed companies in the FTSE 300. Barclays, which commits 1% of UK pre-tax profits to community activities every year, spent £32 million on community projects last year.

Set the pens free

1690
John Freame and his partner Thomas Gould establish as goldsmith-bankers in the City of London.

1736
The name Barclay becomes associated with the company when James Barclay – who had married John Freame's daughter – becomes a partner.

1896
Twenty private banking businesses form a joint-stock bank called Barclay and Company.

1958
Barclays employs its first female branch manager.

1966
Barclays launches the UK's first credit card: Barclaycard.

1967
Barclays' first ATM is opened for business.

1994
The telephone banking service Barclaycall is introduced.

1997
Barclays becomes the first bank to introduce internet banking in the UK.

2001
Barclays forms a strategic alliance with Legal & General to sell life, pensions and investment products.

2005
Barclays develops customised services such as Barclays Private Bank and Premier Banking.

Ever since Beechams Powders launched 80 years ago, Beechams has been helping consumers deal with their colds and flu. As today's 'cold and flu expert', Beechams boasts a strong medical heritage and an extensive product portfolio covering the whole gambit of cold, flu, cough and sore throat symptoms, available in a variety of formats. Recognising that there is no cure for the common cold, Beechams offers a 'no-nonsense' alternative.

Offerings and Values

The Beechams range has continuously developed and evolved to meet changing consumer needs and it now offers a comprehensive product portfolio, covering many strengths and formats. The range comprises both 'multi-symptom' products: Beechams Flu Plus, Beechams All in One, Beechams Cold & Flu and Beechams Powders, and 'single symptom' products: Beechams Decongestant Plus, Beechams Max Strength Sore Throat Lozenges and Beechams Veno's – each with its own distinct positioning and role.

Innovations and Promotions

Beechams Flu Plus is Beechams' strongest cold and flu relief ever, designed for effective relief from the major cold and flu symptoms. Available in caplet form and as a flavoured hot drink, the hot drinks (Lemon & Hot Berry Fruits) were re-launched in 2005 in easy-to-carry stick packs.

The unique All in One range has been extended since the launch of the liquid in 2000 with a range of tablets, and will be further extended in coming years.

Beechams Veno's for Kids – a chesty cough syrup with guaifenesin suitable for children aged two and over – is the most recent addition to the Beechams Veno's range.

Beechams is supported each cold and flu season by a £6 million media campaign, focusing on core segments of the brand. During the 2005/06 season, advertising was developed to support the Flu Plus and All in One ranges.

For the past five years the advertising has clearly reflected the essence of the brand and communicated that Beechams is the 'no nonsense' remedy to the common cold. The advertising strapline 'Until there's a

cure, there's Beechams' is used to emphasise this. The style of advertising reflects a dry, irreverent British humour, to further demonstrate the no-nonsense approach of Beechams.

Market Context

Beechams, including the Beechams Veno's cough brand, has grown to be worth over £46 million at retail. This is driven by the core multi-symptom remedies, All in One and Flu Plus ranges (Source: ACNielsen).

Beechams owns 12.2% value share of the overall category, and has 29.6% share of the multi-symptom sub category – where Beechams is dominant (Source: ACNielsen).

Beechams is currently the number two brand in the overall cold and flu category, which is worth £376 million per year in total and growing at 3% year-on-year (Source: ACNielsen).

Achievements and Future Prospects

Beechams was voted Most Trusted Brand in the 'cough/cold remedy' category in the 2005 annual Reader's Digest Trusted Brand survey. The survey, which sets out to recognise brands that inspire the most trust among consumers, is conducted online and by post across 14 countries in Europe.

The results show that Beechams is used by 79% of those questioned and obtained a significant 22% share of vote in its category. Reader's Digest asked consumers to score brands according to attributes such as quality, value, brand image and understanding of consumer needs.

Beechams has been named as Winner of the OTC Marketing Awards 'Best OTC Consumer Advertising in Other Media' for the 2005/06 cold and flu season with the use of innovative outdoor media to support Beechams All in One. The brand was also Highly Commended in the SnapshOTC Awards 2005 for 'Best consumer winter seasonal advertising' for Beechams All in One.

Into the future, Beechams is constantly striving to bring innovation to the cold and flu category. Its plans involve building upon the core strengths and heritage of Beechams and delivering new products that meet real consumer needs.

1842
Thomas Beecham starts selling his 'all cure' pills for 6d (2.5p) from a market stall in Wigan.

1859
To keep up with growing demand for the pills, Thomas Beecham builds the world's first factory solely to manufacture medicines.

1913
Beechams pills are now being produced at a rate of one million per day.

1926
Beechams Powders cold remedy is launched.

1989
Having acquired brands such as Macleans and Lucozade, Beechams merges with SmithKline to become SmithKline Beecham.

1990s
SmithKline Beecham launches Beechams All in One liquid.

2000
The company merges again with Glaxo Wellcome to become GlaxoSmithKline.

2002
The company builds on All in One with launch of Tablets.

Powerful Solutions™

After creating the world's first portable electric drill for consumers 60 years ago, Black & Decker decided to make tools specifically aimed at the home tools market, a major decision that was to change the face of the company and create what is now known as the DIY market.

Offerings and Values

Black & Decker is a global manufacturer of power tools, accessories, outdoor tools and household cleaning products. Over the 96 years since the company was first established, many other successful global brands have been acquired, expanding the Black & Decker portfolio.

Black & Decker uses the knowledge gained from extensive consumer research to create powerful and practical solutions that make it easier and quicker for people to achieve great DIY results. This process has led the company to being the number one brand in all four of its core product groups: power tools, accessories, garden products and household cleaning products.

Innovations and Promotions

Black & Decker constantly strives to create everyday power tool solutions for consumers. Products launched over the years include the award-winning Mouse® compact decorating tool, the Workmate® workbench and the Scorpion® powered handsaw.

Three years ago, Black & Decker launched a range of patented self levelling lasers, innovation that excited and grew the spirit level market – in which Black & Decker are the number one branded supplier with 27.7% market share (Source: GFK Marketing Services MAT March 05 – Feb 06).

Over the past three years, laser technology has continued to develop and Black & Decker recently launched the Laser roller measure, with Accu-space™, which not only allows consumers to achieve straight lines, but also allows accurately measured distances between shelves and paintings. 2005 also saw the launch of the TV advertised Autotape™ powered tape measure, which provides consumers with a faster more convenient way to measure.

Black & Decker's garden range includes hedge trimmers, grass trimmers, chainsaws, shredders and blower vacuums. Continuing

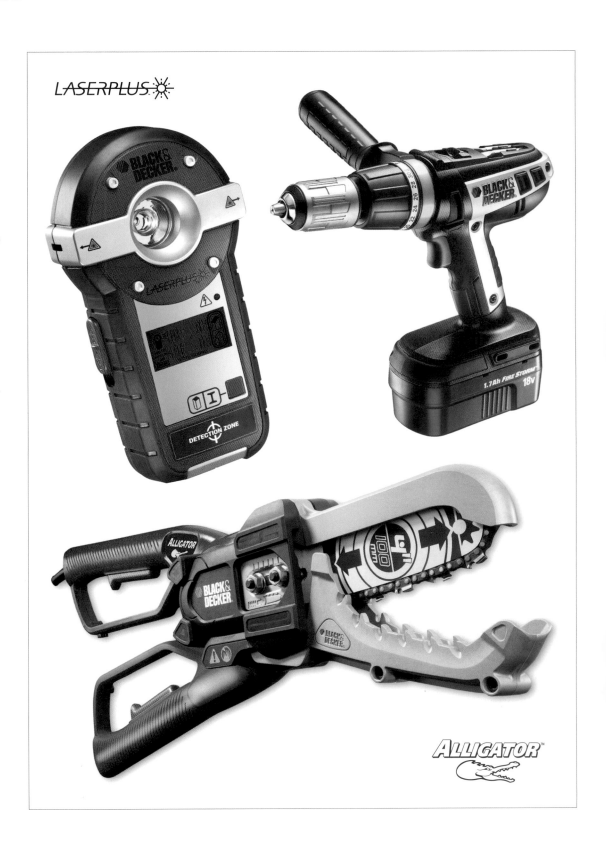

with its innovative culture, Black & Decker has recently launched the award-winning Alligator® powered lopper, which combines the power and results of a chainsaw with the safety of a manual lopper. Black & Decker owns the sub-brand Strimmer® typically used to describe grass trimmers and has released its latest range with an innovative mid-mount design, ensuring balance and maximum comfort for the consumer.

For the home, Black & Decker's Dustbuster® handheld vacuum cleaner range, invented in 1979, has constantly been upgraded with improved technology, including cyclonic action. Black & Decker entered the cylinder vac market in 2004 with its Click & Go™ range and reached the same share as a major competitor, who had been in the market for over 10 years. This year Black & Decker launch the innovative Dustbuster® vacuum cleaner with pivoting nose, allowing the consumer to reach into very small spaces.

Black & Decker recognises the importance of successful communication plans when launching new products. Further driving the DIY market forward, Black & Decker has continually invested in TV and radio campaigns to maximise its product launches in the power tool and outdoor categories.

In 2004 its range of cordless drills featured on the Talk Sport Radio breakfast show, which targeted over 1.9 million listeners. 100 regional radio stations across the UK were used to communicate the features and benefits of new products,

including the laserplus™ laserlevel and the 18V cordless range of outdoor tools comprising of a hedge trimmer, Strimmer® grass trimmer and sweeper, which reached 13 million listeners. E-mail campaigns and interactive microsites have also been created to provide up-to-date information on all new innovative products which are sent to the new and existing consumers.

Market Context

There are many factors that affect the health of the DIY market, from the state of the housing market and the performance of the economy, to weather conditions and the media. The total DIY market has nearly doubled since 1998 from £4.9 billion to £8.1 billion (Source: GfK Marketing Services). However, over the past couple of years, the DIY market has begun to stabilise and recent trends suggest that as DIY tasks become less cosmetic and start to become more like renovations, this trend will generate new growth in the market.

Achievements and Future Prospects

Black & Decker has won many awards both for its products and in recognition of its

business operations. Most recently, it has been awarded Gold for the Alligator® powered lopper in the 2006 DIY Industry Awards, Silver for the Autotape™ powered tape measure in the House Beautiful Awards, and has been named one of the UK's top 50 'Best Workplaces' by the FT.

1910
Two young Americans, Duncan Black and Alonzo Decker, form their own manufacturing company with US $1,200 initial capital.

1914
Black & Decker patents the first handheld power drill with a pistol grip, trigger switch and universal motor.

1946
Black & Decker introduce the world's first portable electric drill for consumers.

1962
The world's first cordless outdoor product, a hedge trimmer, is introduced.

1985
The Automatic Shut-Off™ Electronic Iron sets a new standard for iron performance.

2001
The Scorpion® Powered handsaw hits the market and globally sells 800,000 units in its first year.

2003
An innovative range of patented self levelling lasers is launched.

2006
Black & Decker launch the Alligator® powered lopper and win gold at the 2006 DIY Industry awards.

www.brita.co.uk

The benefits of water filtration sometimes can't be seen, but BRITA consumers have trusted BRITA to be the custodians of their drinking water for the past 40 years. As the original inventor of jug water filters, and the leader in research and development, BRITA leads the way in quality, and enjoys the trust of consumers. BRITA is the UK market leader in domestic filtration and its success has resulted in a brand synonymous with filtered water.

Offerings and Values

BRITA makes a range of water filter solutions for both household and professional use. BRITA filter products significantly reduce limescale, chlorine, heavy metals such as lead and copper, and organic impurities, which can affect the smell and taste of drinking water, and cause the oily film often found on hot drinks.

Over time, BRITA has become a worthy contender to bottled water. With increasing awareness of the health benefits of drinking more water, BRITA has positioned itself as the smarter solution – not only offering

excellent tasting water, but no heavy bottles to carry around, and great value at only 4p per litre.

For household use, BRITA offers a range of filter jugs, kettles and replaceable cartridges, along with a new electric chiller dispensing chilled BRITA filtered water.

For professional use, BRITA offers a range of filters servicing the coffee, vending and catering sectors. Here the benefits are twofold: Firstly, less limescale build up in machines, resulting in fewer breakdown costs and more consistency of drink quality for the end user. Secondly, in some sectors,

particularly vending, the use of the BRITA brand has been seen to increase appeal and hence sales of vended drinks.

Innovations and Promotions

Since the launch of the first domestic water filters in the 1970s, BRITA has led innovation in the market, constantly redesigning and improving its products. Key innovations include the 1994 development of filters for professional applications such as coffee machines, vending machines and catering equipment, the 2001 launch of Acclario – the world's

first water filter and kettle in one and in 2005, the launch of a new generation of water filter jugs with a new filter cartridge, Maxtra, for BRITA's best-ever performance offering an extra 20% limescale reduction. 2006 has seen the launch of the BRITA Breville Aqua Fountain – an electric water chiller with a BRITA filter cartridge inside; and in the summer of 2006, BRITA launched its first range of water filter taps, in conjunction with British tap specialist Francis Pegler, offering consumers the chance to get BRITA filtered water straight from the tap.

In February 2006, and in line with BRITA's international strategy to harmonise brand appearance across the world, BRITA UK introduced a new logo and design guidelines to its consumer and trade materials. This will ensure that the presentation of the brand remains consistent, modern and design orientated. Following the 'BRITA Couple' and 'How do you like your water?' advertising campaigns, which had generated both significant sales uplifts

and broader awareness for the brand, 2005 saw BRITA launch a new campaign: 'Hands', which was developed specifically to support the launch of BRITA's new generation of water filters and cartridges such as Maxtra.

Market Context
In the UK, the water filter market focuses on the sale of water filter jugs, water filter kettles, and replacement cartridges.

More than 70% of the population are familiar with water filter jugs, and of the 24.9 million households in the UK, 24% (almost six million) own a water filter jug (Source: BRITA Usage and Attitudes Study). As a result the UK water filter market is worth over £96 million per year.

Ownership has been in steady growth since the mid 1990s and BRITA remains the leading brand in household water filtration in both the UK and worldwide (Source: BRITA Usage and Attitudes Study).

With recent innovations, BRITA now has a presence in the 'small domestic appliances' market via links with partners

in products such as kettles, chillers and coffee machines.

Achievements and Future Prospects
BRITA has developed partnerships with a number of household brands, including Bosch Siemens, Breville, Bush, Hinari and Magimix, for the creation of appliances featuring an integrated BRITA filter cartridge inside. The brand partnerships have resulted in coffee makers, kettles and chillers with BRITA water filter technology. The inclusion of integrated BRITA filter cartridges in household appliances such as kettles adds value to the proposition and in recent research by BRITA, consumers stated that one of the main reasons they chose the Breville filter kettle was because of the BRITA-branded filter cartridge inside.

BRITA recently took a leading role in the development of a standard for water filters via the British Standards Institute. The aim of the standard was to provide quality assurance and consistency for the consumer.

1966
BRITA founder, Heinz Hankammer begins to experiment with the demineralisation of water in his back garden.

1967
BRITA launches its first water filter product, designed to produce demineralised water for car batteries and laboratories.

1970
BRITA's first household water filter jug is born.

1982
BRITA UK is launched as an independent distribution company.

1992
BRITA UK is bought back by BRITA GmbH. BRITA moves to new offices and production warehouse in Sunbury-on-Thames.

2004
BRITA moves its UK operation to Bicester, north Oxfordshire, investing 15 million euros in a state-of-the-art production facility and new office building.

2005
BRITA UK is voted 28th Best Small Company to Work For (Source: The Sunday Times).

2006
BRITA celebrates its 40th birthday year and 25 years in the UK.

www.brylcreem.com

Brylcreem has been at the heart of men's grooming products since 1928 and is renowned worldwide for its years of male hair care expertise. With its years of experience and insight into men, their hair and hair styling products, Brylcreem understands exactly why men want to have great looking hair.

Offerings and Values

While the Brylcreem Classic range, in its iconic red pot, remains an important part of the brand, the Brylcreem portfolio now includes a much wider range of products addressing specific needs. In order to be seen as different from 'old Brylcreem', it was essential that the new product range reflected modernity and innovation.

Brylcreem's Styling range is the modern face of the brand, representing 80% of its revenue through the 12 products. The gel range, comprising of five products, is the UK's leading gel range, out-selling the closest competitor by nearly half a million units each year (Source: IRI 52 w/e March 18th 2006). New product development and innovation are vital for the brand to remain the number one male hairstyling brand, so staying on top of consumer trends is vital. Tapping into a recent consumer trend, three key Brylcreem gel products are now water-resistant, as well as non-flaky and fast drying, and two Brylcreem waxes are now easier to wash out.

Innovations and Promotions

Brylcreem keeps delivering new products that work hard with the aim of helping real men look and feel really sharp. In September 2005, Brylcreem added a shampoo to its hairstyling range. Brylcreem Head Clean is a revolutionary shampoo designed to strip styling product build-up from mens' hair, leaving them ready for a re-style. It's specifically designed for men who don't want silky soft hair or extra volume, but simply clean, manageable hair in one wash and without any fuss.

In February 2006 Brylcreem launched its reformulated and repackaged range. The new-look range features an 'easy-to-navigate' design, with refreshed Brylcreem logo, highlighting Brylcreem's British Grooming heritage (since it was established in 1928). The range includes improved formulas which aim to ensure men continue to look their best, no matter what they put their hair through.

BRYLCREEM
THE PERFECT HAIR DRESSING

To help consumers navigate the range and find the right Brylcreem product for their requirements, the new-look Brylcreem features an easy-to-use, colour coded 'strengthometer', a four-point scale that immediately highlights each individual product's strength and attributes.

Brylcreem is all about British style – smart looks with a bit of edge and a knowing

confidence. Brylcreem is a British brand, standing out from European competitors and as such, its brand communications remain very down-to-earth and straight-talking.

To reflect this, sponsorship of Sky Sports football programme 'Soccer AM' leads Brylcreem's promotional activity for the second year, with 39 individual 'bumper break' commercials to communicate the brand message.

Each advert features the strapline 'Soccer AM with Brylcreem', in addition to an individual shot of one product from the Brylcreem range. The bumper breaks capture the essence of both the Brylcreem and Soccer AM brands, communicating 'All you need is Brylcreem' in an irreverent and entertaining way.

The sponsorship is supported by a mix of other above- and below-the-line activities. Press campaigns are used to support new products in key male publications and PR activity is also being used to amplify the Soccer AM sponsorship.

Market Context

The UK unisex hairstyling market is worth £175 million but is declining at a rate of 5.6% year-on-year (Source: IRI). By contrast, the UK male toiletries market is worth £402.3 million, and is growing at a rate of 4.1% year-on-year (Source: IRI). Brylcreem accounts for 9% of the UK unisex styling market (Source: IRI). Brylcreem can be found on the male toiletries fixture in most grocery outlets, although unisex styling brands such as Wella Shockwaves, Fructis, VO5 and L'Oréal Studio Line are its key competitors.

Achievements and Future Prospects

Brylcreem is the UK's number one men's hair styling brand (Source: IRI) and is targeted at men aged 16-28. The brand has a global presence, and is available in 46 countries including Brazil, India and the US.

Over its 78 year history, Brylcreem has collected an array of awards. Most recently it has won awards from men's lifestyle magazines including FHM, MAXIM and Front.

1928
Brylcreem is established with the launch of Brylcreem Original – a hair cream for mature men.

1935
Brylcreem's first advertising agency is appointed, with the objective to 'secure the goodwill of the barber'.

1961
Brylcreem Original is re-launched in red plastic tubs with TV advertising to support the change.

1988
The Brylcreem 'Black' range – male hair and body grooming products targeting 16-24 year-olds – is launched.

1993
Sara Lee acquires the Brylcreem brand and aims it at 16-30 year-old men, putting the sole focus back on hair styling: Brylcreem sales rise by 33% as a result.

1997
Sara Lee rekindles the 'Brylcreem Boy' heritage and chooses David Beckham to represent this.

2005
Brylcreem begins its association with Soccer AM.

2006
Brylcreem re-designs and re-launches its Styling Range.

www.bt.com

BT's vision is to be dedicated to helping customers thrive within a rapidly changing environment where individuals and businesses increasingly need to connect and communicate whenever and wherever they happen to be, using whatever device they choose. By designing everything it does around customers, BT will help them succeed on their terms, at their pace and in their own unique context and environment.

Offerings and Values

BT is one of Britain's best-known companies and is a brand that's recognised and understood throughout the world.

The company has transformed itself in recent years. It has evolved from being a supplier of telephony services to become a leading provider of innovative communications products, services and solutions. Its customers range from multinational corporations to residential householders, of which there are more than 20 million in the UK.

For consumers, BT offers an extensive portfolio of telephony, broadband and mobility products and services. Late in 2006, it will begin using its communications network to deliver next-generation TV to customers.

Towards the end of 2005, BT conducted a thorough review of its brand. This resulted in the articulation of a new company vision. 'Bringing it all together' has been introduced as a unifying message to be used across all of BT's customer communications. It is designed to help create a more cohesive and consistent message across each of BT's three core communications themes: value, customer care and innovation.

Innovations and Promotions

BT's developments in products and services for consumers are consistent with the company's focus on meeting the requirements of today's and tomorrow's customers. Its recent innovations include: BT Fusion, an intelligent mobile service that switches calls to a BT broadband line when the user is at home, offering customers the convenience of mobile in combination with the lesser cost and higher call quality advantages associated with a fixed-line phone.

Set for launch later in 2006, BT Vision will combine access to digital terrestrial channels, an extensive video-on-demand library, catch-up TV and a range of interactive services offering customers choice, convenience and control over their home entertainment services. BT has already signed content deals with BBC Worldwide, Paramount, Warner Music Group, Endemol and many others.

Underpinning BT's range of innovative services is its national network. The company is committed to investing more than £10 billion to transform its network to become an IP-based '21st Century Network' across the UK by 2009. When complete, it will carry all voice, video and data traffic on a single state-of-the-art network giving consumers optimum capabilities to be able to communicate wherever they may be using whatever device they choose.

In October 2005, BT launched a major new TV and radio advertising campaign pulling together all of BT consumer communications with a consistent theme and tone of voice, following a period of

and so, in an increasingly competitive and rapidly evolving market, BT's brand becomes an absolutely critical differentiator and is compelled to work harder than ever before.

Achievements and Future Prospects

BT has been a driving force behind the successful take-up of broadband internet services across Britain. Indeed there are now around eight million BT wholesale broadband connections. And in April 2006, the company announced a new 'ultra-fast' consumer broadband service set to take the broadband experience to a whole new level for millions of customers across the UK. Capable of delivering broadband download speeds of up to 8Mb, the new service enables the entire family to enjoy watching movies, making calls over the internet, online gaming, downloading music and faster web surfing – all at the same time and for no extra cost.

BT has been named as the leading telcoms company in the Dow Jones World Sustainability Index for five consecutive years and is the holder of the prestigious Queen's Award for Enterprise for Sustainable Development.

separate campaigns for BT consumer products. The campaign introduced a thoroughly modern, albeit everyday, family using BT products to help them navigate through life's ebbs and flows.

The ads are designed to reflect the increasing converged world of communications we now live in and focus on a range of BT products and services from Wi-Fi to phonebooks, from 118 500 directory enquiries to landline texting.

Market Context

The UK telecoms market is worth tens of billions of pounds and is characterised by intense competition, whether for traditional voice services, mobile telephony or broadband.

Just as this is the age of convergence, it is also a period of market consolidation,

where some major communications companies are joining together in a bid to be able to offer customers more than one service, for example, 'triple-play' (broadband, TV, landline telephony) services to customers – or 'quadruple-play', where mobile services are added.

A number of powerful brands have set their sights on succeeding in this arena

1981

British Telecom is created from Post Office Telecommunications and then privatised in 1984.

1991

The company unveils a new trading name, BT, together with the 'piper' brand identity.

2001

BT re-brands its mobile business as O₂ prior to its de-merger.

2006

The BT Group plc is structured so that it provides a holding company for the separately managed businesses that make up the organisation.

BUPA is a brand truly guided by its mission statement: 'Taking care of the lives in our hands'. Its well-defined values guide its business and brand behaviour. As a provident association, it has no shareholders and re-invests profits back into its health and care businesses. The organisation is committed to being ethical, accountable and respectful. In communications, BUPA endeavours to project a leading and expert brand that is warm, friendly, open, accessible, caring and empathetic.

Offerings and Values

BUPA is renowned for private medical insurance but has expanded into many other areas. For example, BUPA is now the UK's second largest provider of care homes, has a network of private hospitals and provides health assessments and occupational healthcare.

BUPA Membership, market leader for private medical insurance, provides cover to over three million people in the UK including staff in over half of the FTSE 100 companies.

Annually, BUPA spends over £800 million on its members' healthcare including around £100 million on cancer treatments.

BUPA Hospitals perform a wide range of procedures and continue to attract increasing customer numbers from the NHS.

BUPA Wellness offers health assessments and treatment in 47 Wellness Centres across the UK, equipped with cutting-edge technology to assess fitness and detect early signs of disease and illness, as well as private GP, dental and musculoskeletal services.

BUPA is increasingly involved in the provision of residential and nursing care for the elderly. BUPA Care Services is the UK's second largest private provider of care home places, with 299 residential and nursing homes with over 20,000 residents.

BUPA International is another fast-growing part of the group, caring for over three million customers worldwide in places as diverse as Australia, China, Denmark, Hong Kong, India, Ireland, Malaysia, Saudi Arabia, Singapore, South America, Spain and Thailand.

BUPA can help you choose when and where you want to be treated. We believe that being able to make an appointment that's convenient for you is a start to making you feel better

0800 600 500
bupa.com

feel better BUPA

BUPA can help you see the right person for the job All the consultants we work with have at least seven years' clinical experience, so you will get the specialist support you need to make you feel better

0800 600 500
bupa.com

feel better BUPA

clear health

putting you in touch with our professionals

issue 2 • autumn 2005

breast cancer revolution

how one of the biggest advances for years could save thousands of lives

feel better **BUPA**

sports injury lowdown • secrets of the Mediterranean diet • count on dancing

BUPA Wellness

"Helping our employees with pressures they face makes them **feel better** and makes business more productive"

BUPA Employee Assistance Programme

In Spain, BUPA owns Sanitas, a leading private medical insurance company with over one million members which has expanded to provide care homes in addition to its hospitals and clinics. In Australia, BUPA has one million members, representing over 10% of the market.

Innovation and Promotions

The UK health and care market has been changing dramatically recently and further developments are likely due to both NHS structural and attitudinal changes and the expansion of the private sector, which is seeing new entrants and different types of policies. Consequently, new models of private care are burgeoning.

BUPA's marketing challenge is continually to remind people of the benefits of private health and care in a way that positions BUPA as the only and obvious brand to choose, both rationally and emotionally.

BUPA's current advertising strategy conveys the simple and powerful idea that people will 'Feel Better' with BUPA. This promise is being used across BUPA. All its businesses are dedicated to making people feel better, both physically in terms of the standard of treatment and care they receive and emotionally because of the reassurance and peace of mind provided.

Market Context

With scientific progress, overall public health is improving. Yet, with an ageing population, an expanding range of treatments and a more affluent society, the need for healthcare services is increasing and consumer demand often exceeds what the NHS can offer.

Spending on UK health and care cover products, including private medical insurance, health cash plans, dental benefit plans and long-term care insurance reached £4.2 billion in 2004, according to healthcare analysts Laing & Buisson.

The number of people covered by private medical insurance policies in the UK, or enrolled in medical schemes self-insured by employers, was 7,576,000 at the end of 2004, up 0.5% on the previous year.

Private healthcare is primarily funded by private medical insurance, the market for which has boomed since the beginning of the 1980s. Of this market, BUPA has a 41% share representing £1.2 billion in revenue.

Achievements and Future Prospects

BUPA established the concept of private medical insurance in the UK, leading the market right up to the 1980s when rapid expansion attracted new competitors. However, it has retained its strong

market lead and remains the pre-eminent brand in the sector.

BUPA has also developed new NHS relationships, opening the first privately run NHS Diagnostic Treatment Centre at Redwood in Surrey and performing thousands of operations every year in its other hospitals on behalf of the NHS.

BUPA pioneered the development of health screening and specialist occupational health services in the UK and is now the biggest provider of screening services conducting over 100,000 health assessments annually.

In almost 60 years, BUPA has grown to become a leading international health and care company with bases on three continents and more than eight million customers.

1947

BUPA is formed when 17 regional provident associations amalgamated to form The British United Provident Association, soon to be called BUPA.

1981

BUPA's first purpose-built hospital opens in Manchester.

1987

BUPA's international ambitions take a huge leap as it acquires Sanitas, Spain's largest private health care organisation.

2005

BUPA establishes its 'Feel Better' communications platform across the business. It also expands its international operations by acquiring the US-based insurer, Amedex Insurance Company, which serves Latin America and the Caribbean and International Health Insurance Danmark (IHI) which provide health insurance products to expatriates.

2006

BUPA's worldwide business has undergone rapid growth since the late 1980s and it now has 40,000 staff globally.

Chelsea Football Club's rise as a brand has been rapid and is driven by a simple vision: by 2014 Chelsea wants to be recognised internationally as the world's number one football club. Feted for winning trophies, Chelsea also aims to be recognised as the best in every other area of its business, including customer service, sponsorship and corporate social responsibility. The foundations for this are embodied in the club's brand values of excellence, style, leadership, integrity, pride and unity.

Offerings and Values

The Chelsea FC brand aims to offer fans success, style, passion and loyalty, which are the values that underpin their relationship with the club. Chelsea's fundamental product and service is playing – and selling tickets – for first-team matches at Stamford Bridge, and for matches involving the club at other grounds.

So fan loyalty, and ultimately customer satisfaction, is dependent on the successful execution of this offering.

Allied to this is a series of competitive, innovative and modern services, which are designed to build on fans' affinity to the club. These range from the True Blue and Junior Blue membership packages with exclusive offerings, to financial services, merchandise and media packages combining traditional and new media.

Since 2004, Chelsea has developed a corporate social responsibility (CSR) programme, which is interwoven into stakeholder relationships. The key CSR

initiative is a national charity partnership with CLIC Sargent, the UK's leading children's cancer charity. Chelsea engages all its players, management, staff, fans and partners in its activities with CLIC Sargent. In the 2004/05 season, Chelsea helped raise £1 million for charities and good causes.

Innovations and Promotions

Since the takeover by Roman Abramovich in 2003, the Chelsea brand has been transformed. Under the leadership of chief

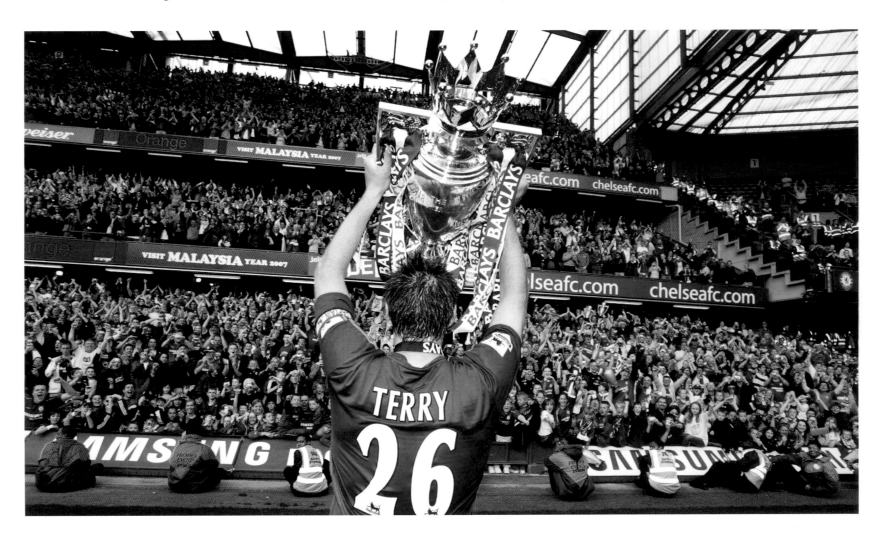

executive Peter Kenyon, there has been a high-profile re-branding around the core business of football. Previously Chelsea had diversified into other businesses such as hotels, restaurants, a travel company and a leisure club under the Chelsea Village identity. Now only the name Chelsea FC is used for business activities.

As this transformation was happening, the club's identity was also revolutionised. The unpopular club badge, introduced in the 1980s, was abandoned. Chelsea has returned to its original badge design from the 1950s, but this has been repositioned in a retro style to universal fan acclaim. This also had a key business function in terms of copyright and protection of marks in the international market.

Virtually every department was revamped and every major area of the business overhauled, from the first team and academy structure to ticketing, CRM, traditional media (match-day programmes, monthly magazines, TV), new media (website, mobile, online TV) and the sponsor/partnership programme. This has led to a whole host of modernised and innovative offerings, such as football's first financial portal, www.chelseafcmoney.com.

Market Context

The accelerated development of Chelsea FC has only been possible against the backdrop of English football since the Premier League began in 1992. The English Premier League has become the most popular in world football, beamed every week to 195 countries, and two teams – Manchester United and Arsenal – had previously dominated. Simultaneously, the creation of the UEFA Champions League meant there were European rivals too, such as Barcelona, AC Milan, Real Madrid and Bayern Munich.

After the takeover of Chelsea FC by Abramovich in 2003, a period of rapid investment was needed in the football side of the club, not just to catch up, but to overtake its rivals as any vision was reliant on sustained success. The £400 million plus investment has since catapulted Chelsea onto a global level, but the club has never lost touch with its heritage.

Achievements and Future Prospects

Chelsea FC is experiencing an unprecedented period of success in its 100th season. In the past three seasons, Chelsea has become the most successful team in British football,

with two successive Premiership titles garnered under the management of Jose Mourinho.

Without such a successful performance on the football field, Chelsea's ambitions to develop its brand as a world force would be impossible. The business plan is based on global visibility through traditional and new media penetration, market-leading sponsor partners, fan engagement and market legacy.

Going forward, Chelsea has identified three key target markets – London, North America and Asia, specifically China – which are all also vital markets to the club's partners, Samsung and adidas.

In these markets Chelsea has embarked on significant local partnerships. In London, Chelsea was the first Premiership team to back the 2012 Olympic bid and was recently nominated an official ambassador for London by the Mayor. In China, Chelsea is entering into a co-operation agreement with the Chinese Football Association and with the Asian Football Confederation. In America, there is an alliance with AEG, the operator of four teams in Major League Soccer and one of the world's leading sports and entertainment companies.

1905
Chelsea FC is founded.

1955
Chelsea wins the First Division title for the first time.

1970/71
Chelsea wins the FA Cup and European Cup Winners' Cup, repeating the same sequence in 1997 and 1998.

2003
Roman Abramovich buys Chelsea FC.

2004
Peter Kenyon, formerly of Manchester United, is appointed chief executive of Chelsea FC and recruits Jose Mourinho as manager.

2006
Of Chelsea's 24-man first-team squad, 16 were chosen to represent their countries at the 2006 World Cup, encompassing 10 different nationalities.

www.cosmopolitan.co.uk

British Cosmopolitan launched in 1972 and has since remained one of the dominant magazine brands in the UK. UK Cosmo attributes this success to the brand DNA, consistency of its voice and the constant ability to innovate and evolve for its generation. Relevance counts for more than heritage because a consumer purchase of a magazine is an act of trust – 'you know something I don't'.

Offerings and Values

The Cosmopolitan mission is to celebrate fun, glamour and a passion for life, and to inspire young women to be the best they can be. A magazine for a 'Fun, Fearless, Female'. It achieves this via eight core editorial pillars: relationships and sex, men, real life stories, beauty and shopping, careers, emotional health and well-being, issues and campaigns. Of these editorial pillars, relationships is unique to Cosmo and is the crucial element which enables a trusted and more intimate relationship with its readers.

As the voice of young British women, Cosmopolitan attracts a very broad church of readers, for all of whom the brand resonates. They fall into three clearly defined reader groups: The Rite of Passage reader, aged typically between 15-17 years who reads Cosmo as a window on her future. Her need state is open to everything, expecting Cosmo to tell her "everything I am going to need to know". The Core reader, aged 18-35, is living an independent and full-on life. Her need state is do everything, expecting Cosmo to "provide the guidance, know how and confidence". The Nostalgic reader who is 36-45, who today behaves no differently from her early thirties, enjoys the "reassurance from Cosmo that she is still in the know".

Cosmo's core business is the magazine which now has an extended family with CosmoGIRL! and Cosmopolitan Bride. Building on the strengths of its magazines, the brand also retails a range of licensed merchandise carefully selected to fit with the personality. The Cosmopolitan Collection includes a successful range of handbags, swimwear, bedding, soft furnishings and beauty accessories. Cosmopolitan has also published a significant number of books on relationships, sex, beauty and emotional well-being, including a book entitled 'Was it good for you' – a celebration of the brand's

give your
relationship
the kiss of life

COSMOPOLITAN
bring out the Cosmo in you

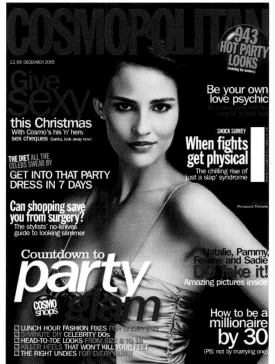

dominance in the UK to coincide with its 30th birthday in 1992.

Innovations and Promotions

Cosmopolitan remains the industry benchmark in magazine publishing. To its readers, Cosmo is as relevant today as it was in the 1970s, 1980s and 1990s. In the 2000s Cosmo has an all time high subscriber base of over 42,000 readers and a Travel Size version which offers consumers choice and convenience at the newsstand. In 2005 Cosmo launched its first above-the-line advertising campaign since 1972 to help protect the unique position of the brand. The campaign introduced a new ad-line 'bring out the Cosmo in you', designed to reinforce Cosmo's 'Fun, Fearless, Female' positioning.

In such a dynamic market place, a business strategy which keeps the brand fresh, modern and relevant is essential. Recent innovations have included the launch of a brand new editorial property – the Fun, Fearless, Female Awards. More than just your average celebrity awards, Cosmo will reward the most fun, fearless females in all walks of life from celebrities to readers, bound by their inspirational qualities.

The Cosmo Beauty Awards, launched in 2003, have become the ultimate buying guide for the consumer and are used extensively by the trade as a powerful brand endorsement of best in class. In 2006,

Cosmo celebrated the 10th anniversary of the Naked Centrefold, a famous editorial and event property which supports Everyman – the testicular and prostrate cancer charity – raising invaluable research funds and awareness.

Now a truly multi-platform media brand, it can connect with its readers over and above the magazine, through online, events, surveys, reader polls, subscribers, e-subscribers, text and email.

Market Context

The magazine market has come a long way since Cosmopolitan launched in February 1972.

Today, despite the unprecedented levels of competition, Cosmo consistently delivers an average circulation over 460,000 every month. Cosmo's female readership is over 1.7 million, 37% greater than its nearest competitor (Source: NRS July-Dec 2005). What's more, 844,000 female readers are unique to Cosmo, choosing not to read any other magazine on the market (Source: NRS July-Dec 2005). The Cosmo reader accounts for £1 in every £10 spend on beauty and fashion in the UK. Cosmo also generates the highest retail sales value of all monthly magazines in the market.

Achievements and Future Prospects

In February 2002 Cosmopolitan celebrated its 30th birthday and was praised highly in the comment of the day in The Times leader

column. "Cosmo is bigger than a magazine, it is a brand, an empire, a state of mind."

Since 1972 Cosmo has established an enviable campaigning heritage on a variety of issues, from equal pay and sexual health to motivating political engagement and the rights for rape victims. In 2005, as the voice of young women, for a three week stretch leading up to the May General Election, Cosmo was never out of the headlines. The strength of the magazine's 'high heel vote' campaign saw editor Sam Baker featured on the cover of The Observer, putting the 6.8 million young women in the UK who were unlikely to vote in the spotlight. The campaign was subsequently nominated for a Channel 4 Hansard Society Politics Award.

Cosmo has been recognised with a number of prestigious awards including British Society of Magazine Editors (BSME) Innovation of the Year in 2003, for the magazine's Rapestoppers Campaign. The magazine has also been awarded the BSME Women's Magazine Editor of the Year in 1991, 1993, 1999, 2001 and the Periodical Publishers Association Consumer Magazine of the Year in 1992. In 2003 Cosmo was voted 'Favourite media for Beauty' by Tesco customers and awarded the Proctor & Gamble Beauty Award in 2004 for the magazine that has 'Best supported the Beauty Industry'.

1972
British Cosmopolitan launches. The first issue is supported by a TV ad by Saatchi & Saatchi.

2001
CosmoGIRL! and cosmogirl.co.uk launch.

2002
Cosmopolitan celebrates 30 years at number one. In the same year, Cosmo launches a Travel size format – offering consumers choice.

2004
Sam Baker is appointed as Editor. In addition, Cosmo appoint London ad agency CHI for the first ATL campaign since launch.

2006
Cosmopolitan launches its Fun, Fearless, Female Awards. Cosmo also celebrates the 10th anniversary of the Naked Centrefold.

Also in 2006, the new cosmopolitan.co.uk launches – a content rich and community driven site.

Originating in Wilf Handley's Newcastle workshop in 1929, Domestos bleach was first sold across the North East in stoneware jars which were refilled by door to door salesmen from the back of their bicycles. Today it is the UK's number one selling bleach brand sold across all major supermarkets and independent stores.

Offerings and Values

In the 1950s Domestos led the way in British health education through its introduction of public awareness campaigns to educate consumers in the prevention of typhoid, dysentery, gastro-enteritis and other illnesses. That pioneering approach and concern for public health stayed with the brand when Domestos Ltd was acquired by Lever Bros in 1961 and has continued to be a key focus ever since. The change in ownership soon led to an investment in the brand's first ever advertising campaign and a move to its distinctive and iconic blue bottle with red cap. It was followed in the 1970s by its first major formulation change with a move from thin to thick bleach. There are many types of disinfectant product but only bleach has the power to kill all known types of germs including bacteria, viruses and fungi.

Over the years the Domestos range has expanded from its first product, the 'Original' blue variant to a comprehensive portfolio of bleach-based products, offering consumers the most appropriate product for different cleaning jobs in the home. Alongside this, it has produced a wide range of literature to help consumers understand the importance of home hygiene and provide advice on situations where people need to take extra care with cleaning. In addition the brand has introduced 'Hotspot Hygiene', a way of focusing cleaning efforts where they make the most difference – the times, places and situation where consumers can actually help reduce the risks of infection.

All of this information has also been communicated to healthcare professionals such as Heath Visitors and Infection Control Nurses to provide them with the correct information and advice to pass on to their patients. As a result, the brand has earned the trust of consumers, many of whom have been loyal to it for years and believe in its promise to kill all known germs and keep their homes clean and safe.

Innovations and Promotions

Domestos continually invests in research and development to ensure that consumers are being offered the best possible products to protect them from germs in the home. The most recent addition to the portfolio is Domestos 5x which has been specifically designed to fight germs that are found in the toilet bowl and rim. Made using a revolutionary formulation containing C-TAC it coats the toilet killing germs on contact and continues working flush after flush, five times longer than any other bleach or toilet cleaner. In addition, Domestos has been quick to respond to the changing communication needs of a more discerning and sophisticated consumer audience. Recent work has included a series of

webtorials on major websites such as Channel4.com and itv.com.

The Domestos 'Millions of germs will die' campaign launched at the beginning of 2005 with the aim of communicating the indomitable strength and power of Domestos in a way that created a functional and emotional point of difference. Four TV ads, each of which focused on a specific element of the brand's range, used animations of walking, talking and slightly scary germs to convey the germ killing power of Domestos bleach. Radio, national press and outdoor executions were also used during the campaign. In addition, www.millionsofgermswilldie.com was created in the style of a Hollywood action blockbuster to introduce the characters used in the ads and provide an overview of the brand, including the importance of practising good hygiene around the home.

Market Context

The Household Cleaning and Bleach market is worth £509.3 million. Of this amount £95.9 million is made up of bleach. The household bleach sector historically has had two leading branded players Domestos and Parozone bleach. Domestos is represented by Domestos regular bleach, Domestos fragrance bleach and Domestos Bleach spray. ROB has 51.5% of the market with the new player Reckitt Benckisers Cillit Bang Stain & Drain entering at 1.1%.

The Household Cleaning market is worth £413.4 million and consists of Bathroom/Shower, MPK, Specialist and Toilet sectors.

The Specialist sector which is worth £108 million is made up of segments like Oven Cleaners, Window Cleaners, Hob Cleaners, Limescale Removers and Drain Cleaners.

The Drain segment as a total is worth £16.5 million. Domestos Sink & Pipe Unblocker has now been on the market for a year and has become the number two player in this segment behind Mr Muscle and is the only brand in growth (Source: IRI 52 w/e Apr 15th 2006).

Achievements and Future Prospects

Domestos has been working with health experts for generations to help educate consumers about the importance of hygiene. The brand sees this as an important role that it will continue to play moving forward.

Domestos recently gained a Highly Commended Award for 'Experiential Marketing Away from Point of Sale' at the ISP Awards 2006. This was for 'Germaphobia' – an educational roadshow that toured the country during June and July 2005, teaching consumers about germs and the importance of home hygiene, with microbiologists on hand to offer expert advice.

1929
Domestos is first sold in stoneware jars across the north east of England.

1950s
Domestos leads the way in British health education with public awareness campaigns.

1961
Domestos Ltd is acquired by Lever Bros which is followed by the first ad campaign and introduction of the iconic blue bottle with red cap.

1970s
The first major formulation change takes place, with a move from thin to thick bleach.

1984
The brand is re-launched with an even thicker formulation.

1990s
The angle-necked bottle is introduced as well as a toilet specific range and fragrance variants.

2003
Domestos bleach becomes thicker still.

2004
Domestos Bleach Cleaning Spray, for cleaning areas frequently touched by different people and hard to reach areas, is launched.

2005
Domestos Sink & Pipe Unblocker, which has the power to remove blockages in as little as 15 minutes, is launched.

2006
The launch of Domestos 5x, a revolutionary toilet cleaner that attacks germs for five times longer than any other toilet cleaner or bleach, takes place.

www.drmartens.com

From the time the first Dr. Martens were created in 1960, form and function became linked and known as Dr. Martens – or Doc Martens, Docs or DM's. The boots would go on to become a design icon and a part of the social fabric of the UK subculture scene. What started as workman's boot would grow into a brand with a unique offering of boots, shoes and sandals for men, women and children.

Offerings and Values

Designed to be durable, functional and tough, the original Dr. Martens boot evolved to become a mainstay of the working classes. Dr. Martens first developed footwear for British workers from the docks to the police force to the postal workers. Later, Dr. Martens grew from its humble origins to a brand that resonates with youth culture, decade after decade.

Having started out as a company that produced just one style of boots nearly a half-decade ago, Dr. Martens now sells more than 300 styles in 80 countries. The US is the largest market, accounting for in excess of 50% of all sales, followed by the UK and France.

The consumers who have adopted the brand have in part been responsible for the success of Dr. Martens. From early on, youth cultures gravitated toward DM's as a symbol of rebellion and a form of self-expression. Personalised by its wearers, the boot enabled members of these groups to express their individuality and creativity. In fact, Dr. Martens was a brand for customisation long before the current trend of mass customisation. From how they were laced, to what colour the laces were, DMs said a lot about their wearer.

Innovations and Promotions

Dr. Martens has grown to become an important part of footwear history, proving that industrial work boots can be comfortable as well as stylish. It also helped define a new category of footwear: 'rugged casual'.

While several marketing campaigns, which played up the Dr. Martens heritage, have certainly played a role in the growth of the brand, the real growth is attributed more to a grass roots, peer-to-peer phenomenon.

The Dr. Martens brand has always had a strong association with music. In fact, Pete Townshend of The Who was the first high-

profile celebrity to be seen wearing Docs. He was such a fan of the footwear that he wrote about the boots in his song 'Uniform'. Many other bands, both past and present, have also been seen wearing Docs in press photos as well as in concert. A testament to the true popularity of the brand among musicians is that the company has never paid money for celebrities to wear them.

Market Context

Dr. Martens has recently been over-shadowed by the rise of the trainer as the epitome of comfortable and fashionable footwear. Just as the trainer has its roots in athletic performance but has captured the middle ground, so Dr. Martens has moved to the middle ground from its roots in industrial performance.

Consumers, particularly men, are keener than ever to find the smart-casual shoe that will allow them flexibility of wearing the same footwear for different occasions. Dr. Martens still serves the technical, industrial market but also the casual and outdoor markets. Most important is the personality of the footwear, which is spirited and always slightly edgy.

Achievements and Future Prospects

Dr. Martens was the original cult brand that defined who you were by what you wore on your feet. In a sense, those who adopted the brand helped create and develop it. Self-expression and youth culture are a key part of the Dr. Martens heritage.

Dr. Martens has taken its heritage of individual self-expression and has made it relevant to

today's consumer. Individual self-expression is no longer about anti-establishment outsiders, but rather creative, inspirational insiders.

Like the many different subcultures and social groups that have adopted it over the years, the brand always has been and always will be many different things to many different people. The brand is scruffy, smart, sexy, macho, fashionable, classy, classless, uniform, and unique.

1945
After breaking his foot while skiing, Dr. Klaus Maertens, a 25-year-old German soldier, designs an air-filled shoe sole that he could comfortably wear while his foot healed.

1946
Dr. Maertens partners with old university friend Dr. Herbert Funck to create a boot utilising the air-filled rubber soles.

1947
The boot is so comfortable that it becomes popular enough for the pair to begin handmade production in Germany.

1959
Griggs, a family company of English shoemakers, acquire the exclusive licence to produce the air-cushioned sole from Maertens and Funck.

1960
On April 1st, the first Dr. Martens production boot rolls off the factory line in the small village of Wollaston, England. Taking its name from its date of birth, the eight-eyelet 1460 boot is born.

1990s
Dr. Martens begins exporting its footwear to the US. Originally carried by small independent retailers, the brand quickly explodes into the mainstream.

1994
Half of all Dr. Martens wearers are now women.

2003
The brand collaborates with illustrators, artists, fashion designers and street artists to make their mark on the original '1460' boot. The collection is showcased around the world, from Tokyo, to London, New York and Paris.

Elastoplast®

Elastoplast® offers uncomplicated and innovative solutions to everyday problems and pains to helping people to get on with enjoying their lives. The brand has built a solid reputation as the most recognisable and trusted first aid dressings brand in the UK, with 97% of people recognising the brand and 81% of people having bought an Elastoplast product (Source: IPSOS Brand Image Monitor).

Offerings and Values

While the traditional adhesive fabric plasters remain the brand's most recognised product, Elastoplast now encompasses a portfolio of wound care solutions, ranging from core plasters to advanced wound care.

The core range of Elastoplast plasters includes everything to meet the needs of an everyday cut and graze: from traditional fabric plasters, water resistant plasters, and cushioned plasters for extra padding, to plasters for sensitive skin.

With children being the most susceptible to cuts and grazes, Elastoplast was the first brand to introduce the character plaster to the market – designed to ensure that small misfortunes are quickly forgotten – with the launch of Mickey Mouse©Disney plasters in 1989. Over the years, a series of character

plasters has followed, including other familiar faces from Disney.

Following the success of new additions to the Elastoplast range such as Burn Relief Spray and Burn Plasters as well as Scar Reduction Patches, Beiersdorf has extended the Elastoplast brand into the Sports Supports market with the launch of Elastoplast Sport in September 2003. Less than two years after its launch, the Elastoplast Sport sub-range was one of the leading brands in the Sports Supports market, with its range of tapes, elasticated and adjustable neoprene supports.

Innovations and Promotions

As market leader Elastoplast is seen as a strong innovator, thanks most recently to the Elastoplast Spray Plaster, launched in

February 2006. The Spray Plaster delivers a transparent, breathable film that seals the wound to block out water, dirt and germs. The formulation dries quickly to provide a safe and flexible means of covering cuts and grazes on awkward areas such as knuckles and elbows, as well as other parts of the body for more than two days, gradually disappearing as the wound heals. It has the added benefit of being waterproof and transparent, so that wounds can be observed without disturbing the healing process.

At the beginning of 2005, Elastoplast launched SILVERHEALING™, the first range of mass-market plasters and dressings in the UK to harness the natural antiseptic power of silver. Adapted from silver technology used in hospitals, the wound pad contains

New plasters containing silver.
They kill germs.

Life happens. Elastoplast helps to heal.

Things you didn't know

The gutta-percha plaster (1882) was the first plaster to offer an accurate dosage of medication for skin treatments.

Hansaplast First-aid bandages – the earliest available for consumers to treat their wounds without a doctor – became available for the first time in 1931.

When asked, unprompted, to think of a first aid dressings brand, 42% of people named Elastoplast first (Source: IPSOS Brand Image Monitor).

To date, Beiersdorf has produced more than 16 billion metres of Hansaplast and Elastoplast plasters – enough to circle the globe 400 times.

---

silver under a polyethylene net. On contact with moisture in the wound, silver ions are released, destroying bacterial cell structures and inhibiting their functions, killing germs and bacteria.

Elastoplast has a strong promotional heritage with campaigns such as the hugely popular 'There, there, there' campaign in the 1980s. In 2005 Martin Johnson was the ideal celebrity endorsement for the Elastoplast Sport range; and the current Plasterman campaign supporting the launch of Silverhealing features the distinctive voice of Brian Blessed in its TV ad. While Elastoplast's brand values remain the same today, technological progression has led to the development of the advanced wound care market. This means that education is more important than ever in ensuring that consumers are fully aware of the scope of products available to treat their everyday wounds.

Consumer education is achieved via an integrated marketing strategy incorporating above and below-the-line advertising, PR, online, ambient media and point of sale.

The first aid dressings category, which includes plasters, dressings, bandages and tapes, is worth £60.9 million, with plasters or 'strips' constituting 60% of all category sales (Source: IRI).

The market is seasonal, peaking during the summer months when children are most susceptible to injuries and people stock up to go on holiday. Although new product development accounts for a small proportion of the category – around 5% of value sales – innovation is key to driving growth and interest in what is already a mature market.

There is a high degree of overlap between first aid dressings purchasers and purchasers of antiseptics, foot care and supports (Source: IPSOS Brand Image Monitor Study).

Achievements and Future Prospects

Acquired by Beiersdorf from Smith & Nephew in 2000, Elastoplast has built an enviable reputation as the leading brand in the first aid dressings market and as such the brand is synonymous with plasters. Although own-label dominates the category, with a 47.9% share, Elastoplast is the number one brand in the market, with a 29.1% share (Source: IRI).

The brand's SILVERHEALING fabric plasters won the award for best health product at the 2006 Product of the Year Awards – an award voted for by a nationally representative, independent survey of 12,593 individuals. In addition, 2005 saw the

SILVERHEALING range win the Boots Health & Beauty magazine Customer Healthcare Award Scheme (first aid category).

2006 sees Beiersdorf UK celebrate its 100th anniversary.

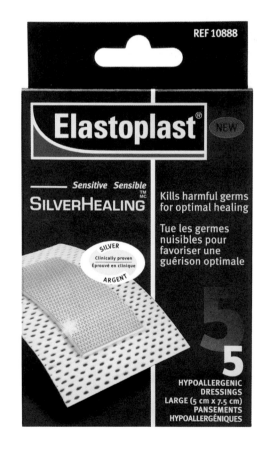

1882
Paul Beiersdorf takes out a patent to protect the manufacture of his medicated plaster, which soon grows to a range of 105 products.

1886
Lohmann AG invents Elastoplast (Tensoplast) Fabric – an innovative cloth spread with adhesive.

1927
The British patent and the rights to the trademarks of Elastoplast in all countries that were part of the British Empire are bought by Smith & Nephew.

2000
Beiersdorf buys back the rights to sell and manufacture Elastoplast products in the UK and Commonwealth countries.

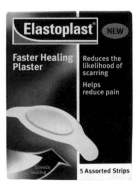

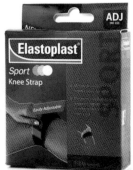

For more than 115 years, Energizer has played a vital role in how people live, work and communicate. In the early 21st century, Energizer is better placed than ever to offer consumers the batteries required for their power-hungry devices such as digital cameras and MP3 players. With the widest range of batteries, including Energizer Ultimate Lithium and Rechargeables to power these high-tech devices, Energizer will continue to build its brands and market to consumers to continue raising awareness of the range.

Offerings and Values

Energizer, a leading manufacturer of batteries and torches, has been powering devices for the past century.

Today Energizer's extensive range caters for every need from standard household devices to high-drain digital devices, such as portable DVD players and digital cameras. Energizer's battery product portfolio spans lithium, alkaline, carbon zinc, miniature, rechargeable, hearing aid, watch and electronic batteries, with more than six billion battery cells produced annually.

Innovations and Promotions

Launched in June 2005, Energizer Ultimate Lithium, the world's longest lasting battery in high-tech devices (Source: ANSI/IEC Industry approved device tests), is proven to last up to seven times longer than standard alkaline batteries in digital cameras, that's 630 photos versus only 90 from ordinary alkaline batteries and up to 5.5 hours longer in an MP3 player. Energizer Ultimate Lithium is not only unique to Energizer but also unique to the market place. Available in the two bestselling sizes, AA and AAA, the new Energizer Ultimate Lithium battery is aimed at those that want to get the very best out of their high-tech devices.

The Energizer 15 Minute Charger, launched in 2005, provides the fastest and most economic way to charge 2200 mAh rechargeable batteries that power high-drain battery-operated devices such as digital cameras and MP3 players.

The 15 Minute Charger was awarded 'Product of the Year' at the 2006 Product of the Year Awards, which recognise and reward new FMCG product innovation in the UK through a TNS survey of over 12,500 consumers.

Following on from the success of the 15 Minute Charger, Energizer has launched the Ultra Compact Charger, which is not only the smallest charger on the market (shrinking to half the size when not in use) but it also takes both AA and AAA batteries, making it versatile.

Throughout 2005 and 2006, Energizer has sponsored the Gadget Show on Five, which attracts an audience of key battery consumers and gadget lovers. The opening and closing credits and break bumpers, feature an enthusiastic young inventor pitching new ideas for gadgets to his boss.

FOR TODAY'S HIGH-TECH GADGETS

Sponsors of The Gadget Show

This year, to underpin Energizer's market-leading position in Photo Lithium, the credits will close with brand icon Mr Energizer catching an Ultimate Lithium battery and the strapline: 'Energizer Ultimate Lithium. For Today's High-Tech Gadgets'.

The sponsorship is a demonstration of Energizer's aggressive growth strategy focusing on high-tech devices and gadgets within the UK and will be fully supported in-store through point of sale material carrying the message 'Energizer. Powering The Gadget Show'.

Market Context

The total UK battery market is worth over £317 million (Source: ACNielsen & GfK combined data). Whilst Energizer is a strong number two in the overall battery marketplace with over a quarter of the total

market (Source: ACNielsen), Energizer also holds number one positions in rechargeables, electronic cells, carbon zinc, photo lithium and within the impulse channel of trade (Source: ACNielsen). In addition, Energizer also holds a number one position in torches, and in the high street 'super premium' battery sector with Energizer Ultimate (Source: GfK December 2005).

General purpose batteries (such as AA and AAA cells) continue to dominate the battery market with 85% share of sales (Source: ACNielsen & GfK March 2006), whilst the specialist/electronic battery sector is growing rapidly at 35% growth year-on-year (Source: ACNielsen MAT March 25th 2006); driven primarily by the rapid increase in high-drain, high-tech devices. Devices such as digital cameras and MP3 players have high-drain characteristics, requiring quick bursts

of power, while simultaneously requiring consistent and constant power.

Achievements and Future Prospects

In 1959, Energizer revolutionised the battery industry, introducing alkaline battery technology that is still powering the majority of devices today. Energizer Holdings, Inc. became an independent, publicly held company in 2000 and today is one of the world's largest manufacturers of dry cell batteries and torches. In 2003 Energizer acquired the worldwide Schick-Wilkinson Sword (SWS) Company, adding world class brands in the personal care category to the Energizer portfolio.

In total there are 10,000 Energizer associates who manufacture and sell batteries and torches in 150 countries across the world. Six billion battery cells are produced annually by Energizer, powering equipment in all corners of the world.

1886
Brush Electric Company executive W. H. Lawrence forms the National Carbon Company (NCC), which later becomes The Eveready Battery Company.

1896
Energizer markets the very first battery for consumer use. 'The Columbia' is six inches tall and used to power home telephones.

1958
Energizer launches the first batteries for use in transistor radios and rechargeable nickel-cadmium batteries.

1959
Energizer launches the first standard alkaline battery.

1960
Energizer introduces the first silver oxide button cell for use in miniature hearing aids and watches.

1986
Ralston Purina, Co., headquartered in St. Louis, Missouri, purchases The Eveready Battery Company, the holding company of Energizer brand batteries and torches.

2000
Energizer Holdings, Inc. becomes an independent, publicly held company.

2003
Energizer acquires the worldwide Schick-Wilkinson Sword (SWS) Company, adding world class brands in the personal care category to the Energizer portfolio.

2004
The Energizer Ultimate battery – the company's 'best ever alkaline' is launched.

2005
Energizer Ultimate Lithium is launched.

www.uk.pg.com

The Fairy name first appeared in 1898 on a pale yellow bar of soap. Today the brand represents a range of products renowned for their cleaning ability and caring nature. Over 13 million UK households buy 150 million bottles of Fairy each year, 57% of the total market (Source: ACNielsen 2005), making it the nation's favourite washing up brand. In 2005 turnover topped £100 million.

Offerings and Values

The Fairy brand has stood for 'sparkling performance' for over 100 years, with principles built upon cleaning and its caring nature. Fairy's dishwashing brand, an iconic household emblem for nearly 50 years, has maintained market leadership through its performance; lasting up to 50% longer than any other brand (Source: Laboratory Testing).

Brand communication is simple, highlighting performance through mileage or cleaning messages. The customer comes first, with Fairy operating a free-phone advice line and money back guarantee. Furthermore, Fairy does not produce products for other brands.

Over the years, the 'mild green Fairy liquid' slogan, made famous by Nanette Newman, has given way to a more dynamic brand position, featuring celebrity chef Ainsley Harriott. In addition, new products have been developed to combat stubborn, burnt on stains or for quick cleaning.

Fairy supports a number of charities and in 2005 became the UK's biggest fundraiser for 'Make-A-Wish', which grants children with life-threatening illnesses special wishes. Its corporate social responsibility policy means it donates products for use during natural disasters; it is recognised by wildlife experts as the best product for cleaning birds following oil spills.

Innovations and Promotions

During the 1950s, most people used powders and crystals to wash dishes. After conducting vigorous tests, Fairy launched a dish washing product, Fairy Liquid. By the end of its first year six out of 10 people in the UK had bought it. The first Fairy Liquid TV advertising campaign soon followed leading to a host of celebrity endorsements, including actresses Leslie Ash and Nanette Newman and, more recently, chefs Ainsley Harriott, Anthony Worrell Thomson and Gary Rhodes.

To fit in with modern kitchens and times, Fairy changed its signature white bottle to an ergonomically designed transparent bottle which is easier to control and contains concentrated washing up liquid.

2003 saw the launch of Fairy Powerspray, a leave on cleaner that removes tough, burnt on food. Fairy Active Foam was launched in 2005, an everyday washing up foam in a pump bottle with grease-cutting performance enhancers. Fairy Liquid, meanwhile, remained powerful enough to tackle grease yet mild enough to be certified by the British Skin Foundation.

In 2006 Fairy introduced two new products to the Dishwasher cleaning range: Fairy Active Bursts and Fairy Powder Bursts. Fairy Active Bursts was the first all-in-one detergent plus liquid product, requiring no unwrapping prior to use.

As part of the Fairy Active Bursts launch promotion Fairy poked fun at its traditional 'Hands That Do Dishes' campaign, replacing it with the slogan 'For Hands that Don't Do Dishes' and glamorous celebrity endorsers such as model Jodie Kidd, and home design expert and TV presenter Naomie Cleaver. It also featured photography by Helena Christensen.

Market Context

The dish cleaning market is divided into sink and dishwasher sectors, with Fairy leading sink and Finish dishwasher.

The sink washing sector is a mature market with over 300 million bottles sold annually. Its value has increased in the last year by 7% with volume increasing by 2%, driven by trends for specialist products such as Anti-Bacterial liquids and Fairy Powerspray. These trends have offset a previous decline in the market, fuelled by the increase of dishwasher penetration. Fairy defines the UK's washing-up detergents market with a 57% share, over six times more than competitors Persil and Morning Fresh.

Dishwasher tablet sales are led by Finish. Fairy joined the market in 2006 and is now the second largest brand. The market is split between detergent only and multi-benefit products. Recent introductions, such as the 'no need to unwrap' sector already make up over £35 million of the £200 million market (Source: ACNielsen May 2006).

Achievements and Future Prospects

Fairy has grown in recent years to become the UK's top selling brand across the household category (Source: ACNielsen April 2006). Following the launch of Fairy Active Burst and Fairy Powder Burst, it is the only national brand to offer a complete range of products in both sink and dishwasher categories.

Turnover has been driven in recent years by Fairy Powerspray and Fairy Active Foam launches, which added £9 million revenue, driving Fairy to top £100 million. This looks set to rise further following the growth in sales of Fairy Active Bursts.

In 2005 all Fairy products became certified by the Good Housekeeping Institute and accredited by the British Skin Foundation whilst new Fairy Active Foam was voted Product of The Year by UK shoppers (Source: TNS).

In early 2006 new Fairy dishwashing 'pods' took a 12% share of the dishwasher market. Meanwhile four new Fairy scents were launched for the sink; Lemon Twister, Apple Quake, Strawberry Flame and Passion Flower Storm. In the laundry stakes Fairy Non-Bio rivalled Persil Non-Bio for market leadership and Fairy Fabric Softener was launched.

1898
Fairy Soap launches through Thomas Hedley & Sons.

1930
Procter & Gamble acquire the brand and Fairy Baby trademark.

1987
Lemon scented Fairy Liquid is introduced alongside Fairy Original.

1989
Fairy non-bio laundry product launches, for sensitive skin.

1997
Fairy Liquid with anti-bacterial agents is introduced.

2003
Fairy Powerspray launches, for tough burnt on stains.

2005
Shoppers vote Fairy Active Foam Product of the Year (Source: TNS).

2006
Fairy Active Bursts launches and sales top £100 million.

GE&RGE

George is a fashion brand that designs affordable, stylish ranges for the whole family. On average, eight million customers shop at George every week in the UK, generating sales in excess of £1 billion. George clothing is sold in 302 UK stores and more than 3,000 stores across the world, including Germany, Japan, Korea, Mexico, Puerto Rico, Argentina, the US, Brazil and Canada.

Offerings and Values

The George range is designed in-house by a team of designers who keep abreast of the forthcoming trends and influences from the world of fashion. Their inspiration comes from trade fairs, buying trips, celebrity influences and listening to George customers.

The core George product range is aimed at the 25-44 age group and includes womenswear, menswear, childrenswear, schoolwear, footwear, nightwear and lingerie. G21 is a range aimed at the fashion conscious female aged 16-21 years and offers new products in stores every four weeks. Fast Fashion is aimed at women in their 20s and features products that go from design to store in eight weeks.

George also offers maternity wear, swimwear, petites, skiwear and a childrens' dressing up range.

Style, quality and value are the principles that define the George brand. As a value fashion retailer, George customers expect value for money, but the proposition is not just about price – customers demand quality and style. Listening to customers is key for George marketeers, who hold regular focus groups to understand customers' preferences.

Innovations and Promotions

The George brand is famous for innovation. In February 2006, George became the first supermarket to design a bridal range offering wedding dresses, bridesmaids' dresses, wedding shoes and wedding lingerie. The fact that people could buy a wedding dress from George for £60 created a lot of interest and generated extensive PR coverage both in print and broadcast media.

In March 2006 George launched a range of 'Must Haves' for womenswear, menswear and childrenswear, bringing customers the latest key pieces at incredible prices.

George invests £8 million in marketing and promotional activity in the UK, which

includes TV and press advertising, in-store marketing, ASDA magazine's 16 fashion pages per month, Mini-Magazine, PR, website and customer research.

George uses TV advertising to support each season. In Spring 2006, it focused on the launch of George's 'Must Haves', which are the latest womenswear trends, updated every month. The ads featured one model wearing the three 'Must Have' outfits for April.

George Home launched in April 2006, taking George's style credentials from fashion into furnishings. The George Home collection comprises 2,000 new products, ranging from bedding to bath accessories, cushions to candles.

George is committed to cause related marketing. Together, George and ASDA are the biggest fundraisers for breast cancer in the UK. George and ASDA are celebrating 10 years of 'Tickled Pink' this year. Each year George designs a range of 'pink' clothing including T-shirts, lingerie, footwear and accessories. Liz Hurley, Jennifer Anniston, Jerry Hall and Scarlett Johannsen are amongst the many celebrities who have donated their time to the campaign and been photographed wearing a George 'Tickled Pink' T-shirt by world-renowned fashion photographers including David Bailey and Bryan Adams who kindly waived their fees in support of the campaign.

Market Context

Putting clothing in the shopping trolley next to the weekly groceries has become commonplace to British shoppers. Indeed, in 2005, 57.9% of all shoppers had bought an item of clothing or footwear in supermarkets, compared to 45.5% in 2002 (Source: TNS Worldpanel Fashion, Total Clothing, Footwear & Accessories 52 w/e March 5th 2006).

Of all shoppers, 35.5% have bought an item of clothing or footwear in George, and this has risen from 26.5% in 2002 (Source: TNS Worldpanel Fashion, Total Clothing, Footwear & Accessories 52 w/e March 5th 2006).

The total UK market for fashion, clothing, footwear and accessories is worth £30.3 billion and George's value share is 3.4%, while its volume share is 8.9%, making George the second biggest retailer by volume (Source: TNS Worldpanel Fashion, Total Clothing, Footwear & Accessories 52 w/e March 5th 2006).

Achievements and Future Prospects

George is a brand that has continually evolved. In the 16 years since the first George department launched in an ASDA store, the brand has evolved to become a high street retailer and stand-alone store in the UK and a global fashion brand in 10 countries.

Today one in 12 people in the UK own a piece of George clothing (Source: Mintel). As testament to the brand's popularity, it has won many accolades, including Best Value for Money Retailer and Childrenswear Retailer of the Year by Prima High Street Fashion Awards and Best Childrens' clothing brand by Tommy's Parent Friendly Awards.

When William Grant, founder of Glenfiddich®, began building his distillery more than a century ago, he could hardly have dreamt that today Glenfiddich would have grown to become the world's favourite single malt Scotch whisky. Sold in 180 countries, Glenfiddich is found in homes and bars in every continent. Five generations on, William Grant & Sons Ltd remains one of the very few independent family-owned Scotch whisky companies, with direct descendants of William Grant driving the company forward today.

Offerings and Values

The Glenfiddich brand has grown to provide a comprehensive range of single malts. Alongside Glenfiddich Special Reserve 12 Year Old sits Glenfiddich Caoran Reserve 12 Year Old, Glenfiddich Solera Reserve 15 Year Old, Glenfiddich Ancient Reserve 18 Year Old, Glenfiddich Gran Reserva 21 Year Old and Glenfiddich 30 Year Old.

The Glenfiddich Distillery has produced some of the world's rarest single malts including the Glenfiddich Vintage Reserve, the Glenfiddich 50 Year Old and the world's oldest single malt Scotch whisky, the 64 year-old Glenfiddich Rare Collection 1937. At the Glenfiddich Distillery there is a single-minded dedication to craftsmanship and quality throughout every stage of production, which ensures that only the finest single malt Scotch whisky is produced.

Glenfiddich single malt Scotch whisky is created using the finest malted barley and a single source of crystal clear spring water from the Robbie Dhu Springs. It is the only Highland whisky to be produced using a single source of natural spring water.

Glenfiddich's whisky-making methods are exactly the same today as they were in 1887. The Distillery still employs the traditional skills of dedicated craftsmen, from the coppersmith who tends the stills to the coopers who build and maintain the casks. The Glenfiddich Malt Master, only the fifth since 1887, ensures that the quality of the Glenfiddich range is never compromised.

Innovations and Promotions

William Grant & Sons remains one of the innovators in Scotch whisky. From the distinctive triangular green bottle to the unique production process used for the

Solera Reserve, Glenfiddich has always been progressive. It has challenged malt whisky conventions and will continue to do so.

The Glenfiddich Distillery, offering tours in six languages, welcomes more than 80,000 visitors each year. A new visitor centre opened in 2005 to accommodate the influx of tourists from around the world who can enjoy the tour free of charge. The centre features a short film created by famous Hollywood director Ridley Scott's firm, Ridley Scott Associates, and has already been awarded a Five Star Grading by the Scottish Tourist Board.

Market Context

Glenfiddich Single Malt Scotch Whisky is the world's biggest selling single malt. It outsells its nearest rivals by two to one (Source: IWSR).

Glenfiddich Single Malt Scotch Whisky created the single malt category more than 40 years ago, when the family exported it to England in the early 1960s. It has remained the world's market leading single malt ever since.

Today, more than three quarters of the bottles of Glenfiddich that leave the Distillery are sold overseas.

Achievements and Future Prospects

The quality of Glenfiddich contributed to William Grant & Sons winning the International Wine & Spirit Competition's Distiller of the Year award in 1999 and 2000, and the International Spirits Challenge Distiller of the Year in 2001 and 2005. Glenfiddich received three gold medals at the 2005 International Wine & Spirit Competition, more than any other single malt Scotch whisky.

Today in the UK, Glenfiddich is involved with a series of high-profile events. The annual Glenfiddich Food & Drink Awards, now in their 36th year, recognise excellence in food and drink writing, publishing and broadcasting. In 2005 celebrity chef Gordon Ramsay scooped Food and Drink Personality of the Year.

The Glenfiddich Spirit of Scotland Awards were established to celebrate Scottish talent. They recognise the

individuals who inspire Scottish people and lead the way in Scottish culture. Winners include author Ian Rankin, tennis star Andrew Murray, singer Sharleen Spiteri and actor Ewan McGregor.

Glenfiddich Independent Mix is a series of music events featuring leading live musicians and DJs. The events provide a backdrop for Glenfiddich Classic Serves, which have been created for Glenfiddich by leading drinks mixologists.

The Glenfiddich Artists in Residence Programme, established in 2002, gives internationally acclaimed artists the opportunity to stay at the Distillery and take inspiration from the unique atmosphere and environment. In 2006, artists from the USA, Canada, Taiwan and Iceland were in residence.

1887

William and his seven sons built The Glenfiddich Distillery with their bare hands and the first spirit flowed from the stills on Christmas Day.

1963

The single malt Scotch whisky category is created when Glenfiddich is first exported to England.

1974

David Stewart is appointed Master Blender of William Grant & Sons. His achievements include the introduction of Glenfiddich Solera Reserve 15 Year Old, the first single malt to use the innovative Solera maturation process.

2006

Five generations on, William Grant & Sons is one of the very few Scotch whisky companies to remain in the hands of the family that founded it.

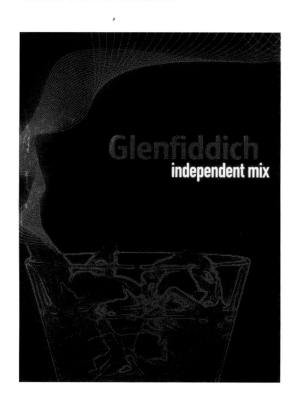

HITACHI
Inspire the Next

www.hitachi-eu.com

The name Hitachi literally means sunrise, reflecting the company's founding philosophy of contributing to people and society through technology. This philosophy has helped Hitachi become one of the world's largest corporations, with a range of over 20,000 products and more than 300,000 employees worldwide.

Offerings and Values

In Europe, Hitachi has 88 companies, employing 5,300 people with revenue exceeding US$6.3 billion. The company's focus in Europe is on seven key growth sectors: digital consumer electronics; power generation; transportation systems; construction machinery; air conditioning; storage systems and automotive components & systems. Its extensive operations include the Hitachi Design Centre in Milan and research & development facilities in France, Germany, Ireland and the UK, as well as a number of manufacturing plants. Although primarily known for its hardware products, Hitachi also offers financial services and solutions, logistics solutions and has recently introduced its expertise in consultancy to Europe. Not all of the Hitachi companies in Europe trade using the Hitachi name. One example is Maxell, a leading supplier of energy and multimedia products, e.g. recordable DVDs.

Innovations and Promotions

Worldwide, the Hitachi Group, which comprises some 956 companies, covers a wide range of business areas, from home electronics, automotive, power and industrial to medical. In order to continue making the industry-leading high-tech products that have always been its hallmark, the company invests millions of dollars in research and development every year.

To support these innovations, Hitachi has launched a new, pan-European corporate brand campaign that incorporates the company's first significant TV advertising for over 10 years. The campaign, which is intended to run over two to three years with a significant investment, focuses on a series of consumer and business benefits that Hitachi can deliver in Europe, communicated around the central theme of how 'Hitachi's technology and know-how improves your

life'. The campaign illustrates this theme through some of its leading edge product areas – consumer electronics, data storage, rail, power, construction and air conditioning – to improve the understanding and appeal of Hitachi's brand.

Designed to create a more unified and consistent brand, the new campaign reflects Hitachi's commitment to significantly expand its overseas business and is the first stage in a three-year corporate brand communication investment.

The media mix comprises press and online activity in Hitachi's four key markets (UK, Germany, France and Spain), supported by TV advertising in France, Spain and the UK. In the future the campaign will be extended into other markets, and will communicate other

benefits which Hitachi delivers. In addition to the Group campaign, future marketing activity undertaken by Hitachi's individual European businesses is likely to adopt a similar look and feel.

Market Context
Most consumers' first experience with Hitachi is via its consumer electronics products. The UK market for TVs, video recorders and camcorders has grown steadily over the past decade and is concentrated into a few multinational companies, with the five largest companies, including Sony, Matsushita and Phillips, accounting for more than 70% of total volume sales (Source: Euromonitor).

The market is forecast to grow by 5% to reach a value of more than £4 billion in 2007 (Source: Euromonitor). Television

will remain the largest sector in 2007, accounting for more than 90% of all value sales (Source: Euromonitor).

Achievements and Future Prospects
Hitachi Ltd, headquartered in Tokyo, Japan, is a leading global electronics company, with approximately 347,000 employees worldwide. Its consolidated sales for the fiscal year 2005 (ended March 31st 2006) totalled 9,464 billion yen (£45 billion) – a 5% increase on the previous year. With a revenue of US$84 billion (£48.3 billon) the previous year, Hitachi is ranked as the 23rd largest company in the world by Global Fortune 500.

Looking ahead, Hitachi has set ambitious targets to improve brand recognition and understanding in the key markets of the UK, France and Germany through its new pan-European corporate brand campaign developed in partnership with Loewy.

1910
Namihei Odaira opens an electrical repair shop in Japan and Hitachi is born. The company succeeds in the first domestic manufacture of three 3.6775 kW electric motors.

1932
Hitachi makes its first electric refrigerator.

1959
Hitachi completes development of electronic computers based on transistors and establishes Hitachi America Ltd.

1969
The company begins developing and mass-producing all-transistor colour televisions.

1974
Hitachi releases its first series of general purpose large-scale computers.

2000
Hitachi establishes its third European lab, Sophia-Antipolis in France, specialising in broadband communications and intelligent transport systems.

2002
Hitachi develops the world's first silent liquid-cooling notebook PC, and the world's smallest (0.3mm) non contact IC chip.

2006
Hitachi is engaged in diverse lines of business and is rapidly exploring new businesses with high potential for enhancing corporate value.

IBM has a fundamental belief in progress, science and the improvability of the human condition. With its unique capabilities, IBM sees it as its responsibility to create opportunity and prosperity for businesses, industries, society and the world.

Offerings and Values

One of the core values collectively defined by IBM today is that innovation matters, and the shape of today's business world reflects this. Over the years, IBM has learned how and where to apply innovation to help businesses get results. And although it has always delivered innovation to clients, today IBM goes much further. Now it helps them innovate and collaborate to reach their goal. As companies realise that their continued success depends on completely re-thinking their approach to innovation, the real role of the technology is to enable business transformation. Furthermore, at the heart of each transformation there has to be a core business insight – and increasingly it's this that is the most important capability IBM demonstrates. In fact, such an insight drove the organisation's own restructuring process, with IBM Global Business Services

also aligned to meet specific customer requirements.

Here are some examples of what this innovation-focused approach has achieved:

Facing increasing pressure to raise productivity and cut drug development costs, a leading pharmaceutical provider, Bayer, was determined to bring new drugs to market faster. Working with IBM Global Business Services, the company replaced its in-house Electronic Data Capture (EDC) application and re-engineered its processes worldwide to extract maximum value from the new system. This reduced the time spent gathering data from weeks to near real-time and made clinical trial information processing more efficient, so drugs can be developed more quickly.

The All England Lawn Tennis Club hosts one of the world's most important sporting events, The Championships at Wimbledon.

For the past 17 years, IBM has worked with The Club to help it meet increasing business demands and to optimise revenue streams through e-commerce and increase the efficiency with which The Championships are organised and run. The result is that more courtside statistics, analysis and insights are available each year, and tennis fans around the world are brought closer to the action.

Innovations and Promotions

Between 1993 and 2004, IBM climbed from the 282nd position in Interbrand's league table of the world's most valuable brands to number three. Here it remained throughout 2005 (Source: Financial World, Interbrand 1994 and Business Week, Interbrand 2004).

It achieved this rise by making huge strides in its marketing strategy. In 1993, IBM was using 70 different advertising agencies. With no central theme and a

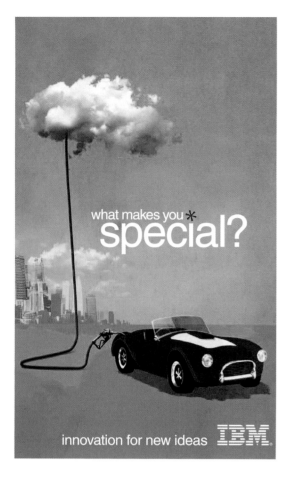

what makes you * **special?**

innovation for new ideas **IBM.**

☎ THE WORLD'S HELP DESK

CALLER: *WIMBLEDON*

PROBLEM: *HOW CAN PEOPLE GET CLOSER TO THE ACTION?*

SOLUTION: *IBM technology sends scores and stats anywhere in seconds. Even to this banner.*

WHAT DO YOU WANT TO SEE?

ON DEMAND BUSINESS **IBM.**

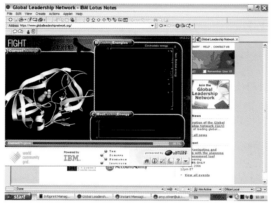

mixture of layout styles, typefaces and even logos, the brand identity had been severely eroded. So, IBM made the decision to consolidate its communications with one core communications partner, around the world.

Ogilvy & Mather was appointed to develop the first global advertising campaign launched by IBM. The result, 'Solutions for a small planet', ran in 47 countries and 26 languages. It was the first step in repositioning IBM as a market-focused, service-orientated solutions provider.

But it was the next development that helped the brand reclaim its leadership. As IBM became aware of the enormous benefits that the internet could provide to businesses of all kinds, the company's solutions and communications had to reflect and deliver this new vision. IBM launched its second integrated global campaign, alerting and educating the market about the potential of 'e-business'.

In 2006, the 'What Makes You Special' campaign was launched, establishing the need for businesses to start thinking differently about innovation, and weaving it into their thinking, their products, and their people.

Market Context

Businesses everywhere, in every sector, have to compete with the ceaseless march of globalisation and the incessant competitive activity it creates. Gone are the days when a decisive cost cutting exercise would help a company regain the upper hand. Today's business leaders must look for new ways to stand out clearly in markets that are constantly in a state of flux.

This new era brings with it a seemingly endless stream of new technological

resources and business solutions that help organisations of every kind identify and grasp the countless opportunities that now surround them. These opportunities will enable them to share knowledge, ideas and share solutions, gain competitive advantage and stay ahead of the game.

Achievements and Future Prospects

During 2005, IBM has again gained an impressive list of innovation credentials. These include receiving more US patents than any other company – an impressive 1,100 patents more. This is the eighth consecutive year that IBM was awarded more than 2,000 US patents. However, it is the results that IBM achieves for its customers that make it the world's third most valuable brand – and gaining in value each year (Source: Business Week, Interbrand 2005).

The company's innovations benefit more than its customers, however, with a fundamental belief in progress, science and the improvability of the human condition, IBM sees it as its responsibility to create opportunity and prosperity for businesses, industries, society and the world. Each year, IBM Corporate Community Relations invests over US$140 million globally in a range of large scale, global programmes focusing primarily on innovative uses of technology in educational contexts to help raise standards of achievement.

For instance, IBM recently announced that two advocacy groups, The Human Rights Campaign and Gay Men's Health Crisis, are now part of its new research effort to help battle AIDS by using the massive computational power of the World Community Grid.

1924
The International Business Machines Corporation is established by Thomas Watson, providing companies with the latest in typewriters and calculating machines.

1935
When the new Social Security Act requires the US Government to keep employment records, only IBM is able to meet the huge demand for punch card data-processors.

1952
IBM develops a range of mainframes, compatible with multiple printers, drives and other peripherals, establishing IBM as an industry leader.

1980
IBM Ireland sets up an international software development centre, one of only four in Europe.

1981
The IBM Personal Computer is unveiled and becomes an overnight sensation.

1993
IBM Global Services is launched.

1995
IBM makes network computing – later to be called e-business – the company's overarching strategy.

2006
IBM celebrates its 50th anniversary in Ireland.

Imodium™

Imodium provides a modern solution to the common problem of acute diarrhoea. Imodium represents an empowered choice for the consumer to get on with their daily activities. With just one dose of Imodium, sufferers can be free from diarrhoea for the rest of the day by slowing their bowel rhythm back to normal.

Users must always read the leaflet.

Offerings and Values

As an expert in diarrhoea treatment, Imodium offers a range of products to specifically cater for sufferers of diarrhoea and their individual symptoms.

The original Imodium Capsules can provide fast relief, as they can stop diarrhoea with just one dose and get the sufferer's digestive system back to normal. Imodium users want to be able to get on and enjoy their lives with confidence. They are looking for control, peace of mind and a positive outlook.

Imodium Instants and Imodium Instant Melts provide the same benefits as Imodium Capsules while also offering convenient and discreet relief, melting on the tongue with a mint taste and no need for water. Imodium Plus Caplets contain an additional ingredient, 'simeticone', to relieve related cramps and stomach discomfort.

Imodium products contain loperamide which works to relieve diarrhoea by slowing the bowel rhythm back to normal and restoring the normal balance of the digestive system, improving the absorption of fluids and nutrients back into the sufferer's body. Thus Imodium can help shorten the bout of diarrhoea and reduce the disruption to the sufferer's life. Sufferers can, therefore, feel better sooner, with the confidence to get on and take control of their day.

Innovations and Promotions

Before 1960, diarrhoea remedies offered by physicians were usually opiates, such as tincture of opium. Most physicians did this with misgivings, as they knew that opium and its derivatives could create addiction

Superbrands

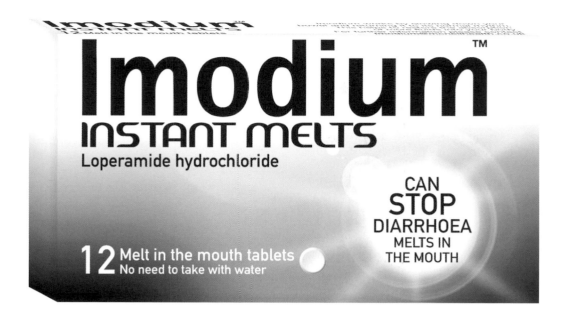

and had undesirable effects on the central nervous system, such as causing stupor and sedation.

Dr Paul Janssen, a Belgian scientist and founder of Janssen Pharmaceutica, set out to separate the anti-diarrhoeal property of opium from the unwanted addictive properties. In 1956 Dr Janssen and his colleagues found a molecule that appeared to have an impact on bowel movements. This compound was diphenoxylate, which worked by slowing down the bowel. It was the first major international drug success for Janssen Pharmaceutica.

Although effective in stopping diarrhoea, diphenoxylate is absorbed into the bloodstream and for this reason it was not felt to be the ideal treatment. From 1956 to 1968 Janssen Pharmaceutica continued in their quest and tested more than 14,000 compounds looking for a more effective and better tolerated drug than diphenoxylate. In 1968 diphenoxin was found to be five times more potent than

diphenoxylate, but the compound was still absorbed into the blood stream and the unwanted side effects on the central nervous system were still present, albeit to a lesser degree.

One year later, in 1969, Dr Janssen and his team of researchers discovered loperamide, a compound that was more effective, well tolerated and longer acting than diphenoxylate and was free of central nervous system effects, even at high dosage levels. The goal of completely separating anti-diarrhoeal and central nervous system activity had been realised.

After nearly five years of further testing and development of this new compound, Janssen Pharmaceutica – by now a Johnson & Johnson Company – launched loperamide as Imodium in 2mg capsules in 1973.

Market Context
Possibly the worst thing about diarrhoea is that it can strike at any time, bringing

inconvenience, worry and often complicating even the most simple of activities. Holidays and business travel can be severely disrupted. It is an incredibly common complaint with almost one third of the UK adult population suffering at one time or another (Source: TGI).

The anti-diarrhoeal market in the UK is worth £42.5 million (Source: IRI). Imodium is the undisputed market leader, with a 58% value share (Source: IRI).

Achievements and Future Prospects
Imodium is sold around the world in more than 120 countries and achieves global sales of more than US$200 million each year.

The Imodium range has collected a wide array of awards over the past decade. Most recently it was named Travel Product of the Year by Boots customers and was highly commended in the 2006 OTC Marketing Awards.

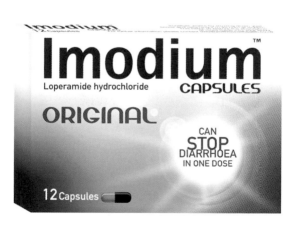

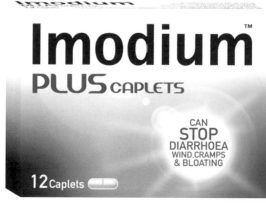

Healthy bowels. Healthy you.

1956	1959	1973	1983	2002	2003
Dr Paul Janssen discovers diphenoxylate.	Janssen Pharmaceutica launches diphenoxylate.	Janssen Pharmaceutica launches Imodium.	Imodium is launched as an over the counter product in pharmacies.	McNeil launches Imodium Instants simultaneously in Germany and the UK.	Imodium Plus Caplets are launched in the UK. Imodium celebrates its 20th anniversary of being available over the counter in pharmacies.

JAEGER

www.jaeger.co.uk

Jaeger began trading in 1884 as a traditional British fashion and lifestyle brand. It now has 51 shops in the UK and Europe, over 25% of which are either new or recently modernised. Jaeger blends heritage with contemporary living to create modern design classics.

Offerings and Values

The Jaeger brand is known for delivering stylish, quality clothing at affordable prices. Its distinctive brand values – Premium, British, Affordable, Elegant, Innovative, Original and Modern Classic – are intrinsic to all it does, from merchandise to store layout.

Positioned as a stylish, premium brand, Jaeger's strategy has taken its characteristics into the 21st century by introducing a modern element that strengthens its appeal. Key to this is delivering relevant merchandise and consistent standards – in every outlet.

The cornerstones of Jaeger's women's collection are its coats, tailoring and knitwear; the majority made from luxurious yarns and fibres such as wool, cashmere, camelhair, silk and angora. True to its British heritage the range also includes timeless fabrics such as pinstripes, herringbones, tweeds and plaids.

Jaeger products are designed to be luxurious, with trims made to the highest specification and attention to detail. Key Jaeger signature colours are black, navy and ivory with strong highlights enhancing the monochrome classics. Although built on modern classics the collections remain relevant, with seasonal trends and key items playing an essential part of each range.

Jaeger's modern classic styling and high quality fabric and make, ensure that each style becomes an investment – a vintage piece of the future.

Innovations and Promotions

The Jaeger strategy is designed to maximise brand potential and drive profitability. It is based around four key values: ensuring the customer is central to decision making; delivering consistency; strengthening and widening the appeal of the brand and aggressively entering new markets. This strategy has been developed to build on the strengths of Jaeger's past and utilises future opportunities in the retail sector.

Jaeger's website (transactional from autumn 2006) has been designed as a virtual store to enable customers to shop online. A further

aid to the business and Customer Relationship Marketing (CRM) is the Jaeger account card, used to communicate to existing and new customers.

September 2005 saw the launch of Jaeger London, a new collection of women's clothing and accessories, featuring supermodel Erin O'Connor as its face. Many of the iconic pieces have been influenced by the Jaeger archive. Distribution of the collection will double in September 2006 when supermodel Jade Parfitt becomes the new face of the collection. At the same time Jaeger London Men's collection will launch, initially in just 10 stores. Both collections support the brand strategy of broadening its appeal and demonstrate that Jaeger's in-house design team creates clothing relevant to modern lifestyles.

In a changing world, casual wear is seen as the new growth area for the menswear business, with 'smart casual' set to complement the formal wear business. Adhering to traditional values the company aims to maintain its drive to produce functional quality products with modern production methods, keeping pace with trends.

Market Context

Jaeger's flagship store was set up after World War II and is still the company's top performing store. Located on Regent Street in central London, it trades on 16,000 square feet spread over four floors.

In addition to its free-standing shops the Jaeger brand is sold through 50 'shop-in-shops' including Harrods and Selfridges in London. Jaeger was the first British brand to operate on a concession basis when it opened in Selfridges in the 1930s.

Jaeger's expansion internationally has accelerated over the last two years providing a solid backdrop for further growth. Japan has been identified as a major burgeoning market; with a flagship store in Tokyo, 11 'shop-in-shops', and a further 20 shops scheduled to open during 2006. Hong Kong, China, and the US are also being assessed as potential new Jaeger markets.

Accessories and gifts are Jaeger's fastest growing product areas. New developments in the last year include the expansion of handbags and jewellery and the launch of the Jaeger beach collection. In spring/summer 2006, the Jaeger Barcelona bag became the season's 'must have' accessory, selling out within days. 2006 sees the launch of the first Jaeger shoe collection, an exclusive range manufactured in Italy.

For autumn 2006, the Jaeger flagship store will undergo major refurbishment, launching the Jaeger Café, designed to be a key meeting place on London's Regent Street.

Achievements and Future Prospects

Jaeger's 122-year history provides it with a solid platform for future growth. Its key

unique selling point is the brand's in-house design team that promotes product development and the use of luxury fabrics. By investing in this team Jaeger stands at the helm of premium fashion retailing.

Historically, tailoring was always at the forefront of a gentleman's wardrobe. Jaeger menswear retains its prime position in the market place today, despite a changing manufacturing landscape – like many of its contemporaries the brand has moved production 'offshore' to compete successfully within a complex marketplace.

Jaeger's aggressive expansion programme is central to its growth strategy, targeting both domestic and international markets. A new store-opening programme will see a total of 118 retail outlets in the UK and Europe by the end of 2006, increasing Jaeger's global network by 50% over the next three years.

1844
British accountant, Lewis Tomalin, sets up Jaeger's first store, Doctor Jaeger's Sanitary Wollen System.

2003
Entrepreneur Harold Tillman, acquires the brand.

2004
Belinda Earl (previous head of Debenhams) joins as chief executive.

2005
Jaeger London, a new collection for women, launches.

2006
The Barcelona bag sells out within days of launching.

Also in 2006, Jaeger café opens in Regent Street's flagship store.

Celebrating 100 years in existence in 2006, 'the original sunshine breakfast' of Kellogg's Corn Flakes is the oldest and one of the most well-known cereals in the UK. Almost three million bowls of Kellogg's Corn Flakes are eaten every day in the UK (Source: TNS 2005). The brand has been driven to such success by a belief first perpetuated by founder W K Kellogg that cereals provide an integral part of the diet as a high carbohydrate, low-fat food.

Offerings and Values

Kellogg's Corn Flakes are golden flakes of toasted corn that provide 25% of an adult's daily allowance of vitamins and minerals such as B1, B2, B6, B12, folic acid and 17% of the RDA of the mineral iron.

The founding principle of the company was to make quality products for a healthier world. This remains as true today as it was 100 years ago. When Kellogg's started trading in the UK in 1924, a cooked breakfast was very much the norm and people had very little awareness of cereal and its benefits. Within a period of 10 years, Kellogg's succeeded in revolutionising people's breakfast eating habits and cereal has remained a firm favourite over the decades.

Today Kellogg's is committed to providing wholesome, nutritional and tasty products for people of all ages and supporting an active lifestyle. It continues this commitment through the WK Kellogg Institute for Food and Nutrition Research, which opened in 1997 in Michigan.

Innovation and Promotions

In 2003, Kellogg's Corn Flakes underwent a comprehensive makeover with an improved taste, crispier flakes and a bold new look designed to meet the ever-changing consumer tastes of the 21st century. More than 100 years after the discovery of the Corn Flake, Kellogg's made modifications to the food and the packaging, which are undoubtedly the first significant changes to one of the world's biggest brands since 1906. The company built further on this in 2004 with the introduction of the re-sealable K-lock pack – the first of its kind.

Kellogg's Corn Flakes has rarely been away from UK television screens, with the most recent campaigns being centred around the theme 'Wake Up', with Kellogg's promoting Kellogg's Corn Flakes as the best

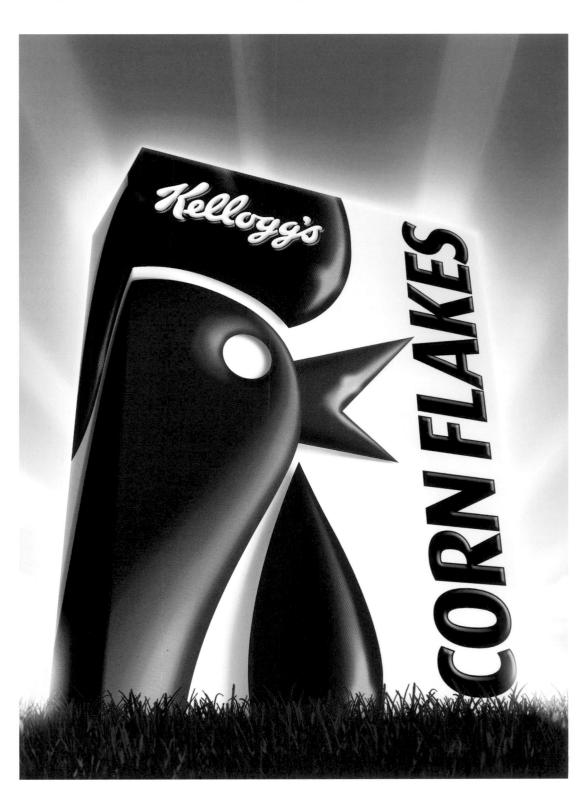

way to wake up in the morning. This has been communicated through the use of metaphors such as the Dawn of Man campaign where early man evolves into modern man thanks to his bowl of Kellogg's Corn Flakes. The Back to School campaign introduced in 2005 focused on children being more alert at school after a breakfast of Kellogg's Corn Flakes.

Away from TV, 2006 sees Kellogg's expand its sponsorship of the Amateur Swimming Association (ASA). Since the sponsorship began in 1998 more than nine million UK children have learned to swim through the ASA Award scheme.

This year also sees Kellogg's extend its partnership with education charity ContinYou to further develop school Breakfast Clubs. Kellogg's has invested over £400,000 in breakfast clubs throughout the UK since the sponsorship began in 1999.

Market Context

Britain spends £1.4 billion a year on cereal and it is found in 96.8% of UK households (Source: IRI/TNS). Despite this, consumption of breakfast is declining, with one in five children and one in four adults skipping the most important meal of the day.

Nearly 90% of the nation eats cereal each morning, firmly establishing it as the preferred breakfast of choice (Source: TGI Data 2005). Today the cereal industry is worth £1.43 billion in the UK and key players are Kellogg's, Weetabix, Nestlé, Jordans and Quaker.

With a market leading 42% share of the total UK cereal market (Source: IRI) Kellogg's has almost 40 brands in the UK and manufactures seven of the top-selling cereal brands (Kellogg's Corn Flakes, Crunchy Nut, Coco Pops, Special K, Fruit 'n Fibre, All-Bran and Bran Flakes) and has the

largest share of the ready-to-eat cereal market in all outlets (Source: IRI).

Achievements and Future Prospects

If a brand value of £64 million (Source: IRI) for Kellogg's Corn Flakes alone was not a good enough reason to celebrate, Kellogg's 100th anniversary in 2006 is providing the brand with a very good excuse for a party.

In recognition of the centenary, Kellogg's is using Kellogg's Corn Flakes as the flagship brand to celebrate. It is producing special packs of Kellogg's Corn Flakes that include a promotion to collect a gold heritage Kellogg's van. A similar promotion in 1984 for Rice Krispies saw more than one million people request the van, making it Kellogg's most successful promotion ever.

1906
The Battle Creek Toasted Corn Flake Company is founded on February 19th by WK Kellogg with 25 employees.

1924
Kellogg's Corn Flakes and Kellogg's All-Bran cereals are introduced to the UK.

1930
Kellogg's become the first company to print nutrition messages and recipes on packs.

1936
UK sales top £1 million – with Kellogg's Corn Flakes priced at five old pennies a pack. This equals more than 50 million packs sold.

1940
Kellogg's is one of the first companies to add vitamins and minerals to its products in order to help the population meet their nutritional requirements.

1955
Cornelius the Cockerel first appears on the front of Kellogg's Corn Flakes.

2003
New bold pack design and foil liners to seal in the freshness are introduced.

2005
As part of a salt reduction programme begun in 1998, Kellogg's reduces salt in Kellogg's Corn Flakes by 25% and consumers vote them 'even tastier' than before.

KFC's vision is to bring people of all ages, races and backgrounds together to enjoy 'Soul Food' – 'proper food at reasonable prices' – within bright and fun interiors. KFC is designed to be perceived as a fun and inclusive brand.

Offerings and Values

KFC's 'Soul Food' strategy, introduced in 2003, was established at the very heart of KFC's business – the product. The company's core products are Buckets, Burgers and Twisters and Colonel's Crispy Strips chicken with home-style side dishes. But little had occurred in terms of new product development within KFC since 2001.

The 'Soul Food' proposition gave new focus to the new product strategy. The first 'Soul Food' product to hit the stores was 'Warm Chicken Salad'. The success of this salad has led to new variants being developed, and more 'Soul Food' products continue to feature on KFC's menus.

The new positioning also impacted on the pricing strategy. This was an offering for real people and as a result, it needed to be proper, wholesome food, offered at a reasonable price. Prior to repositioning the brand, the lowest priced item on KFC's menu was £2.99, which was a barrier to purchase for many consumers.

'Soul Food' meant that pricing was looked at in a different way and the case for a value product at less than £1 was put forward. The Mini Fillet Burger launched in 2004 and has had a positive impact upon sales and perceptions of the KFC brand.

The 'Soul Food' philosophy has also made a real impact upon KFC's retail estate, manifesting itself in all aspects of communication, from window posters to the menu boards and staff uniforms. Stores have been designed along the key elements of the philosophy, and the bright reds, blues and yellows, which are generic and expected within quick service restaurants (QSRs) have been replaced with more natural colours and materials to make the atmosphere less plastic and more real.

Innovations and Promotions

At the beginning of 2003, KFC's business was in a challenging situation. Its market was in decline, struggling in the face of increasing competition from pizza, ethnic

takeaways, supermarket ready meals and a raft of sandwich retailers. Moreover, the media focus on the evils of fast food had fuelled concerns over healthy eating. Consequently, the major players in the QSR sector were all experiencing significant declines.

In order to rise to the challenge, KFC needed to overhaul not only its product and high street presence, but also its image.

At the heart of this was the 'Soul Food' concept, which was most visibly and dramatically brought to life by advertising, created with advertising agency BBH. In fact, 'Soul Food' proved to be an effective creative springboard and led to TV executions that amplified the holistic 'Soul Food' experience. Each execution was able to communicate individual product messages, to different targets, on different occasions.

In striking contrast to the conventions of the category, products were shown being consumed in the midst of the action. Gone were the generic cutaways to flying drumsticks, raining lettuce and bouncing buns. Soul music has been an important component of the advertising, providing KFC with a specific media property that has helped to make KFC ads famous.

Market Context
The British food-service industry has posted positive growth, increasing by 25% since 1999 and reaching value sales of £26.5 billion in 2004 (Source: Mintel). The number of consumer foodservice units stood at 177,600 in 2003, representing a rise of 6.8% on 1999. A total of 5,224 million transactions were achieved in 2003, representing an increase of 15.6% on 1999 (Source: Euromonitor).

Achievements and Future Prospects
Through its 'Soul Food' strategy, KFC has effectively changed public perception of its brand and built an emotional relationship with its consumers, without compromising the immediate sales requirements of retail marketing. Over the course of 2004 and 2005, KFC successfully launched a new 'Singing Soul' campaign. This followed the success of the 'Soul Food' campaign in 2003 and 2004 and takes the brand essence throughout the business, communicating it at all consumer touch-points.

In the UK, KFC operates 680 stores. Globally, KFC is owned by Yum! Brands Inc. (formerly Tricon Global Restaurants), which operates more than 33,000 restaurants in more than 100 countries and territories. Four of the company's brands – KFC, Pizza Hut, Taco Bell and Long John Silver's – are global leaders in their categories. Internationally, Yum! Brands opens about three new restaurants each day, ranking it among the restaurant industry's fastest growing international retailers.

1939
Colonel Harland Sanders creates Original Recipe Kentucky Fried Chicken.

1964
With more than 600 franchised outlets for his chicken in the US and Canada, Sanders sells his interest in the US company for US$2 million, but remains a spokesman.

1966
Kentucky Fried Chicken Corporation grows rapidly, going public on March 17th.

1971
More than 3,500 franchised and company-owned restaurants are in worldwide operation as Heublein Inc. acquires KFC Corporation on July 8th for US$285 million.

1982
Kentucky Fried Chicken becomes a subsidiary of R J Reynolds Industries (now RJR Nabisco), when Heublein is acquired by Reynolds.

1986
KFC is acquired from RJR Nabisco by PepsiCo for approximately US$840 million.

1997
PepsiCo Inc. announces the splitting of its brands – KFC, Taco Bell and Pizza Hut – into an independent restaurant company, Tricon Global Restaurants.

2002
The corporation name is changed to Yum! Brands, which is the world's largest restaurant company in terms of outlets, with nearly 32,500 in more than 100 countries and territories.

La Senza is a specialist high street retailer providing women's lingerie and nightwear at affordable prices. It aims to consistently be at the forefront of market trends. The combination of attentive, knowledgeable customer advisors, an intimate, boutique shopping environment and the La Senza gift-wrapping service is all designed to add up to a memorable and outstanding shopping experience.

Offerings and Values

La Senza's primary objective is to provide affordable lingerie products that are comfortable, romantic and sensual. The La Senza range primarily consists of lingerie, nightwear and swimwear, which is designed to make real women feel fabulous and feminine every time they wear it.

La Senza's designers regularly scour the catwalks for key trends to translate into fashionable and wearable styles at affordable prices. The brand boasts an extensive range of frontless, backless and strapless bras as well as the Dreamshapers range, which includes everything from stick on cups to nipple covers. Fabrics, colours and prints are carefully selected with the customer in mind.

La Senza prides itself on bringing fashionable lingerie and nightwear to women of all ages and sizes. It aims to plug the gap in the market for bigger bras in high-fashion styles without the penalty of higher prices. Its sizes go up to 38F in most styles and size 18 in many garments.

La Senza's bra measuring and fitting service is free and available at all stores, without the need to make an appointment. This service is recommended with every new bra purchase, because it is reported that more than 70% of women could be wearing the wrong size bra. As soon as they commence employment, La Senza customer advisors are expertly trained to provide accurate bra fittings and to give authoritative advice on style, colour and fit.

The retailer's free gift-wrapping service, which comes with all purchases, is extremely popular with La Senza's loyal customers. Garments are wrapped in delicate tissue paper with scented beads and presented in a gift box to make every purchase special.

Innovations and Promotions

The La Senza website – www.lasenza.co.uk – was launched in November 2002 to offer customers an up-to-the-minute way of ordering lingerie quickly. The entire operation from inception to delivery is facilitated by a dedicated in-house team. Lasenza.co.uk is now a multi-million pound operation in its own right, with sales doubling every year since launch.

La Senza has supported breast cancer charities for the past five years and in 2005 entered into a partnership with Breast Cancer Care, to raise £50,000 for the charity, which is the UK's leading provider of information, practical assistance and emotional support for those affected by breast cancer. Throughout the UK, La Senza called on women to dump their old bras in a national 'Bra Amnesty'. For each bra handed in, a donation was made to Breast Cancer Care, and all the bras collected were given to Oxfam. Donators could also show their support for the charity by wearing the Breast Cancer Care pin badge, which is available from La Senza stores nationwide.

La Senza launched its first ever national advertising campaign in summer 2004 in women's magazines and billboard sites. This was followed in November 2005 by large poster sites and a London Underground campaign in 2006.

Market Context

The 1960s and 1970s heralded a liberal approach to underwear with the advent of the sexual revolution. Furthermore, developments in technology and fabrics during the 1980s and 1990s brought more intricate designs to the mass market.

New styles such as the famous Wonderbra, giving a 'push up and plunge' effect, became popular and fashionable. Now fashionable underwear has been developed for all situations including padded, gel filled, air filled, strapless, backless, multiway and bodycontrol. Gone are the days of purely functional underwear, women today have an underwear wardrobe to suit any occasion.

In 2005, the total bra and pant market was worth £1.174 billion, of which La Senza currently has a 6% share (Source: Mintel). There are now 77 standalone La Senza stores in the UK, 17 concessions within Debenhams, three concessions in Northern Ireland, 11 franchises in mainland Europe, and nine stores in Ireland.

Achievements and Future Prospects

In the 10 years since its UK launch, La Senza has won countless awards, both in the fashion trade press and from women's consumer magazines. Most notably, the brand has been named Company magazine Underwear Retailer of the Year for the past three consecutive years and has won More magazine's Most Sexy Lingerie Award for the past two years.

Looking ahead, La Senza is intent on continuing its ambitious expansion programme throughout Europe and the UK in 2006. It is currently considering sites in Spain, Italy, Greece and Germany as well as prime locations throughout the UK.

1996
Having originated in Canada, La Senza is launched in the UK market.

1998
La Senza is bought by Xunely Ltd and becomes a privately owned company, headed by Theo Paphitis.

2004
La Senza enters the European market with its first store in Reykjavik, Iceland and now also operates in Denmark, Norway, Estonia, Malta and Gibraltar.

2006
La Senza has evolved into a leading contender in the lingerie market with a turnover in excess of £100 million.

YOUR M&S

For more than 100 years, the Marks & Spencer brand has been recognised by customers for offering products and services that genuinely meet their needs. Founded on offering excellent products at great prices, over the years the M&S brand name has become synonymous with quality, value, service, innovation and trust. These values are the bedrock of the Marks & Spencer brand proposition.

Offerings and Values

M&S aims to excel in offering its customers a broad range of superior products – whether that be high-quality food for every occasion and every appetite, stylish and easy to care for clothing, home accessories or financial services products that offer peace of mind as well as quality and value.

Innovations and Promotions

The M&S brand has built a strong reputation for innovation. Its focus has been on understanding what customers really need and want, then finding innovative ways of delivering it. The M&S passion for innovation has led to breakthroughs in the development of fabric, cooking techniques and flavours.

For example, M&S announced in January 2006 that it would become the first major UK retailer to sell clothing made from 100% Fairtrade cotton. From March 2006, Fairtrade T-shirts and socks were being sold in M&S stores and online.

In food, M&S continues its salt reduction programme and has removed 250 tonnes of salt across its food ranges over the past year, including cutting the salt content of its sandwiches by 15%.

These innovations have more recently been communicated via Marks & Spencer's 'Look behind the label' campaign, designed to tell customers about the way its products are sourced and made. As part of the campaign, all M&S stores, including windows, and in-store graphics, featured clear and strong messages with striking imagery about M&S products and their health, quality and environmental aspects including: 'We're committed to reducing salt faster than you can say 'sodium chloride'' and 'It's not just our green dyes that won't harm the environment'. A series of advertisements ran in the press to support the campaign.

It's not just our green dyes that won't harm the environment.

Our policy on dyeing clothes is black and white. We've banned all our suppliers from using 56 chemicals in the production process that put either their employees or the environment at risk. We also insist that all remaining dyes are removed from effluents before releasing them back into the environment. To ensure they meet our stringent standards regular factory audits are conducted. So, it doesn't matter whether our dyes are blue, red or yellow, they're as kind to the planet as the green ones. www.marksandspencer.com

YOUR M&S
look behind the label

The new 'Your M&S magazine' is the highest read women's lifestyle magazine in the UK (Source: NRS 2006), representing one of the most trusted and iconic British brands. With four issues a year and a readership of over 3.3 million, it aims to offer engaging editorial, whilst providing solutions and guidance as well as ideas and inspiration across clothing, home, beauty and food.

Market Context

M&S has a wide variety of competitors, from the main supermarket groups, to specialist fashion and home retailers. The rise of home shopping has also changed the competitive landscape, with more and more consumers buying a wider range of products from catalogues and the internet. High street retailers including Marks & Spencer have to compete, not only in store, but also through online offerings, to meet consumers' rising expectations for better price and convenience. Against a difficult trading environment, Marks & Spencer has responded with more stylish product in clothing, a greater focus on value, more competitive pricing, a flow of innovation in food and continued promotion of its '&more' credit card and loyalty scheme.

Achievements and Future Prospects

The 'Your M&S...' re-launch in September 2004 unified all the Marks & Spencer business units under one brand idea and creative look and feel. Instead of a disparate collection of different communication ideas and creative material, everything was now designed to look like it belonged to the M&S family. As well as womenswear, the launch campaign featured menswear, lingerie, childrenswear and food, using iconic imagery to communicate the quality of M&S products.

In food, M&S developed 'monthly food festivals' to re-engage customers with the brand by creating real excitement and interest in-store – for example, using tastings and demonstrations to highlight newness and innovation. Furthermore M&S would treat customers to some of the unique products in the range – such as a bottle of wine or an Oakham Chicken – when they spent over a certain amount in the food hall. The first ad, featuring a sumptuous (and now famous) melting middle Belgian chocolate pudding, aired at Easter 2005; within a week, the pudding factory had gone into overdrive as customers responded to the new campaign at an unprecedented level.

In autumn 2005 this was followed by Marks & Spencer's most successful ever Womenswear TV campaign featuring four models dressing up in the new season's clothes. Starring Twiggy, Erin O'Connor, Laura Bailey and Noemie Lenoir, the campaign was a huge success for the brand.

In addition to simplifying advertising imagery and presentation, M&S improved its store environments, resulting in new-look stores that are sleek and stylish, easier to navigate and more inspirational.

The vision for M&S stores is to deliver a step change in its customers' shopping experience by creating stores with a great environment, offering great product and a service that exceeds all expectations. By the end of this year, M&S will have revamped a third of its chain, in the biggest store refurbishment programme ever undertaken in the UK.

1894
The Marks & Spencer partnership is formed by Michael Marks, a young Russian refugee, and Tom Spencer, a cashier at IJ Dewhirst.

1920s
Marks & Spencer buys stock directly from manufacturers, forming long-lasting relationships with suppliers, some of which survive to the present day.

1930s
The flagship Marble Arch store opens.

1940s
Marks & Spencer is one of the first retailers to experiment with self-service shopping.

1950s
The St Michael own-label fashion label first appears.

1970s
Extensive expansion takes place in both the product range and new stores.

1980s
Out-of-town stores arrive, while M&S introduces furniture and financial services.

2000s
M&S launches Simply Food store format and introduces contemporary new ranges such as Per Una, Autograph and Blue Harbour. The process of modernising store estate begins. M&S introduces successful new marketing campaigns, 'Not just Food' and 'Your M&S'.

Ray Kroc developed his brand vision for McDonald's around a simple but effective consumer-driven premise: quality, service, cleanliness and value. These values have remained the cornerstones of the company, and today McDonald's is the largest food-service company in the world, with more than 30,000 restaurants serving nearly 50 million people each day in 119 countries and territories, from Andorra to The Virgin Islands.

Offerings and Values

McDonald's is committed to providing its customers with food of the highest quality. This is achieved by using the best quality raw ingredients, sourced only from approved suppliers and ensuring that food is prepared to a consistently high standard. The menu is continually reviewed and enhanced to ensure that it meets – and wherever possible exceeds – expectations.

To help customers make informed decisions about their whole diet, McDonald's was the first quick service restaurant to provide a complete ingredient listing and detailed nutritional analysis of its menu. Recently this has been supplemented with the 'Happy Meal Choice Chart', which contains the nutritional information for each one of the 108 different Happy Meal combinations, as well as practical advice for parents to help their kids live active, balanced lifestyles.

This evolution has continued unabated, with 2004 seeing the launch of the new Salads Plus range across key markets around the world – a range of fresh salads, mineral water, yoghurt and fresh fruit. 2004 also saw the introduction of porridge, fruit toast and filled bagels as part of a wider breakfast menu. McDonald's also responded to consumer feedback by offering fruit bags that could be swapped for fries as part of a Happy Meal.

Innovations and Promotions

In 2005 McDonald's evolution continued with the introduction of Toasted Deli Sandwiches, an entirely new range of freshly prepared sandwiches developed around the introduction of 'impinger' ovens, allowing restaurants to produce a wider variety of meal options, while still delivering these new and varied choices within the timeframe people know and expect from McDonald's.

2005 also saw McDonald's continue to distribute a series of 'Brand Books' with each one going to more than 23 million homes throughout the UK, in order to tell people about some of the new choices

Market Context

McDonald's operates within an increasingly competitive marketplace, but through a combination of quality, value, fast and friendly service, clean and pleasant surroundings, insightful marketing and high street profile, McDonald's continues to have a strong presence in the market.

By the end of 2005, McDonald's had 1,250 restaurants and directly employed 42,963 restaurant staff in the UK, as well as another 25,000 employed by McDonald's franchisees. The chain provides food and drink to around two million Britons per day, and upwards of £400 million is spent annually in its supply chain, much of which is spent on British ingredients.

Achievements and Future Prospects

The strength of the McDonald's brand is recognised by journalists, marketers and analysts. Recently it was named one of the best global companies by Global Finance magazine, while Fortune ranked it number one in the social responsibility category of its Most Admired Companies listing.

The company is committed to customer satisfaction that competitors are unable to match and recognises that well-trained and motivated staff are key; the development of all employees at every level of the organisation is a high priority. Training is a continuous process and employees attend courses in the restaurants as well as at the company's six Management Training Centres.

Things you didn't know

McDonald's is now the UK's biggest retailer of pre-prepared fruit.

In India, where the cow is a sacred animal, McDonald's opened its first restaurant that did not sell beef. Instead, mutton is used and the Big Mac is known as the 'Maharaja Mac'.

In the UK, McDonald's uses 100% free-range eggs for its breakfast menu.

The first drive-thru McDonald's was created in 1975 to serve soldiers from an army base in Sierra Vista, Arizona, who were forbidden to leave their cars while in uniform.

available and giving them discount vouchers to encourage them to try the new items.

The McDonald's brand is extremely high profile and its advertising expenditure corresponds. 2003 saw the launch of a worldwide marketing initiative; the 'i'm lovin' it' campaign. This is a global push that continues to connect the McDonald's brand with its customers around the world.

McDonald's has demonstrated a strong commitment to sports sponsorship and nowhere is this more evident than in the UK, where the brand has long been successfully linked with football – one of the nation's favourite sports. 2006 will see McDonald's sponsor the FIFA World Cup tournament and, as part of this involvement, will give 35 young children a day to remember when McDonald's will recruit them to be one of the children that escorts the players onto the pitch before each match.

McDonald's actively encourages its restaurant managers to put time and resources back into the local community. Supporting local football teams has proved an effective way to do this. Hundreds of youth teams play in kit donated by McDonald's across the country, taking the brand into the heart of everyday British life. Throughout the UK, more than 300 youth teams and 500 restaurants are involved in McDonald's sponsored leagues.

Alongside its successes as a business, McDonald's contributes to the communities it belongs to. In the UK it has been involved in a range of good causes from fundraising work with local schools, youth groups and hospitals to supporting environmental and anti-littering campaigns.

Aside from all this, the real achievement of McDonald's is self-evident. No matter how unfamiliar the surroundings, there is always a McDonald's nearby.

1954
Ray Kroc starts supplying milkshake mixers to Dick and Mac McDonald's restaurant in San Bernardino, California.

1955
Kroc buys a franchise from the brothers and sets up his own McDonald's restaurant in Des Plaines, Chicago.

1959
The chain sells 100 million hamburgers in its first three years of trading and the 100th branch is opened.

1961
Kroc pays US$2.7 million to buy out the McDonald brothers' interests.

1963
The billionth McDonald's hamburger is served live on primetime television.

1965
The McDonald's Corporation goes public and was listed on the New York stock exchange the following year.

1974
The first McDonald's in the UK opens in Woolwich, south east London.

1977
The 5,000th restaurant opens in Kanagawa, Japan.

2001
McDonald's acquires a minority interest in the UK sandwich chain Pret A Manger.

2006
McDonald's UK turnover is in excess of £1.6 billion a year.

Microsoft®

Microsoft, whose software is widely held to power more than 90% of all the world's personal computers, has been a leader in the wave of personal computing innovation that has created new opportunity, convenience, and value over the past three decades. During that time, it has created many new products, added new lines of business, and expanded its operations worldwide. Microsoft's corporate mission is to enable people and businesses throughout the world to realise their full potential.

Offerings and Values

Microsoft prides itself on providing software and services that help people communicate, do their work, be entertained, and manage their personal lives. Over the past 31 years of Microsoft's lifetime, innovative technology has transformed how people access and share information, changed the way businesses and institutions operate, and made the world smaller by giving computer users instant access to people and resources everywhere. Microsoft's business continued to grow in 2005, increasing its total revenue by US$2.95 billion, or 8% year-on-year, to US$39.79 billion.

Yet Microsoft's mission extends beyond making and selling products for profit. Through its business activities and community support,

it aims to leave a lasting and positive impression on the communities and society in which it works. Years ago, it was convinced that its original vision of 'a PC in every home' could change lives. It remains convinced of the broad and positive power of giving people better technology. It takes corporate responsibilities seriously, and in its interactions with its employees, customers, partners, suppliers and the communities where it works, it aims to reflect its broader awareness and ambitions.

Today, Microsoft is the largest contributor in the high-tech industry and the third-largest among all businesses in the US. Annually, Microsoft donates more than US$47 million in cash and US$363 million in software to non-

profit organisations throughout the world. In the UK, Microsoft gives to a range of major charity projects both financially and through the donation of software. Charities including NSPCC, Childnet International, Leonard Cheshire, AbilityNet and Age Concern have all benefited from Microsoft's giving programme.

Bill Gates and his wife Melinda, who have three children, are also known for their charitable work. As well as investing millions in research for an AIDs vaccine, their foundation has established a scholarship scheme to enable the brightest students to go to Cambridge University. The Bill and Melinda Gates Foundation is currently working on a global health programme in the developing world.

Innovations and Promotions

Microsoft believes that delivering breakthrough innovation and high-value solutions through its integrated platform is the key to meeting customer needs and to its future growth.

2004 saw Bill Gates deliver Microsoft's vision of digital entertainment anywhere, unveiling Windows XP Media Center Edition 2005, and showcasing a variety of sleek new computer designs, portable media devices, and digital content services.

In a step towards that vision, May 2005 saw the launch of Windows Mobile 5.0, the newest instalment of Microsoft's software for mobile devices, designed to power a new generation of phones, personal digital assistants and media players for people who want to customise devices to fit their needs.

In the same month, Microsoft launched Xbox 360, its 'future-generation' video game and entertainment system designed to place gamers at the centre of the experience. Xbox also enables gamers to link up and play against each other through Xbox Live.

Microsoft's marketing has come a long way since it kicked off its first television advertising campaign in 1992.

Now no stranger to high-profile launches, Microsoft linked up with MTV Europe to showcase the Xbox 360 game system. Elijah Wood, Scarlett Johansson, The Killers and Snow Patrol hosted a half-hour star studded European premier of the new product with performances from The Killers and Snow Patrol airing exclusively on MTV channels across Europe.

Windows Vista™, the next generation of the Windows® client operating system, will be launched towards the end of 2006 and will continue to deliver on Bill Gates' vision of digital entertainment everywhere. Every day, millions of people around the globe rely on their Windows-based PCs to manage the increasing amounts of digital information in their lives. While the tools currently used for managing this information are powerful and familiar, Windows Vista aims to cut through all the clutter. Today's digital generation will be able to explore entertainment such as TV and music and stay connected to people and information on their Windows Vista-based PC safely and easily.

Market Context

Microsoft is a worldwide leader in software, services and solutions designed to help people and businesses realise their full potential. It generates revenue by developing, manufacturing, licensing and supporting a wide range of software products for many computing devices. Its software products include operating systems for servers, personal computers (PCs) and intelligent devices; server applications for distributed computing environments; information worker productivity applications; business solutions; and software development tools.

Microsoft provides consulting and product support services, and trains and certifies system integrators and developers. It sells the Xbox video game console and games, PC games, and peripherals. Online communication services and information services are delivered through its MSN portals and channels around the world. It also researches and develops advanced technologies for future software products.

Achievements and Future Prospects

Microsoft now does business almost everywhere in the world. It has offices in more than 90 countries, which are grouped into six corporate regions: North America (the US and Canada); Latin America (LATAM); Europe, the Middle East, and Africa (EMEA); Japan; Asia Pacific (APAC); and Greater China. It also has operational centres in Dublin, Ireland; Humacao, Puerto Rico; Reno, Nevada, USA; and Singapore. Microsoft believes that over the past few years it has laid the foundations for long-term growth by making global citizenship an integral part of its business, delivering innovative new products, creating opportunity for partners, improving customer satisfaction, putting some of its most significant legal challenges behind it, and improving its internal processes.

1975
Microsoft is founded in Seattle by two young men, one of whom was a college dropout.

1983
Microsoft Community Affairs – one of the first corporate giving programmes in the high-tech industry – is founded.

2005
Microsoft's founder Bill Gates is granted an honorary knighthood by Queen Elizabeth II. As an American citizen he cannot use the title 'Sir' but is entitled to put the letters KBE after his name. Now the world's wealthiest man, Bill Gates, is worth an estimated £28 billion.

2006
Gates announces that his foundation will donate US$691 million towards life-saving vaccines for millions of children in poor countries.

Miss Selfridge

Over the past four decades, Miss Selfridge has proven itself to be one of the most tenacious and durable brands on the British high street. Despite numerous changes in ownership, some of which would have spelled the end for weaker brands, Miss Selfridge has proven that its name, reputation and brand power have stood the test of time.

Offerings and Values

Miss Selfridge is one of the smaller brands in the Arcadia Group, with a UK chain of 152 stores, 93 of which are standalone outlets. The brand's individuality has been heightened by boosting its in-house design team, from two to nine designers over the past two years.

As a boutique brand, Miss Selfridge works hard for its customers, always trying to give them something different. Whether it is using designs from vintage print collections, sourcing its cloth from Rajasthan and Russia, or using its own graphic design team to create unique prints, Miss Selfridge takes its inspiration from a variety of sources. The aim is to eliminate homogeneity, and create a distinctively feminine, confident and contemporary style.

Aside from its main collections, Miss Selfridge collaborates with designers to reach particularly fashion-savvy consumers and, in 2005, the non-conformist British designer Bella Freud launched an exclusive collection, 'Bella' at Miss Selfridge.

Featured in the flagship Oxford Circus store is the Miss Vintage Concession, which comprises clothing, accessories and shoes. Other regional boutiques such as Birmingham, Leeds and Edinburgh also boast local vintage concessions with a loyal following.

As part of its 40th Anniversary celebrations in 2006, Miss Selfridge launches an exclusive Decade Collection in the Autumn, designed by Bella Freud. The collection makes reference to iconic Miss Selfridge favourites, such as

the 'lips' kimono from the 1980s and a reinvented shift dress and coat inspired by the original collection from the 1960s.

The 'Kiss and Make Up' range, with its witty colour names that reflect the spirited and fun nature of the brand, also enjoys a resurgence, with limited edition box sets available in autumn 2006, including such favourites as 'Iron Lady', 'Berry Wogan' and 'Copper Knockers'.

Innovations and Promotions

Miss Selfridge is proud of its reputation for being an innovator and of its ability to help customers put outfits together. It is seeing success with its in-store 'destination boutique' driven by brand director, Sim Scavazza and

her growing team of designers and buyers. The concept was launched in March 2004 and limited edition boutique items are helping Miss Selfridge increase its average selling price by 8% year-on-year. The media has responded enthusiastically to the initiative, with additional product placement and brand features helping boost overall press coverage to the advertising equivalent of more than £1.1 million per month. Favourable media comment has come from the national press, as well as a range of women's magazines including Vogue and Harpers & Queen.

Miss Selfridge supports Breast Cancer Care's Lavender Trust. Co-founded by Vogue contributing editor Justine Picardie, The Lavender Trust raises money specifically to fund information and support for younger women with breast cancer.

Miss Selfridge has helped to support the charity through various projects, including the sale of limited edition Lavender Trust T-shirts and an embellished bag, all exclusively designed by Bella Freud for Miss Selfridge, and through the sale of two unique colourways of Havaianas, the cult Brazilian flip flops. All of the stores and head office employees are also supporting the charity through a 'Charity Challenge' programme in 2006, aiming to raise at least £40,000 in its 40th year.

Market Context
Britons spend around £30 billion every year on clothing (Source: KeyNote), with womenswear accounting for around half of all garment sales. Women are now, as always, looking to keep up with the latest trends, but also being careful with their budgeting.

Miss Selfridge successfully distinguishes itself in this highly competitive sector. Although a few years ago the brand was linked with the younger end of the market, it has now re-established its historically broad appeal, targeting confident, independent women whose age matters less than their attitude to life. Miss Selfridge aims to offer a specially edited range that appeals to fashion-aware mothers and daughters alike.

Achievements and Future Prospects
Miss Selfridge also offers its customers the chance to experience the brand on the internet with its online boutique, launched in 2003. With the website's ability to sell both the product and the destination boutique brand concept to consumers, online sales have grown 68% this year with a 900% growth versus two years ago, with visitors numbering 65,000 every week. Miss Selfridge continues to develop its profitable multi-channel approach, with an emphasis on integrating the stores with the website to achieve maximum results in both channels. Loyal Miss Selfridge consumers from the remotest regions of the British Isles can now buy London Exclusive clothing and Limited Edition collections

from the online boutique, as well as sought-after vintage items, sourced from around the globe by the buying team.

Miss Selfridge supports up and coming designers and, since 2002, has partnered with the Royal College of Art's School of Fashion. A competition conceived through this collaboration challenges young designers to create a collection for Miss Selfridge, with the winner not only receiving £1,500 towards the development of their own collection, but also the opportunity for a paid work placement, during which time they can be involved in their garment going from design to production. The winning collections open the RCA's Graduates Gala catwalk, elements of which can then be seen in Miss Selfridge stores nationwide.

With the demise of Biba, Miss Selfridge is the sole surviving and thriving 1960s fashion brand on the British high street. From June 2006 to January 2007, Miss Selfridge sponsors the 'Sixties Fashion' exhibition at the prestigious V&A.

To celebrate its 40th Anniversary and highlight the heritage and authenticity of the brand, Miss Selfridge produced a book covering the four decades of fashion and events that the brand had a major influence over. This includes archive material and passionate behind the scenes anecdotes from famous models to renowned journalists who have worked with the brand over the years and who still love it.

As one of the UK's largest grocery brands and the leading manufacturer of short life dairy products (Source: ACNielsen), Müller Dairy has enjoyed success across its portfolio of brands, and continues to celebrate yogurt brand Müller Corner as its bestseller. With the help of a committed workforce of 1,200, Müller produced more than 1.6 billion pots in 2005, and aims to increase this further for 2006 with a series of new product developments.

Offerings and Values

Müller's diverse offering caters for all markets with brands including Müller Vitality, number two in the dynamic drinking yogurt market (Source: ACNielsen), Müllerlight, Müller Corner, Müllerice and Müller Amoré.

In November 2005, Müller Vitality became the first range of functional yogurts and yogurt drinks to be boosted with the benefits of very long chain Omega 3 fatty acids. The range was launched with the aim of increasing consumer consumption of Omega 3 as, despite the fact that Omega 3 is essential for good health, dietary surveys show that most people are not getting enough.

The UK's leading healthy yogurt brand, Müllerlight, (Source: ACNielsen) was revamped in 2006 with the 'Best Ever... Even Fruitier' Müllerlight range and a range of Smooth Style yogurts. All 15 flavours are now thicker and creamier with more fruit as well as added probiotics to set a new standard for the healthy category. Appealing to both the health conscious consumer and those focused on quality, the 'Best Ever' Müllerlight provides the consumer with the highest quality product, added benefits and a diverse range of 15 fruit and dessert flavours.

Müller's luxury dessert brand Müller Amoré has continued to optimise its range of premium yogurts made with ingredients from continental destinations, with the addition of three new fruit flavours, Italian Lemon, Mediterranean Peach and Strawberry & French Vanilla. The Amoré range has been re-launched with a new design, to give the whole range a luxurious, indulgent appearance.

The Müller Corner range is to be completely revamped in 2006, not only improving the fruit integrity of the product, but also increasing the fruit quantity. Müller Rice is also undergoing improvements to deliver a more natural taste and a refreshed range with new flavours.

Innovations and Promotions

During 2006 Müller pushes forward with continued product innovation and dynamic marketing campaigns.

Indeed, Müller's marketing activity has taken a leap forward with high-profile media activity including Müllerlight's sponsorship of 'Will & Grace' on LIVINGtv and Müller Amoré's sponsorship of Channel 4 programme 'A Place in The Sun'. The success of the 'Lead a Müller Life' campaign resulted in Sony BMG releasing a Groovefinder remix of the hugely popular soundtrack 'Ain't Got No, I Got Life' by Nina Simone.

In May 2006 an overall re-design, including new logos and refreshed

packaging, has afforded all Müller brands greater on-shelf recognition and coherency ensuring that individual brand representations don't become too disparate. A further reason for the re-design was to bring to life Müller's 'goodness code' via a new on-pack tick system highlighting the relevant benefits of particular products such as 'No Artificial Colours or Preservatives', '35% of Calcium RDA' or 'Probiotic Yogurt'.

Market Context

The short life dairy products market continues to be one of the largest and fastest growing grocery sectors, worth £1.9 billion in 2005, an increase of 6% on 2004 (Source: ACNielsen). The yogurt drinks market alone has grown from a market worth £203 million in 2004 to £270 million in 2005, an annual growth rate of more than 35% (Source: ACNielsen).

In an extremely successful 2005, Müller increased its share of the market by 8% to a total share of 23.2% (Source: ACNielsen). Müller boasts the two most successful brands in the market, Müller Corner and Müllerlight, with a combined value in excess of £300 million (Source: ACNielsen).

Achievements and Future Prospects

Growth from Müller's core range, as well as successful new product development with brands such as Müller Corner Healthy Balance, Müller Vitality with Omega 3 and Müllerlight dessert style flavours, have helped Müller become over twice as big as its nearest competitor, Danone (Source: ACNielsen). A number of recent accolades for Müller have further established the company's position as market leader. Marketing magazine named Müllerlight and Müller Fruit Corner as the two top yogurt brands and Müller as the fifth biggest grocery brand overall, while The Grocer announced Müller Vitality as 'Star Product' in the dairy drinks sector.

1896
The Müller company is established by Ludwig Müller, grandfather of the present owner.

1970
Theo Müller takes control of the company and recognises the opportunity to expand the products from small popular regional brands to those with nationwide appeal by improving the recipe.

1988
Müller launches in the UK with a test market of three Müller Corner flavours – Müller Corner has gone on to become a £178 million brand.

1989
Müllerice is launched in the UK.

1990
Müller launches Müllerlight, now the UK's leading healthy yogurt brand with a value of £127 million (Source: ACNielsen).

1991
Construction begins on a state-of-the-art production facility in Market Drayton, Shropshire.

1992
Müller becomes market leader – a remarkable feat that took the brand just five years to achieve.

1993
The Müller Community Trust is set up to allocate funds to local organisations, to date totalling over £150,000.

2000
The launch of Vitality, takes Müller into the probiotic market with its Feel Good Bacteria™.

2005
Müller Vitality is boosted with the additional benefit of Omega 3.

Nationwide is 'proud to be different'. This is more than a marketing strapline and has become Nationwide's mission statement. Nationwide has mutual (as opposed to Public Limited Company) status – which means that it is owned by and run for the benefit of its members as opposed to shareholders – and estimates that since 1996 this 'mutual' benefit amounts to more than £4 billion.

Offerings and Values

When Nationwide creates products and services these are always developed with its members' needs in mind. Each product it provides is designed to offer the customer a point of difference, from savings to current accounts, from mortgages to investments. For instance, in 2001 Nationwide introduced its fair mortgage pricing strategy, which means no big discounts for new borrowers and better long-term rates for all customers. Nationwide also makes all of its mortgage products available to all of its borrowers, both new and existing. Nationwide does not charge for the use of debit or credit cards abroad and has developed a passbook based account for those 65 and over, which guarantees to track the Bank of England base rate.

As a mutual society run for the benefit of its members, Nationwide has a responsibility to keep in touch with its members and customers. Since 1997, more than 800,000 members have been invited to meet senior Nationwide executives and discuss issues that affect the running of their society at its series of TalkBack events held around the country. In addition, every month Nationwide invites more than 30,000 members to comment on the service they receive from Nationwide and their perceptions of the organisation generally.

Nationwide employees record more than 120,000 pieces of member feedback – from casual remarks to formal complaints – at the point of engagement, helping the organisation to understand and respond to members' views.

Innovations and Promotions

Nationwide promotes the 'proud to be different' tagline throughout its advertising as this underpins what Nationwide is about. This is particularly manifested through the current television ads starring actor Mark Benton.

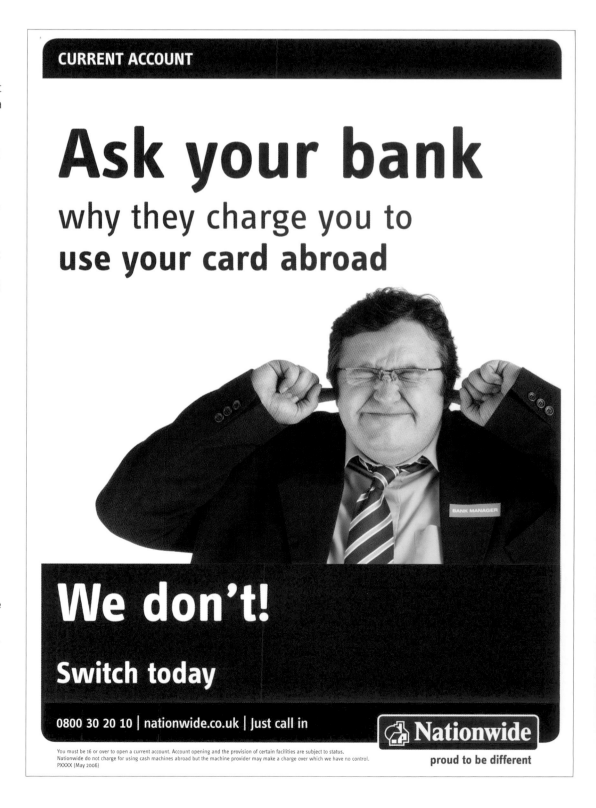

The ads show a 'bad bank manager' highlighting the poor service that can be experienced through a bank and contrasts this with the disgruntled customer going to a Nationwide branch and receiving excellent service. The most widely known execution was 'brand new customers only', where Mark Benton's bank manager character keeps saying the customer can't have anything (including a pen) as he is an existing customer. The ad makes the point that Nationwide's products are open to both customers and non-customers. Using the same theme, a new set of ads has been produced and is being aired throughout 2006.

Nationwide's branch posters, press and internet advertising also use Benton and aim to differentiate Nationwide from high street banks.

The radio ads follow the same train of thought but are more exaggerated due to the nature of radio. The ads originally starred 'Little Britain' TV comedy duo David Walliams and Matt Lucas and now feature Walliams with Welsh comedian Rob Brydon.

Outside advertising, Nationwide sponsors the Nationwide Conference and the Northern Ireland, Scotland and Welsh national football teams. It is also the sponsor of one of the most prestigious and respected music awards in the UK – The Nationwide Mercury Prize – until 2007.

Market Context

The financial services market has undergone rapid change over recent years. In the past decade there have been many new entrants to the market, from online banking operations to supermarkets and other businesses with large customer bases, and wide-scale consolidation.

Nationwide is the UK's fourth largest mortgage lender and second largest savings provider and is also the largest building society in the world (Source: Nationwide Financial Results).

Achievements and Future Prospects

Nationwide takes pride in championing the rights of its consumers. It has fought for honesty and transparency in the credit card market and was the first provider to publish a Summary Box on all its credit card information, enabling consumers to compare cards from different providers, and allowing them to make a more informed choice. The Summary Box highlights all fees and charges, which most providers had previously hidden in their small print. As a result of Nationwide's leadership, all credit card issuers are now required to provide a Summary Box. Nationwide has now launched a similar Summary Box for its current account and personal loan products.

In addition, it has campaigned vigorously against cash machine charges, and for early warning signs on those machines that do charge. Early warnings are now compulsory on 23,000 'convenience' cash machines that make a charge for withdrawals. As a result of Nationwide's campaigning, withdrawals from most cash machines owned by banks remain free.

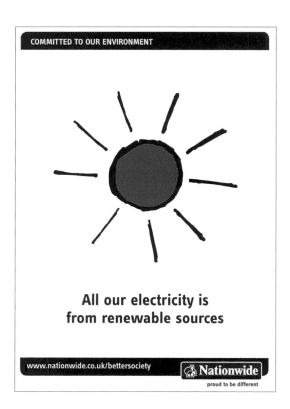

1987
Nationwide launches the first full-service current account to pay interest.

1997
Nationwide launches one of the UK's first internet banking sites.

2001
Nationwide becomes the first organisation in the UK to sign Age Concern's Business Pledge – designed to rid business of age discrimination – and has increased its maximum retirement age to 75.

2006
Nationwide improves its FlexAccount to offer a higher rate of interest, comparable with most savings accounts.

Caring for skin is at the heart of the NIVEA brand and the emotional values associated with the brand have changed little over the past 95 years. Consumers consistently reaffirm their perspective that NIVEA is a timeless, uncomplicated, trusted, honest brand that understands its consumers' needs while offering quality and value.

Offerings and Values

NIVEA Creme is an iconic beauty classic used by millions of women all over the world. It was the first true cosmetic moisturiser and is still the brand's signature product. Yet to best meet consumers' evolving requirements in skincare, NIVEA has expanded significantly to offer a comprehensive choice of moisturising, protection and care expertise in the face, body, hand, lip, men's, sun and deodorant markets.

NIVEA's brand values have changed little over the decades and are encapsulated in the phrase 'Trust NIVEA to care for your skin'. These values are communicated via clean, fresh, healthy and positive imagery in all NIVEA's promotional material and advertisements. NIVEA is dedicated to protecting the skin of the entire family, therefore family values form a vital part of its brand character. Each NIVEA product is formulated to meet specific consumer skin needs, while keeping their skin looking and feeling healthy, soft and well cared for.

NIVEA's consistently strong brand imagery ensures that it remains classically stylish. By creating products that fit in with the latest cosmetic trends and meet changing consumer needs, it retains its contemporary appeal within each generation. It is a tribute to the strength of the NIVEA brand that it can appeal to a wide range of consumers on so many levels.

Innovations and Promotions

New product development and innovation is at the heart of NIVEA's long-term brand development. The Research Centre at NIVEA's headquarters in Hamburg, Germany, which opened in August 2004 is devoted to helping identify and develop the latest products. 2006 has seen the launch of several innovative new products. Firstly, NIVEA has transferred its nourishing, tanning and firming expertise into the new and rapidly growing gradual tanning segment with the launch of NIVEA body Sunkissed Skin, a daily moisturiser with a hint of tan, which also helps firm the skin.

Secondly, NIVEA body Age Defying Lotion, formulated to replenish the levels of Creatine in skin, helping boost the skin's natural anti-ageing process. Thirdly, NIVEA Deodorant Pearl & Beauty, a deodorant offering 24-hour protection along with pearl extracts designed to leave underarms feeling smooth and cared for.

Finally, NIVEA For Men Cooling Gel Moisturiser, a light hydro gel, with Iso Magnesium and Mint Extracts, which refreshes and re-energises the skin and boosts skin's moisture.

Also new for the 2006 Sun market is immediate protection for children in spray and lotion formulations, forming part of the new NIVEA Sun Children's SPF 50+ range.

NIVEA has a strong marketing heritage, with campaigns dating as far back as the 1920s focusing on many of the benefits and values that the brand still stands for today. Nowadays, each section of the brand portfolio is supported by a fully integrated multimedia strategy. 2006 will be the fourth year NIVEA has sponsored Cancer Research UK's Race for Life which is a series of women-only sponsored charity events.

IMPRESS IN AN INSTANT.

Race for Life fits perfectly with NIVEA's values of caring for oneself on the inside and the outside, as well as for others through the sponsorship money raised.

Market Context

With more and more people – men and women alike – interested in looking and feeling youthful and healthy for as long as possible, skincare is big business. As the leading skincare brand in Europe, NIVEA has a 16.2% share of the £612 million UK skincare market (Source: IRI). The largest segment in the market is facial skincare, where product sales total £340.4 million, increasing by 6.4% year-on-year (Source: IRI). The fastest-growing segment is body care with an annual increase of 29.0% (Source: IRI), mainly attributable to the new gradual tanning segment, which NIVEA has just launched into.

With ever-heightening interest in their personal appearance, consumers are eager to try advanced new formulas that deliver on their promises. This trend is putting enormous pressure on manufacturers to innovate and all major brand players must maintain a frenetic pace of new product development in order to keep up with one another and sustain consumer interest. However, innovation does not have to come from the latest hi-tech ingredient – it could also come in the shape of a new packaging format or the identification of a simple unmet consumer need or trend.

Achievements and Future Prospects

NIVEA is the world's largest skincare brand with a strong international presence in around 170 countries and an enviable reputation.

In the UK the brand has a retail value of £159 million, which reflects a growth of 8% in a skin and beauty care category that only grew by 1.5% in 2005 (Source: IRI). This is reinforced by NIVEA being voted the UK's and Europe's Most Trusted Skincare Brand for the second consecutive year in a

Readers Digest study. In 2006 NIVEA For Men Active Firming Moisturiser celebrated the status of Product of the Year – an independent survey of 12,593 individuals; and the Marie Claire Prix D'Excellence De La Beauté award in 2006 went to NIVEA Visage Sensitive Calming Day Cream.

1906
Beiersdorf opens its first UK office in Idol Lane, London.

1911
Dr Oscar Troplowitz, a medical researcher, develops a new kind of cosmetic cream.

1922
NIVEA launches the first mass market skincare cream in the UK – the world's first true cosmetic moisturiser.

1950s
NIVEA begins to expand its product portfolio beyond the iconic NIVEA Creme into lotions, Suncare, Shower and basic facecare. This continues through to the 1980s.

1991
NIVEA Visage launches in the UK.

1992
From here until 2000, NIVEA body, Soft, Hand, For Men, and Lipcare all launch in the UK.

2002
NIVEA Deodorant launches in the UK.

2006
Beiersdorf UK Ltd celebrates its 100th anniversary.

NOKIA

www.nokia.co.uk

Since the 1990s, Nokia has focused on superior design and innovative technology to become the world's leading mobile communications company. Its clear leadership in the mobile phone arena has allowed Nokia to constantly challenge traditional concepts of the mobile phone – this 'Human Technology' has led to the manufacture of cutting edge products which not only delight but help to enrich the lives of their users.

Offerings and Values

Nokia is about connecting people – to the people that matter to them and the things they find important. Whether a music lover, photographer, fashionista, business professional, or budding film-maker, Nokia develops mobile devices that support everyone's lifestyle. Nokia is dedicated to enhancing people's lives and productivity by providing easy-to-use, secure products.

At the heart of Nokia's handset design is usability: product interfaces are easy to navigate, keypads are pleasant to the touch and the size and shape is comfortable and appropriate – all adding to the consumer's trust of Nokia as a brand.

Innovations and Promotions

Since the launch of the first hand-held mobile phone in 1987 Nokia has been a technology trailblazer. Nokia handsets were the first to feature text messaging, to access internet-based information services and to include integrated cameras. Today, Nokia is leading the charge into the third generation of mobile telephony, showcased by its Nseries range of high performance multimedia computers, which brings together mobile devices, internet content, mobile music, still and video cameras, email and games.

Nokia Eseries devices are also due to appear in the marketplace in 2006 – offering optimised solutions such as mobile email to business users.

Nokia has also led the way in the field of mobile music – its first mobile phone with a built-in MP3 player was launched in 2002. Since then, music capabilities have become a fixture throughout the Nokia range – headed up by the Nokia N91 which holds up to 3,000 tracks. In 2005 Nokia sold more than 45 million mobile phones with integrated digital music players, making it the largest manufacturer of digital music devices globally.

Design is also a fundamental building block of the Nokia brand. Less than a decade ago, all mobile phones seemed to be black. Then Nokia introduced colour and changeable covers to its products and the mobile phone suddenly became a style statement. Its reputation for iconic design has continued with two Fashion Collections – designed to complement the latest catwalk trends – and the elegant Nokia 8800 which became an instant design classic and one of the most sought after phones of the year when it was introduced in 2005.

Nokia's enduring success is not just down to its products – savvy, innovative and interactive marketing also plays a key role and Nokia continues to communicate with its consumers in an emotive way – using its sponsorships to bring value to its customers, and create desirability for the brand.

Nokia was one of the first technology brands to get involved with the fashion industry, sponsoring London Fashion Week from 1999 to 2004 and working with fashion designers including Kenzo, Louis Vuitton and Donatella Versace.

In the field of music, Nokia first started supporting new talent and live events in 1997 and continues this in 2006 with its third year of involvement with the Isle of Wight Festival and its second year with the Carling Weekend: Reading & Leeds Festivals, where its 'Rock Up and Play' will give aspiring musicians the chance to show off their skills and play on stage alongside big name acts.

In 2006, Nokia UK partnered with the world's leading music promoter, Live Nation, to launch an exclusive new live mobile music service, Ticketrush, which gives music fans the chance to buy tickets to their favourite gigs and festivals – in some cases, ahead of general release or to sold out shows. 2006 also sees Nokia sponsoring ITV's The X-Factor for a third year running – putting musical hopefuls through their paces with celebrity judges Simon Cowell, Sharon Osbourne and Louis Walsh.

Nokia has also grown its film credentials with the Nokia Shorts film competition which has been running for four years. Since its launch Nokia Shorts has created a new frontier for film makers – to tell a story in just 15 seconds – and has carved a niche for Nokia in the crowded film sponsorship arena.

Market Context

Over the last five years, the telecommunications market has become heavily saturated, with a focus on consumers upgrading handsets, rather than buying for the first time. Even in such a market however, Nokia has retained its lead on the competition, with over 50% of brand preference in the UK – more than five times that of its nearest competitor.

Achievements and Future Prospects

Nokia has won over consumers, insiders and journalists, recently winning the highly coveted Mobile News Magazine's 'Manufacturer of the Year Award' for two years running, awards for its flagship devices such as the EISA (European Imaging and Sound Association) European Media Phone for the Nokia N90, plus

awards for its promotional campaigns like its Marketing Week Effectiveness award for the Nokia fashion collection.

Nokia has also recently launched its own online shop, branching out into a new market – selling directly to consumers.

In the future, Nokia will look to reaffirm and consolidate its position as leader in mobile technology and design and focus on becoming recognised as a credible brand player within new domains such as music.

1987
Nokia Mobira Cityman 900 – the first and original hand-held mobile phone is launched.

1994
The Nokia 2100 series is the first digital hand portable phones to support data, fax and SMS (short message service).

2001
The first Nokia camera phone – the Nokia 7650 is launched.

2004
Nokia introduces its first fashion collection of three handsets.

2005
Nokia brings its first 3G device to market – the Nokia 6630.

2005
The Nokia Nseries sub-brand is launched – showcasing cutting edge technology.

Also in 2005, the launch of the first mobile device to allow broadcast-quality mobile TV takes place.

2006
The Nokia N91 – the first mobile device with a hard drive allowing space to store up to 3,000 songs – goes on sale in the UK.

O₂

www.O2.co.uk

O₂ was born in 2002, a re-launch of the former BT Cellnet. Today, O2 is completely different to its troubled predecessor. In December 2005, it overtook Vodafone to become the UK's largest mobile phone operator, with 16 million active customers. In an increasingly commoditised market, O2 has stood out with an award-winning marketing strategy that has not only made existing customers more loyal but also helped it acquire more new users than competitors this year. In January 2006, the success of O2 group was reflected in the £18 billion paid for it by the Spanish telecoms group, Telefónica.

Offerings and Values

Since its launch, O2 has stood apart from its rivals. As its competitors have become embroiled in a 'tariff and minute' battle for customers, O2 has put customer service and rewards at the centre of its brand offering.

This idea means that O2 doesn't force-feed consumers with product information. Instead it wraps its product communications up in the brand. Offers such as 'Bolt Ons', 'Happy Hour', 'O₂ Home' and 'O₂ Friends' are all examples of its customer insight and ability to deliver tangible benefits.

More recently O2 has recognised the need to reward existing customers, as well as acquiring more, and has focused on improving customers' experience of interacting with the brand and rewarding them for their loyalty. This strategy was encapsulated in the launch of the 'O₂: A World that Revolves Around You' campaign, created by O2's advertising agency, VCCP.

Innovations and promotions

Technology is no longer a major differentiator in the mobile phone business. The real areas of innovation and competition seem to be price, service and brand affinity.

In this respect, O2's focus on customer loyalty and retention has been one of its most important innovations, helping it achieve market leadership.

This shift in strategy saw O2 break market convention by offering the same or similar deals to existing customers as new ones. Offering pre-pay customers '10% of Top-ups back every three months', contract customers '50% extra airtime on your bundle for life' and bundles of attractive offers as 'Treats', have all been received as great value, no-catch offers, encouraging incremental usage and boosting brand appeal. This loyalty strategy also saw O2 take a more direct approach, offering customers who deal with it directly online,

o2.co.uk

10% of your Top-ups back every 3 months

Pay & Go™

Text 'reward' to 50202

O₂

Terms and conditions apply.

The O₂ comes alive 2007

YOUR BLUE ROOM

Win your tickets to celebrate the Gunner's final salute at Highbury

Celebrating full-time at Highbury O₂

as opposed to via a third party retail channel, extra value and better deals.

O2 has also broken new ground in enhancing its customers' experience, in new and imaginative ways, putting a new twist on experiential marketing with the O2 'Angels' and injecting new thinking into sponsorship. Through its backing for Channel 4's Big Brother at brand launch, the Arsenal football team and the England Rugby Union team, O2 uses its expertise in mobile interactivity to boost people's enjoyment of an O2-sponsored property. Another example is the Wireless Festival, a highly popular annual music event in London and Leeds. O2 customers can enjoy a 'Blue Space', with free drinks, exclusive performances and massages. They can also send texts to be displayed on a giant message board, and have personalised CDs made with photos taken from their phone.

As with all mobile companies, above-the-line is very important for O2 and while it manages to communicate new products and services in its ads, it does it simply and subtly. VCCP's 2005 campaign, 'A World that Revolves Around You', used a planet theme to visualise the brand's desire to put the customer centre stage. Otherworldly music emphasised that O2 had created a new kind of mobile phone service, removed from the brash and deal-driven image of its rivals.

Market Context

With almost 90% of the UK population owning a mobile phone and more than eight major players in the market competition has intensified. This has further intensified focus on price and service.

The emphasis now is on persuading people to spend more on enhanced services, such as picture messaging, mobile internet and downloading music. All of these are vital in the battle to increase Average Revenue Per User (ARPU) – a key metric of success in the market. O2 is particularly strong in mobile data products, with its O₂ Active mobile internet service having over 8.5 million users.

Rapid advances in technology mean that the mobile phone market is now a multimedia domain, with operators increasingly considering convergence with television, music and the internet. This will play an important part in O2's future, now it is owned by the multimedia-focused Telefónica.

Achievements and Future Prospects

O2 has achieved a lot in its four-year life. Rising to UK market leadership, by customer base size, at the end of 2005, and commanding an £18 billion price tag in its acquisition in early 2006, it is clearly a brand on the ascendancy. Its savvy communications strategy has driven brand affinity, customer loyalty and also sales. Studies show that O2's investment in integrated communications is expected to pay for itself 60 times over. Results such as this helped the company and its agency VCCP win the Grand Prix at the 2004 IPA Effectiveness Awards.

Looking ahead, O2 is set to play a key role in the revival of the former Millennium Dome in London, being redeveloped as a major entertainment venue by AEG. To be renamed TheO₂, the brand will use its technical expertise to add value and enhance customers' enjoyment of the experience. O₂ will provide a fresh experience for O₂ customers through providing exclusive access to tickets before they go on general release, fast track queuing systems and exclusive access to the Blue Room bar within TheO₂ Arena through mobile ticketing.

Another important development is the launch of a new £10 million campaign, using the endline 'It's your O₂. See what you can do'. Again, this sees O2 break though the convention of focusing on tariffs by looking at how the world, and customer use of mobiles, is changing. Whether photos, games, music, video – or just making calls – O2 wants to focus on the limitless possibilities of mobile communication and entertainment.

2002

Following the demerger of mmO2 plc from BT to create a wholly independent holding company, the UK brand BT Cellnet re-launches as O₂.

2003

O2 sponsorship of Big Brother sees the introduction of media messaging and video alerts for the first time on UK TV. In the same year, O2's sponsorship of

Capital Radio's Party in the Park, results in over 60,000 texts being sent from people at the event for the chance to go backstage.

2004

O2 signs a long-term strategic agreement with NTT DoCoMo to exclusively launch the i-mode® mobile internet service in the UK and Ireland.

2005

O2 overtakes Vodafone to become the UK's biggest mobile phone network, with 16 million active users. The company also launches a Mobile TV trial in Oxford.

2006

O2 de-lists, from the London Stock Exchange, on completion of the take-over by Telefónica S.A. It also posts its best-ever quarterly customer growth in the UK.

Panadol is a name that is known worldwide and is synonymous with being an effective remedy against various ailments. It is found in thousands of medicine cupboards in the 85 countries where it is sold.

Offerings and Values

As the most popular brand of paracetamol in the UK (Source: My Pharmacy UK), Panadol aims to provide safe, high-performance pain relief for conditions such as headache, migraine, backache, rheumatic and muscle pain, neuralgia, toothache, period pain, sore throats and for the relief of feverishness and the aches and pains of colds and flu.

Panadol has been in the market for nearly 50 years. The active ingredient in Panadol, which is paracetamol, is recommended by experts around the world as an effective first choice for pain and fever. Paracetamol is the healthcare professional's choice for many patient groups for whom other painkillers may be unsuitable, such as children, the elderly, asthmatics and those with stomach disorders.

Indeed, for some it is the only pain reliever that can safely be taken. For example, when used as directed, Panadol provides fast, effective pain relief without the risk of stomach irritation that can be caused by aspirin and ibuprofen, with the added benefit of not interacting with the majority of other medicines.

GlaxoSmithKline, Panadol's parent company, is one of the world's leading research-based pharmaceutical and healthcare companies, committed to improving the quality of human life by enabling people to do more, feel better and live longer.

Innovations and Promotions

Panadol has expanded beyond the original familiar white tablet and is now available in various shapes and forms catering for the different needs of the consumer.

The Panadol range includes Panadol original, which is a pain reliever and fever reducer suitable for all ages from six years-old; Panadol ActiFast, which is formulated in a special way to be absorbed twice as fast as ordinary paracetamol; Panadol Extra, which contains caffeine for 30% extra pain relief with an extra boost; and Panadol Ultra, which combines paracetamol with codeine for stronger pain relief and fever reduction.

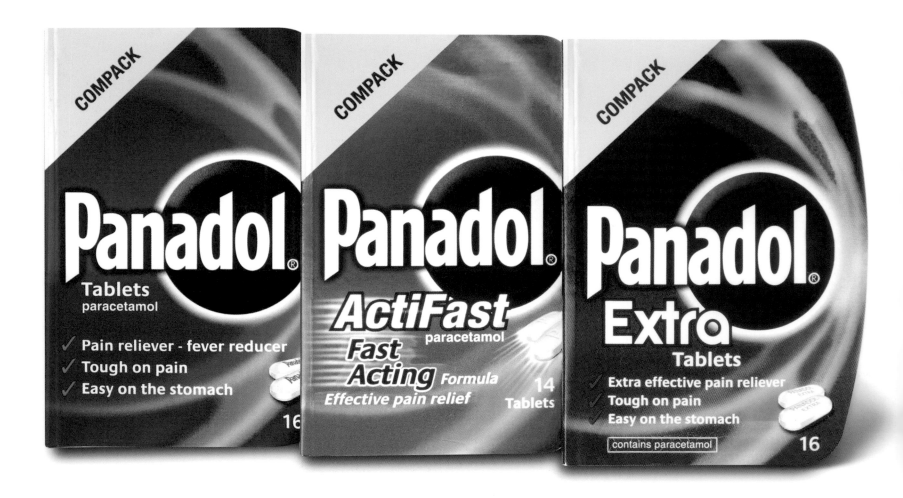

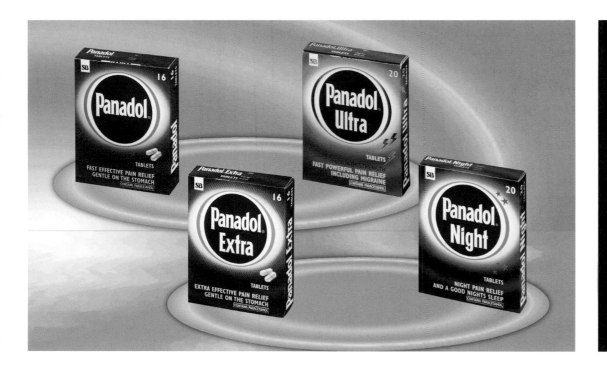

GlaxoSmithKline continues to invest in the Panadol brand, most recently with the focus on Panadol Extra, the biggest selling sub-brand in the range (Source: IRI). A heavyweight outdoor campaign, worth more than £1.2 million, ran during September 2005 with the message '30% Extra Pain Relief' to communicate the fact that, when compared to standard paracetamol, Panadol Extra can give 30% more pain relieving power.

Earlier in 2005, Panadol ActiFast was the focus of a £500,000 national poster campaign, which comprised 2,000 six-sheet poster sites communicating the message: 'Twice as Fast'. The campaign was designed to show that for some consumers, Panadol ActiFast can get to work up to twice as fast as standard paracetamol tablets. The posters also highlighted the new crush-resistant 'compack' packs, designed to be carried in pockets or handbags, which click open to reveal the product and patient information leaflet.

Market Context
Pain relief is the second-largest over-the-counter (OTC) market after vitamins and minerals and is valued at £319.5 million, which represents a 0.9% decline year-on-year (Source: IRI). The decline is attributed to rising price competition and deep cut-price promotions within pharmacy and grocery multiples.

Brand loyalty is high in the pain relief market, with consumers staying with the brands that suit them. Episodes of pain are not generally seen as the time to experiment or change pain killers, although some consumers will buy from a portfolio of accepted brands.

Achievements and Future Prospects
Since its inception, Panadol has proved to be one of the most successful and valuable medications ever created. GSK believes in the highest standards of research and production, and aims to continue to create Panadol products that are relevant to the evolving needs and expectations of consumers.

1955
Panadol is launched as an over-the-counter (OTC) product in the UK by owner Phillips, Scott & Turner, which is later acquired by Sterling Health.

1970s
Panadol has gained enormous popularity and can now be found anywhere from pharmacies to supermarkets and clinics.

1980
Panadol becomes the first systemic analgesic available in mass market outlets in Australia.

1989
Panadol Extra is launched OTC in the UK.

1993
Panadol Ultra is launched OTC in the UK.

1994
Panadol is acquired by SmithKline Beecham as part of its purchase of Sterling Health.

1996
Panadol Night is launched OTC in the UK.

1999
Panadol receives approval for osteoarthritis pain relief in the UK.

2001
Panadol ActiFast is launched OTC in the UK.

2002
GlaxoSmithKline is created by the merger of GlaxoWellcome and SmithKline Beecham.

2003
Panadol is re-branded and re-launched, supported by a £2.4 million marketing campaign.

2006
Panadol Extra is the number one selling oral analgesic variant in the UK (Source: IRI).

RaC

RAC has been meeting the needs of the motorist since the beginning of motoring itself in the late 19th century. Today's RAC aims to satisfy all consumer needs throughout the motoring lifecycle – including financing, inspecting, purchasing, insuring, protecting and repairing cars. A people-centric business, RAC is committed to leveraging its motoring knowledge to help its customers.

Offerings and Values

In the early days of motoring, most drivers joined the Royal Automobile Club, which became the arbiter of matters relating to cars and driving. It promoted and enhanced the new 'motoring movement' by teaching driving, issuing road maps, approving garages and hotels, organising insurance and eventually establishing road patrols to help its members.

Today, RAC's vision is to be the UK's first choice provider of motoring solutions. RAC provides a broad range of services to motorists, including roadside assistance, traffic information, driving tuition, service and repairs, car finance and direct car insurance.

RAC is one of the leaders in developing in-car telematics, working with TrafficMaster to provide traffic and travel information using communications and satellite location technology.

The rac.co.uk website provides online services to members and the general public from live traffic news, through car purchasing advice to downloadable children's games.

RAC also offers bespoke solutions to corporate customers, including the leading passenger car, truck and motorcycle manufacturers, contract hire and leasing companies. In addition to breakdown and recovery, the services offered to business customers include accident management, warranties, driver training, risk management and journey management.

RAC cares for drivers travelling at home and abroad through its provision of travel insurance, route planning, European breakdown assistance and travel

RaC

says RAC Patrolman Andrew Waters. That's why you'll find dozens of free ideas for keeping the kids entertained on long journeys at rac.co.uk

RAC Patrolman EDWARD THOMAS

accessories. Fully qualified RAC engineers conduct vehicle checks for individual motorists, manufacturers and garages.

Innovations and Promotions

RAC has a considerable history as a television advertiser, with campaigns that have for the most part focused on roadside breakdown assistance.

The challenge faced by RAC following its acquisition by Aviva, the parent company of Norwich Union was twofold. Firstly it had to define and differentiate its core Roadside Assistance offering; secondly, it had to articulate and bring to life a clear brand ideology that could be extrapolated across a series of commercial offerings including Direct Insurance.

So, a new advertising platform was required to communicate the brand's broader motoring services offerings. The 'People behind the people behind the wheel' campaign was launched in November 2005 and stems directly from in-depth consumer research into the brand. This research revealed deep customer affection for – and satisfaction with – the competence and reliability of RAC's service. RAC was seen as expert, fair, and driven equally by improvements in technology and customer service. It was also seen as a 'people' brand with a core area of expertise that stretched – at least potentially – a long way beyond roadside rescue.

Market Context

It is a fact of life that cars break down. Most drivers will find themselves let down by

their vehicle at some time or other; new cars may be becoming increasingly reliable from a mechanical perspective, but the incidence of simple faults such as flat batteries and flat tyres remains stubbornly high – supplemented with a host of modern electronics-related incidents.

For most drivers, the answer to these problems is to call for assistance from a breakdown recovery organisation.

There are 27.5 million cars on the road in the UK and 30.6 million licensed drivers (Source: RAC Report on Motoring). Of these, some 75% have membership of a motoring breakdown organisation, either personally or as part of a corporate

scheme (Source: RAC Report on Motoring). RAC's share of the total market is about 30% (Source: RAC Report on Motoring).

Achievements and Future Prospects

The core of RAC's offering continues to be its breakdown service and this is the main benefit enjoyed by the organisation's 6.5 million members. However, whilst today's RAC offers a broad range of services dedicated to fulfilling the needs of motorists, it continues its tradition of being a campaigning body established to take on the role of protecting the interests of the motorist.

The people behind people behind the wheel

1897
The Royal Automobile Club, the UK's oldest motoring organisation, is established.

1970s
RAC's fortunes decline to a near crisis point, mirroring the woes of the domestic motor industry.

1998
The full members of RAC vote to sell its motoring services division, which is bought in June 1999 by Lex plc.

2005
RAC is acquired by Aviva, the parent company of Norwich Union.

www.radox.com

Radox has built on 100 years of expertise in herbs and minerals to develop an expansive core product range to suit a wide variety of everyday washing and bathing needs. Renowned for its ability to help change the way people feel both mentally and physically, Radox has developed its bath, shower and handwash ranges by selecting and blending combinations of natural herbs and minerals to improve the way you feel.

Offerings and Values

Radox recognises that people bathe for many different reasons; to ease aches and pains, to help change their mood, to relax and de-stress, to aid sleep, to revive the senses or to indulge in some 'me time' pampering. As with bathing, Radox also appreciates that people have varying needs from a shower depending on who they are and what they are doing.

In addition to the core unisex shower range, there is also a range of three products specifically developed for men – Transform, Activate and Recharge.

Most recent Radox launches include Radox Heavenly bath liquid and Radox Pampering shower cream products. On top of continuing brand developments and expansions, Radox Salts – the original core of Radox – still have a fond place in the hearts of many consumers. The Salts range consists of two variants, Muscle Soak and Vapour Therapy, which still hold more than 40% share of the overall Salts Market (Source: IRI, 52 w/e March 18th 2006).

Innovations and Promotions

April 2005 saw Radox Shower radically re-launched in a new modern translucent pack with a new convenient hook for hanging in the shower, which tucks away to fit tidily in a wash bag or bathroom cabinet. There are eight shower variants in the core range, each with a unique blend of herbs and minerals and new soothing formulations in softer colours for everyday showering needs.

At the same time, the brand re-launched its handwash range in a modern translucent pack, with improved graphics and clearer communication of benefits. There are six variants to choose from, based on different hand washing needs, and to suit different rooms in the home.

In February 2006, Radox added three new pampering shower creams to its range. Each one has been formulated with natural luxurious ingredients, such as pearl extract,

cashmere, and milk – renowned for their caring and indulgent properties – to give a truly pampering shower experience.

TV advertising remains a key activity for Radox, with new campaigns aired every two years to communicate the key brand messages. TV advertising is also supported by a mix of below-the-line activities based on strategies for the year ahead. The strategy includes an ongoing public relations campaign to deliver a consistent, integrated and continual brand presence throughout the year, and to support new product launches.

Market Context
The parent company of the Radox brand, Sara Lee, is the number-one manufacturer in washing and bathing with a 19% share of the total market (Source: IRI, 52 w/e March 18th 2006). Radox, the UK's favourite washing and bathing brand, accounts for 14% of this, and has shown growth of almost 200% during the past 10 years (Source: IRI). The brand's core Radox Herbal Bath range is the market leader with a 20% share, while Radox Shower leads in its category with 14% (Source: IRI). Radox has also achieved success internationally, holding leading positions in South Africa and Australia, with consistent year-on-year growth.

Achievements and Future Prospects
Radox is also number one with regard to innovation. For example, it was the first in the market to develop the 'Proven-To-Relax' formulations found in Radox Herbal Bath. Radox was also first to market with shower gels and hook-shaped bottles for shower products. It was also the first to introduce a non-drip valve to ensure that the product doesn't drip in the shower.

Consumer and trade magazines accredit the brand year-on-year for its innovation and quality. Pure Beauty and Beauty magazines voted Radox Shower 'best new shower product' in their 2005 awards, and Relax Shower has been voted 'best value shower gel' in the 2005 Prima Beauty Awards.

1957
By this point Radox is known as a relaxing bath – still in a salts format – to be enjoyed after sport, gardening or other physical activities.

1969
Liquid Radox is developed as an easier and more effective format to use in the bath. It was voted one of the 10 most successful products to be launched in the grocery trade in its first year.

1975
A move towards showers heralds the launch of Radox Shower with its defining hook pack – specifically developed to hang upside down in the shower.

1993
Radox is first to introduce the innovative non-drip valve to its shower packaging.

2004
The Radox Herbal bath range is re-launched comprising the six favourite Bath variants in a new modern bottle shape.

2006
Radox launches caring and pampering products into its range with Pamper cream shower range and Heavenly bath silks and velvets.

Ribena has been quenching the nation's thirst for nearly 70 years with its unique blackcurrant taste. Over those seven decades, Ribena has developed exceptional insight about blackcurrant cultivation and soft drink consumers. This knowledge has helped to make Ribena Original the number one juice drink in 'Out of Home' in the UK today (Source: ACNielsen ScanTrack w/e March 25th 2006).

Offerings and Values

Ribena's range includes Ribena Original Blackcurrant and Ribena Really Light, which was launched in April 2005 and is already valued at £35 million (Source: ACNielsen ScanTrack w/e March 25th 2006).

In 2005 the Ribena brand was re-launched with new pack graphics and a new pack shape for 500ml and 330ml bottles. This launch has been an unprecedented success, with sales of 500ml bottles growing by 21% over the last 12 months (Source: ACNielsen ScanTrack w/e March 25th 2006).

As part of this re-launch strategy, Ribena Light and Toothkind were replaced with Ribena Really Light, which has the the taste you expect from Ribena but with no added sugar. Ribena Really Light is available in 600ml, 1 litre and 2 litre squash, as well as ready to drink in 500ml, 330ml and cartons plus a new 6 x 330ml multi pack for the fridge.

Ribena's value is derived from its long heritage of making a high quality product range made from the juice of real fruit.

This quality is ensured by a unique supply chain which means Ribena uses 95% of the UK's blackcurrant crop and takes most of it from bush to juice in 24 hours.

Ribena works very closely with its 41 blackcurrant growers, some of whom have had a relationship with the brand for three generations. Ribena also passionately believes

95% OF ALL BRITAIN'S **BLACKCURRANTS** MAKE IT

Things you didn't know

95% of all Britain's blackcurrants are grown for Ribena.

Ribena has been bottled in Coleford in the heart of the Forest of Dean since 1947.

Blackcurrants are grown especially for Ribena by its network of 41 growers across England, Scotland and Ireland.

Ribena was rationed during World War II as a vitamin C supplement for children because the supply of oranges to Britain dried up.

Ribena grows 5,000 acres of blackcurrants, producing 13 billion blackcurrants every year. If all of these blackcurrants were put side by side they would stretch more than three times around the equator (40,074km).

in sustainable and wildlife friendly agriculture and has formed a partnership with The Wildlife Trusts to ensure all of its farms implement individual action plans to help local wildlife flourish.

Ribena began to publicly tell the story of its relationship with its growers through new television advertising in 2005.

The narrative follows the journey of one of the 5% of unlucky blackcurrants that don't make it into Ribena. Just as he can see the gates of the Ribena factory, he gets 'squished' and the David Bellamy voiceover provides the end line: '95% of all Britain's blackcurrants make it into Ribena.'

Innovations and Promotions
Ribena Really Light Blueberry was launched in April 2006. As Ribena's newest product, it is designed to drive growth by appealing to consumers who already know and love Ribena as well as attracting new consumers. Ribena Really Light Blueberry has no added sugar, is low in calories and is a source of vitamin C. It broadens the Ribena range and uses the brand's expertise to provide a sophisticated adult taste.

The launch was supported with a £1.5 million marketing spend. This included outdoor advertising, PR and sampling campaigns across the UK.

The Blueberry flavour is available in 500ml and Ribena's new six pack 330ml, which is available in four flavours: Ribena Original Blackcurrant, Ribena Really Light Blackcurrant, Ribena Blackcurrant and Cranberry and Ribena Really Light Blueberry.

The new multi-pack competes in the adult lunchbox sector and can be kept in the fridge or taken out and about for on-the-go consumption.

Ribena launched its largest ever through-the-line campaign in 2005 with a '95%

chance to win' on pack offer. This reinforced the brand's strapline: '95% of all Britain's blackcurrants make it' and its unique relationship with the British countryside.

The promotion gives Ribena drinkers a 95% chance to win 'The Best of British Prizes' including a Mini Cooper, tickets to The V Festival or, with typical Ribena tongue in cheek humour, their very own blackcurrant bush cutting so they can grow their own Ribena.

This was supported with an integrated marketing campaign, including bespoke advertising, PR and online activity.

An innovative new valve cap was also launched in 2005, to replace the previous sportscap bottle. The concept behind the new design was to create a sleeker, more modern bottle with a spill-proof closure.

Market Context
Ribena's 2005 re-launch was a deliberate effort to appeal to a young adult audience. Historically, the brand has talked directly to mums, but market research indicated that the key Ribena consumers were actually

16-34 year-olds (Source: TNS Worldpanel). Subsequently, the primary audience for all brand and marketing activity has been this group of consumers.

Achievements and Future Prospects
Ribena has a strong 70 year heritage and today is a £152 million brand (Source: ACNielsen ScanTrack), producing more than 750 million bottles and cartons per year. Ribena is the sixth biggest soft drinks brand in the UK (Source: ACNielsen ScanTrack) and number 26 in ACNielsen's Top 100 grocery brands listing. Ribena is sold in more than 20 countries around the world.

1933
Dr Vernon Charley and manufacturer H.W.Carter & Co start production of a blackcurrant syrup.

1936
It is discovered that the blackcurrant syrup retains an exceptionally high vitamin C content.

1937
The blackcurrant syrup is developed further and named Ribena from the Latin for blackcurrants – Ribes Nigrum.

1938
Ribena is first developed for sale mainly through hospitals and maternity homes.

1947
A site at Coleford in the Forest of Dean is chosen for the new Ribena factory.

1982
The Ribena carton is launched.

2005
Ribena launches a new graphics and advertising campaign along

with Ribena Really Light, which has 15 calories per 500ml.

Established in Switzerland 1895

www.rotarywatches.com

Established in La Chaux-de-Fonds, Switzerland in 1895 by Moise Dreyfuss, Rotary Watches is a fourth generation, family run company offering contemporary classic dress watches in the mid-market price bracket. Rotary is extremely proud of the reputation it has built up over the years for quality and innovation combined with value for money. In the UK, Rotary is the brand leader in the mid-market, defined as watches that retail for between £100 and £200.

ROTARY ROUND REVELATION™ TWO FACES, TWO TIMES... ONE WATCH
THE ROTARY REVELATION'S TWO MOVEMENTS ENABLE YOU TO KEEP TWO DIFFERENT TIMES ON YOUR WRIST AND OFFER YOU TWO DIFFERENT STYLES

GS02910/32/06 £299
Swiss made stainless steel case, with leather strap, two quartz movements and scratch resistant sapphire glass.
For a copy of our latest brochure call 08705 100846 or visit www.rotarywatches.com

Offerings and Values

Rotary offers consumers a wide choice of dress watches with a range of 200 models in order to cater for all ages and all tastes. The models enjoy high specifications that guarantee longevity and reliability at affordable prices. From diamond-set watches with matching bracelets to the hugely popular Limited Edition series (production limited to 500 worldwide) of Swiss automatics in their special watch winding boxes, Rotary is a household brand name that engenders trust and confidence in consumers and retailers alike.

The launch of the waterproof Dolphin Standard in 2005 marked one of the most important technological breakthroughs in watch making for the past decade. For consumers the new standard offers peace of mind thanks to a simple promise: 'Swim and Dive All Day'. The standard marks a move away from the complex system of water resistance to which the rest of the industry subscribes. Unlike competitor brands, which reserve water-resistance features for a limited number of chunky sporty models, Rotary has applied the Dolphin standard to virtually its entire range.

In 2006, Rotary has joined forces with the Royal National Institute for the Blind to donate £1 for every 'Easy to Read' watch sold, in recognition of the fact that there are more than two million visually impaired people in the UK who struggle to find a watch that meets their needs.

Innovations and Promotions

In 2006 Rotary launched the first ever round rotating case as an extension to the very successful Rotary Revelation™ family. With two movements and two different dial designs, the Rotary Revelation offers the wearer the ability to maintain two different time zones simultaneously and – if not travelling – to have the choice of two different dials to suit different outfits or occasions.

Above-the-line advertising in 2006 naturally focuses on this exciting and stylish new product, which at £300 for a Swiss made, stainless steel watch, epitomises the value for money credentials for which Rotary is renowned.

Rotary does not sell direct to consumers. Rather, the company supplies the trade and as such is committed to a major programme of trade marketing encompassing teams of field trainers who use state-of-the-art multimedia training CDs to make staff training fun and interactive.

In terms of above-the-line activity, Rotary uses a combination of press advertising and PR to communicate to its target audience, choosing to focus creative executions on anchor products such as 'Rotary Revelation'.

Market Context

According to GfK's UK consumer panel, the watch market is worth £744 million and the average price paid for a watch is £46. Growth in the market is being driven by an increasing incidence of multiple ownership as accessorising for both men and women becomes more and more important. The most significant growth is being seen in the higher price brackets, notably £100+ as consumers become more aware of the benefits of investing in a watch that will last a lifetime rather than a lower priced disposable model. Rotary's key competitors in the mid market are Seiko and Tissot.

Achievements and Future Prospects

In the annual UK Jewellery Awards administered by RJ Magazine, the leading trade title for the watch and jewellery industry, Rotary has been a consistent victor, winning the Volume Watch Brand of the Year title in 1998, the Watch Supplier of the Year award for two consecutive years in 2002 and 2003 and was a finalist for the Watch of the Year Award in 2004.

The same trade title, RJ Magazine, runs a monthly retailers' poll by telephone of 200 retailers to ascertain the bestselling brands. Rotary has topped this retailers' poll for 24 consecutive months.

In addition, Rotary Revelation™ was voted 'Watch of the Year' by the duty free title TFWA in 2004, while Rotary was runner up in the watch category of MAXIM magazine's Style Awards in 2004 and 2005.

Already present in some 35 countries worldwide via a distributor network, future plans include the development of a portfolio

of brands for the Rotary Watches Group via standalone propositions, each with their own unique selling point, designed to sit alongside Rotary but targeting different audiences.

1895
Moise Dreyfuss begins making timepieces in a small workshop in La Chaux-de-Fonds, Switzerland.

1907
Georges and Sylvain, two of Dreyfuss' three sons, open an office in Britain to import the family watches.

1925
The now-famous Rotary logo, the 'winged wheel' is introduced.

1985
The Swiss business and its trademarks, with the exception of the rights for the UK and Gibraltar, are sold to the Hirsch Group.

1992
Rotary UK buys the trademarks back and now owns the right to use the trademark worldwide.

2006
Rotary invests heavily in staff training, information technology and new product development, with recent highlights including the launch of the Dolphin Standard in 2005 and the Rotary Round Revelation™ in 2006.

ROYAL DOULTON

ENGLAND

Having earned a reputation for excellence, creativity, skilled craftsmanship and distinctiveness of design, The Royal Doulton Company is valued for its sense of heritage and quality. Prized by collectors the world over, The Royal Doulton Company has an international reach extending way beyond its English roots.

Offerings and Values

Each of the company's principal brands – Royal Doulton, Minton, and Royal Albert – enjoys a long association of royal patronage, and holds at least one Royal warrant. They are also trademark registered. When drawing up new product design, Royal Doulton's Design Studio studies the market, analyses consumer research, and often refers to Royal Doulton's own museum and archives – dating from 1815 to the present day – for inspiration.

Today, Royal Doulton provides a wide selection of domestic tableware manufactured in bone china and fine china. The brand also features in an extensive range of crystal stemware and giftware. Royal Doulton lists among its products extensive giftware offerings, character jugs, china flowers, and an array of collectable figurines often known as the Royal Doulton 'pretty ladies'.

Royal Albert, which traces its origins back to 1896, has become an internationally recognised brand, offering domestic tableware and gift items. Equally famous, with an illustrious heritage dating back to its inception in 1793 is the Minton range, best known for its most popular pattern Haddon Hall, which is particularly favoured by the Japanese market.

Innovations and Promotions

The Royal Doulton Company is undergoing an important period of change in its long history as it implements a three-brand master strategy as a first step in developing the company's brands. New global merchandising systems, an e-commerce website, product packaging, point of sale and designer endorsement have all been identified as keys to the brand's development.

A recent collaboration with Gordon Ramsay, the Michelin-starred celebrity chef, has resulted in the creation of a groundbreaking new tabletop collection launched in May 2006. The design was created by Ramsay and Royal Doulton designers following in-depth research at Ramsay's restaurants with the aim

of helping customers recreate the fine dining experience enjoyed in Ramsay's restaurants.

Royal Doulton is a quintessentially British brand with a strong commitment to craftsmanship and artistic innovation. Spring 2006 saw the launch of both a number of new figurines and gifts as well as additions to hugely popular current ranges.

The Licensing Division, created in the mid 1990s to propel the three brands into new product sectors, has achieved considerable success, not least with the launch of Bunnykins Clothing, Silverware, as well as the Children's Furniture product range. In the UK, licensed products include home textiles, jewellery, candles, stationery, child/baby gifts and accessories.

Central to The Royal Doulton Company, promotional and marketing activities have been the development and rationalisation of the brand and its communication. The introduction of everything from new logos to in-store promotional material and branded fixtures has demanded that the focus of activity be centred on the communication and effective introduction of the recent significant changes.

Market Context

Withstanding market fragmentation, ceramic giftware has enjoyed considerable growth – gift-giving, home decoration, and investment being the main motivations. Despite the introduction of many alternative forms of gifts, the ceramic form is sought after as offering true qualities of heritage, craftsmanship, and real, long-lasting value for money.

The Royal Doulton Company is a market leader within the ceramics and chinaware markets, with a large proportion of all English bone china being supplied by Royal Doulton, as well as almost half of the UK's ceramic sculptures.

The key markets worldwide for premium ceramic tableware and giftware are the UK

and Europe, North America, Asia Pacific and Australasia. In total the global market is estimated to be worth over £1.6 billion.

Achievements and Future Prospects

The Royal Doulton Company is one of the world's largest manufacturers and distributors in the premium ceramic tableware and giftware market. With 200 years of heritage, The Royal Doulton Company is a thriving global organisation, with around £95 million annual turnover, employing approximately 2,500 people across its production sites and numerous distribution operations worldwide. The company currently operates in over 80 different markets and has distribution companies in the US, Canada, Australia, and Japan. Indeed, approximately half of all sales are generated outside the UK.

To sustain its position, The Royal Doulton Company's emphasis for future brand growth centres on its ability to focus on the consumer, to understand its buyers, and then to create products that suit individual tastes and needs. Excellence and distinctiveness of design are values that it intends to build on in order to take the brand forward.

1815
John Doulton begins producing practical and decorative stoneware from a small pottery in Lambeth, South London.

1875
John Doulton's son, Henry, relocates the business to Stoke-on-Trent.

1901
King Edward VII, permits the company to prefix its name with 'Royal', and the company is awarded the Royal Warrant.

1930s
The Royal Doulton Company is involved in the manufacture of figurines and giftware.

1966
The company is the first china manufacturer to be awarded the Queen's Award for Technical Achievement, for its contribution to china manufacturing.

1972
Royal Doulton is bought by Pearson and merged with Allied English Potteries.

1993
The Royal Doulton Company separates from Pearson and becomes a publicly quoted company listed on the London Stock Exchange.

2006
Royal Doulton becomes part of the Waterford Wedgwood Group.

Every single person in the UK, at home and at work, is a Royal Mail customer – making the company unique. The reach of Royal Mail's network makes it a brand that touches everyone. Royal Mail covers 99.9% of the UK's population, with regular, reliable services. That's greater penetration than any other media channel, including TV, radio, mobile and landline phones. Not even the combined coverage of all the mobile phone operators can match the reach of Royal Mail.

Offerings and Values

Royal Mail is the custodian of an immensely powerful human network, derived from the astonishing reach it has, not only geographically (99.9% of all households) but also emotionally (the trust placed in the postman, as well as the emotional power of mail itself).

As a result of Royal Mail's unique universal service offering, anywhere in the UK is accessible for one low price. Royal Mail's first class service delivers items sent in the UK within 24 hours, for 32p – one of the cheapest rates in Europe.

Royal Mail's Special Delivery service guarantees delivery by 9am or 1pm next working day or the customer gets their money back. Royal Mail's business mail services allow bulk mailers to send thousands or millions of items with significant savings on standard rates. But Royal Mail's products don't just start and end with the physical mail, it also offers a range of end-to-end logistics services, data and media services to help businesses find, grow and keep their customers.

Innovations and Promotions

Royal Mail has always been at the forefront of innovation, and in 2005 launched several new products including the successful 'Big Book' service, enabling customers to post large numbers of heavyweight items at one low cost. Royal Mail also introduced one of the world's first digital stamps, SmartStamp, which enables customers to buy personalised postage from the internet and print directly on to the envelope.

Royal Mail's special stamps celebrate what it means to be British and the diverse range has featured The Queen's 80th birthday, the Ashes and London 2012.

August 2006 sees one of the biggest changes to postal pricing in Royal Mail's 370-year history – for the first time size as well as weight will be used to calculate postal prices. Although it is estimated that more than 80% of mail will cost the same or come down in price, Royal Mail still needs to communicate this change to the whole

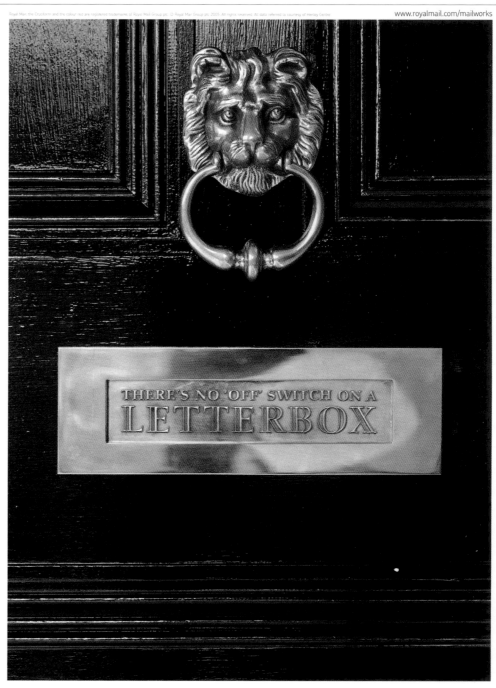

www.royalmail.com/mailworks

THERE'S NO 'OFF' SWITCH ON A
LETTERBOX

A letterbox is always ready and waiting to entertain. No matter when, the sound of the letterbox always gets you to your feet. Quite simply, a letter is impossible to ignore. Nearly 8 out of 10 people open their mail immediately, a third of them will put it to one side to act like an in-home salesman where it can engage, inform and persuade. Again. And again. **With us it's personal®**

Achievements and Future Prospects

Royal Mail's focus on quality in the past few years has seen it deliver its best financial and service results ever. Royal Mail's First Class service remains at target-beating levels, with 94% of First Class stamped letters arriving the day after posting (Source: Research International Dec 2005) – ahead of the 93% national target.

Royal Mail's Special Delivery service continues to provide time-critical deliveries by 9am and 1pm with 99% arriving by the guaranteed time (Source: Royal Mail Track and Trace April 2006).

With nearly 175,000 staff, Royal Mail handles more than 84 million letters, cards and packages every day and its recent growth in the direct mail and goods distribution markets has been heavily influenced by the huge increase in online trading.

The reach of Royal Mail's network does not end in the UK – it is also one of the world's largest international carriers, carrying 1.5 billion items a year destined for over 240 countries.

Royal Mail's corporate social responsibility policies are regularly commended by industry and peer awards. Most recently, Royal Mail was awarded Best European Corporate Social Responsibility programme in the European Risk Management Awards for the second time, an 'Opportunity Now' Silver Benchmarking Award for gender equality and diversity in the workplace, and Best Corporate Social Responsibility programme by the World Mail Awards 2006.

population. The integrated TV, press, radio, outdoor, DM and online campaign will culminate in a door drop to all 27 million addresses in the UK.

Royal Mail's advertising campaign in autumn 2005 was inspired by the emotional power of mail and the emotional responses mail invokes in people. As the only company that delivers to every home and business in the country, every day, Royal Mail is the enabler of millions of personal connections.

Market Context

The postal market in the UK has undergone a complete transformation in the past few years, with full market liberalisation introduced in January 2006. Today Royal Mail faces its biggest challenge, working in a competitive marketplace yet continuing to offer its universal one-price-anywhere service. It has already completed the biggest turnaround in corporate history, from losing £1 million a day three years ago, to making £1 million a day in 2006. Now Royal Mail is competing with other world-class postal services but will continue to provide a comprehensive service to the whole of the UK, remaining dedicated to providing top class business services to its 340,000 business customers.

1635
Charles I allows the public to use his Royal Mail.

1840
Uniform postage introduced with the Penny Black.

1883
Postmen are introduced.

1927
London Underground mail rail opens.

1968
The first 2nd class letter is sent.

1974
Postcodes are designated for all UK addresses.

1981
The GPO splits into the Post Office and BT.

1993
Self adhesive stamps are introduced.

2004
SmartStamp is launched.

2006
The UK postal market is fully liberalised – only the second in Europe. Changes in pricing are made to take into account size as well as weight.

As one of the most recognisable brands in the world, Shell operates the world's largest single-brand retail network with 40,000 outlets. And according to Interbrand's annual survey, it is one of the world's 100 most valuable global brands, worth nearly US$3 billion. But while many consumers might only connect the name 'Shell' with service stations, the brand touches their lives in many more ways through its diverse range of businesses and operations.

Shell and Ferrari

Developed with

World beating performance for your car

Shell's partnership with Ferrari is about much more than just a sticker on the car. We're there for every moment of the race weekend, working with Ferrari, to develop fuel and lubricants that will drive us to victory. The expertise we generate transfers directly to Shell V-Power and Shell Helix - designed to deliver a winning performance every time you put them in your car.

shell.com

Offerings and Values

Shell operates across the broader energy business: for example, as an oil company, in exploring for, producing, and marketing natural gas – a business in which it is a leader; and in the area of new and renewable energy, where it is developing businesses in solar, wind and hydrogen.

Through its retail network, Shell delivers the essential ingredients for personal mobility – vehicle fuels and oils, car-care products, food and drink, groceries, travel-related items and much more, all available at the same point in a single purchase.

Although best known for keeping people on the move, Shell is also present in homes with LPG (Liquefied Petroleum Gas), used for heating, hot water and cooking. In addition, Shell's lubricants plants produce leading lubricants brands such as Shell Helix, Shell Rimula, Shell Tellus, Pennzoil and Quaker State, which are marketed across approximately 120 countries.

Shell's core values of honesty, integrity, and respect for people, define who Shell is and how it works. It is a global group of energy and petrochemicals companies, operating in more than 140 countries and territories, employing around 109,000 people.

Shell is committed to carrying out its business operations efficiently, responsibly, ethically and profitably. To these ends Shell is always seeking relevant and innovative energy solutions that are important to everyone with whom it comes into contact, including the general public, local, regional and national governments, the media, non-governmental organisations and financial analysts.

Innovations and Promotions

Besides main-grade fuels, Shell's range of innovative products is constantly expanding, supported by extensive research and development. Shell is a market leader in branded, differentiated fuels including Shell

**Cleansed. Refreshed.
Revitalised. With Shell Helix.**

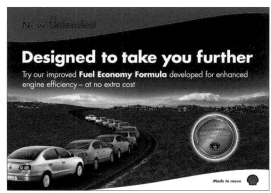

Designed to take you further

Try our improved **Fuel Economy Formula** developed for enhanced
engine efficiency – at no extra cost

Made to move

V-Power, Shell V-Power Racing, Shell V-Power
Diesel, Shell Pura and Shell Optimax, all
tailored to meet growing customer
requirements for improved engine and
environmental performance.

The benefits of fuel and lubricant
technology, developed and proven in motor
racing, are made available to Shell customers
through high-quality fuels that are cleaner,
more efficient, and offer the utmost engine
protection, and with lubricating oils tested
under extreme conditions.

Shell's technical partnership with Ferrari
began in the 1930s with the sponsorship of
the Scuderia Ferrari, and later through
Formula One racing, beginning in 1950.

Together they have won more than 100 F1
World Championship races. Today, Shell
supplies Ferrari with fuels and lubricants,
and a team of specialised Shell engineers
gives Ferrari state-of-the-art analysis at each
Grand Prix.

In order to relate more closely to its
consumers, Shell has embarked on a number
of initiatives. For example, it has formed a
major partnership with Audi Sport to develop
the world's first-ever diesel-powered car
capable of winning the famous Le Mans
24-hour Race, widely regarded as the ultimate
test of performance and endurance and a
showcase for Shell's V-Power fuel technology.

Market Context

Shell is one of the most enduring service
stations brands competing on a global basis
with names such as BP, Esso, Mobil and
Texaco, and in the UK market with brands
as varied as Tesco, Sainsbury's and Q8.

Achievements and Future Prospects

Shell is successfully pioneering synthetic
products such as GTL Fuel and Lubricants from
its proprietary Gas to Liquids Technology (GTL).

GTL Fuel is a clean transport fuel derived from
natural gas rather than conventional crude
oil and can be used in conventional diesel
engines without modification.

GTL can be supplied through existing
infrastructure, which makes it a practical, cost-
effective option. GTL is also a source of pure,
high quality base oils that will mark a step
change in Shell's ability to meet future lubricant
requirements by reducing emissions and
improving fuel economy even further. In some
European countries, Shell has already introduced
GTL Fuel as a special ingredient in its top
performance diesel fuel, Shell V-Power Diesel.

Shell is aiming to create a more emotional
attachment to its customers by making its
marketing activities more relevant and exciting.
At the same time, it is committed to providing
better fuels that address motorists' needs
for greater fuel economy, and are specifically
designed to take drivers further. As a result
of combining these aims, John and Helen
Taylor set a new Guinness World Record for
the most fuel-efficient circumnavigation of the
world through 25 countries ever undertaken
in a standard car (VW Golf FSI1.6).

They used just 24 tanks (of the maximum
50) of the new Shell Fuel Economy Formula
petrol – a tribute to the principles of fuel-
efficient driving.

1833

Marcus Samuel
opens a small shop
in London dealing in
antiques, curios, and
oriental seashells.
His trade in shells
becomes so
profitable that he
sets up regular
shipments from the
Far East.

1890

Marcus Samuel Jnr
starts exporting
Kerosene to the Far
East, sending the
world's first oil tanker
through the Suez
Canal. He pays
tribute to his father's
original business
when he brands the
kerosene 'Shell'.

1897

Samuel calls his
enterprise The
Shell Transport and
Trading Company.
A seashell emblem
was chosen to give
the name visual
emphasis.

1907

Shell forms a close
alliance with Royal
Dutch Petroleum,
also active in the
Far East. Rapid
growth follows.
As with many
other petroleum
companies, the
new motorcar age
fuels their growth.

1950s

Supply and
demand both
boom, and during
this period, Shell
supplies almost one
seventh of the
world's oil
products.

1960s

A boom in the
market for natural
gas leads to the
exploration for and
production of
natural gas in the
North Sea.

1970s

Major oil fields are
discovered in the
North Sea and Shell
becomes a major
player in this area.

2006

Shell makes
automotive history
in the US when the
Audi R10 TDI,
powered by Shell
V-Power Diesel
technology, wins the
'12 Hours of Sebring'
– the first time a
diesel sports car has
won a world-class
endurance event.

SONY®

Sony manufactures audio, visual, video, communications and information technology products for the global consumer and professional markets. With its music, pictures, game and online businesses, Sony is one of the world's leading consumer brands.

Offerings and Values

Sony's most famous product, the Walkman, was launched in 1979. First described as a 'small stereo headphone cassette player', the Walkman introduced the concept of mobile entertainment. At first, retailers reacted badly to the Walkman, arguing that there was no future for a cassette player without a recording mechanism. The public thought differently and Sony sold 1.5 million Walkman players in its first two years on the market.

Today, Sony's product portfolio includes more than 5,000 products. This vast range includes DVD players, cameras, PCs, televisions, hi-fi equipment and semiconductors. These are organised around a brand portfolio that includes Walkman personal audio, BRAVIA flatscreen televisions, VAIO computers, Handycam camcorders, Cyber-shot digital cameras and the PlayStation games console.

Innovation and Promotions

A quarter of a million multi-coloured balls bouncing down the hilly streets of San Francisco is not a sight seen very often, but that's what Sony did to create its recent television advertising campaign for its range of Bravia flat-screen High Definition-ready LCD TVs, launched in September 2005.

The result of the bouncing balls is captured on screen to represent the strapline 'Colour like no other'.

The Bravia advertising campaign was the biggest of 2005 for the Sony Consumer Products group and £4 million was spent on the media campaign, which ran across TV, cinema, radio, outdoor, print, online and in-store.

The agency responsible for creating the campaign, Fallon, received a Gold award for 'Best 60 Seconds Or Less TV Commercial' for the Bravia advert at the British Television Advertising Awards.

In the UK, Sony invests more than £40 million per year in the marketing support of its brands, using a mixture of television, cinema, specialist and consumer magazine press advertising, PR and sponsorship. Indeed, its association with Dame Ellen MacArthur saw the yachtswoman use an all-Sony based onboard media system on her record-breaking round-the-world voyage. This comprised 12 Sony cameras and microphones that could all be operated from below via a simple switching box and video conferencing that helped put the story on national news during the attempt. Three Sony VAIO Centrino-based notebooks were instrumental for navigation, video and still picture editing and communications. According to MacArthur, the VAIO laptops worked without a hitch.

Market Context

The UK market for consumer electronics is made up of TVs, DVD players and audio

products. Despite a softer retail climate, this market continues to blossom – reaching a value of £5.2 billion for the 12 months up to the end of January 2006 – a 10% increase on the previous year (Source: GfK).

Sony is the number one consumer electronic brand in the buoyant UK market with a value share of around 18% (Source: GfK). Sony's key competitors are Samsung, Apple, Panasonic and Philips.

Achievements and Future Prospects

Sony recorded consolidated annual sales of 53.43 billion euros for the fiscal year ended March 31st 2005 and employs approximately 151,400 people worldwide. In Europe, Sony recorded consolidated annual sales of 12.03 billion euros for the fiscal year ended March 31st 2005.

Sony Europe, headquartered at the Sony Centre am Potsdamer Platz in Berlin, is responsible for the company's European electronics business and registered consolidated sales of 8.87 billion euros for the fiscal year ended March 31st 2005.

In 2006, the launch of High Definition (HD) broadcast will be key for Sony from the professional HD recording equipment, through to its new BRAVIA HD ready TVs, as consumers begin to enjoy the viewing benefits provided by High Definition. Sony has made two major developments in this area.

The first is a deal with Sky, which sees Sky and Sony UK co-operate to raise awareness of HDTV in the run-up to the 2006 launch of Sky's package of HD channels, including sports, movies, entertainment, documentary and arts. The marketing campaign will encompass national advertising, direct marketing, demonstrations at events such as the Ideal Home Show and press and radio promotions. The two companies will promote each other's products in their marketing activity and there will be promotions to offer customers savings when they buy a Sony HDTV set and a Sky HD box together.

Sony's second major HD development is the addition of Blu-ray (a next-generation optical disc format) HD technology to its

products. Sony launched the world's first Blu-ray notebook under its VAIO brand in May 2006. Further Sony Blu-ray launches include DVD drives, DVD players and PlayStation 3.

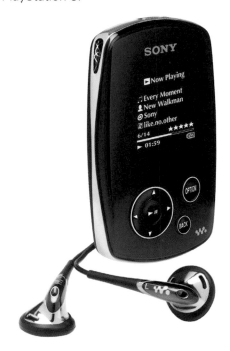

1946

Tokyo Tsushin Kogyo K.K. – later Sony – is established with start-up capital of 190,000 yen for the research and manufacture of telecommunications and measuring equipment.

1950

Japan's first magnetic tape recorder, the 'G-Type', launches.

1968

Sony launches the Trinitron colour TV.

1979

The first personal headphone stereo – the Walkman – is launched.

1982

The world's first CD player is launched.

1990

A High Definition-ready, widescreen, 36-inch television for home-use is launched.

1995

Sony launches the Digital Handycam, the first consumer-use digital video camcorder.

2000

Sony's Personal IT Television 'Airboard' launches.

2003

Sony launches the first 'QUALIA' products.

2006

Sony Corporation celebrates its 60th anniversary.

 **Sony Ericsson**

www.sonyericsson.com

Formed through a joint venture between Sony of Japan and Ericsson of Sweden, Sony Ericsson came into being in 2001. Since then, the company has combined Sony's reputation for quality and design with Ericsson's reputation as a technical innovator. It is now set on a clear path: to establish itself as the most attractive and innovative mobile brand in the world.

Offerings and Values

In order to grow the brand and deliver excellence in consumer devices, Sony Ericsson is leveraging the best of its parents. In 2005 Sony Ericsson licensed the Walkman brand from Sony to enhance the consumer offering of its music handsets. Walkman phones have been developed into their own category, delivering the music mobile experience to consumers. With an enhanced media player, expandable memory and easy to use music transfer software, the Walkman range is fast becoming the consumer choice of music mobile.

In 2006 Sony Ericsson continued its tradition in imaging mobiles by licensing the Cyber-shot name from Sony. The first Cyber-shot phone is available from summer 2006 and will boast a 3.2 mega pixel camera as well as enhanced picture capture to ensure the very best in picture quality from a mobile phone.

These unique offerings appeal and resonate with millions of people enabling Sony Ericsson to deliver an energising experience through the brand.

Sony Ericsson products are well designed from the inside out, with a distinctive, clean approach that is modern yet relevant. Sony Ericsson makes communications products that fuse great applications and great content to create handsets that are trendsetting, easy to use and easily personalised to match the individual's lifestyle. Its latest handsets, headsets and accessories are sources of endless mobile energy that transform seamlessly between imaging, music, gaming, business and self expression.

Sony Ericsson products live this brand promise. The W950i, K800i and M600i are all strong in design as well as rich in benefits, in terms of music, imaging and gaming.

Innovation and Promotions

Sony Ericsson strives to be a cutting-edge provider of applications, forging partnerships with application developers and content providers. A global strategic agreement with Sony BMG Music Entertainment is one way in which the company is bringing the best and latest in entertainment and content to its users.

The company has also activated a major global sports sponsorship deal with the Women's Tennis Association Tour, which was renamed the Sony Ericsson WTA Tour. The six-year partnership is an unprecedented opportunity for Sony Ericsson to offer tennis fans new ways to experience the game through mobile technology, connectivity and content. In 2005 Sony Ericsson launched the first of its Walkman phone range, bringing the first truly music based mobile to market.

In these ways, Sony Ericsson is always thinking a step ahead, anticipating ways to open up appealing new experiences. But innovation is never just for its own sake – innovative thinking must energise consumers, help inspire people and create benefits. While too much technology can be a barrier, Sony Ericsson is committed to demonstrating how energising technology can be. Mobile phones are often seen as generic, functional tools, so the Sony Ericsson difference is that it is not just another mobile phone brand – it is a facilitator to help people experience more. Sony Ericsson handsets aim to energise their users' experiences so they can see more and hear more.

Market Context

The mobile market continues to grow at a vast pace, with saturation running at 106% in the UK, prices are being driven down and consumer expectation are being raised ever higher (Source: Gartner).

In 2005 there was a 21% growth worldwide in the number of handsets sold, totalling 816.6 million (Source: Gartner).

Indeed, the mobile phone has now become ubiquitous, becoming a means of both communication and self expression. Consumers choose handsets that reflect their lifestyles and that are made by companies they trust – but there is a vast number of handset makers, operators, accessory manufacturers, technology companies and retailers, all competing for their attention.

Achievements and Future Prospects

In 2005, Sony Ericsson sold 51.2 million handsets worldwide, up from 42.3 million in 2004, ensuring 2005 was the best year yet for the company. This was on the back of the successful launch of the world's first Walkman phone, the W800i, on August 12th 2005.

Music is a key focus for the business and in 2006 Sony Ericsson has teamed up with some of the biggest names in the world of entertainment; Robbie Williams through T-Mobile and Christina Aguilera with Orange.

The marketplace remains a tremendously challenging one, with saturation beyond 100% in Western Europe, so to achieve stand out, drive purchase and grow market share, Sony Ericsson must continue to focus on its core strengths.

2001

2003

Sony Ericsson launches the T610i, the first handset on the market with an integrated camera.

2004

Sony Ericsson launches the first mega pixel camera phone onto the market, the S700i.

2005

Sony Ericsson launches the world's first genuine music mobile, the W800i. In addition, the company is voted Best Mobile Manufacturer by Mobile Choice magazine.

Specsavers Opticians is the largest privately owned opticians in the world and one of the most successful retailers in the UK (Source: Retail Week 2005). One in three people who wear glasses in the UK buy them from Specsavers (Source: GfK). Still run by husband and wife founders, Doug and Mary Perkins, the company is also a success story abroad, where it has nearly 200 stores in the Netherlands and Scandinavia and has recently opened its first store in Spain.

Offerings and Values

Specsavers Opticians has maintained its founders' philosophy of providing affordable fashionable eyecare for everyone. It offers more than 2,000 styles, including designer ranges such as fcuk, Quiksilver, Monsoon, the excusive Red or Dead collection and its best-selling own brand designer range Osiris.

All Specsavers glasses now include Pentax lenses as standard and pricing is kept as simple and clear as possible so there are no hidden extras.

The largest retail provider of home delivery contact lenses in Europe and one of the top two retailers of continuous wear lenses in the world (Source: VisionTrak Sept 2005), Specsavers was one of the first optical retailers to introduce a direct debit scheme for contact lens wearers. Its own-brand easyvision lenses include daily disposables, monthly disposables and continuous wear lenses, which can be worn for up to 30 days and nights without removal.

Specsavers is still very much a family run company with values to match. Over the past few years, more than £1 million has been donated to various charities. Every two years the company also nominates a national eyecare charity to support – its current relationship with Guide Dogs has seen Specsavers stores raise more than £200,000 to fund the training of 40 new Guide Dog puppies.

Innovations and Promotions

Specsavers has invested heavily in innovative systems and equipment to help ensure that it attains world class standards. For example, in 2005 it introduced high quality Pentax lenses as standard in all its glasses.

TWO PAIRS OF DESIGNER GLASSES FOR £125

Sweden and the Netherlands, bringing its European portfolio to nearly 200, including the opening of its first franchise store in Spain.

As part of its ongoing Drive Safe campaign, Specsavers has introduced a range of lenses especially tailored to drivers, including their own brand UltraDrive lens and a new Polaroid lens, which reduces glare from road surfaces.

Specsavers has also recently launched a store voucher for employers, meaning companies can now offer their staff more affordable corporate eyecare.

Specsavers has been the largest advertiser in the optical sector for many years, with a gross annual spend of £20 million to promote its special offers and build its brand. Indeed, 96% of consumers recognise the Specsavers logo (Source: TNS).

The brand's 'Should've Gone to Specsavers' campaign was the first to win a Retail Week Marketing Campaign of the Year award two years running and the phrase has been adopted by the nation. Specsavers' sponsorship of football and rugby referees has attracted much support as it reflects a sense of humour appreciated by consumers. Specsavers has also recently started sponsoring Channel 4's flagship daytime programme Countdown and launched the first Specsavers Spectacle Wearer of the Year competition to find the UK's sexiest specs wearer.

It also has a duty of care to inform people when their next eye examination is due, which is done through more than 280,000 pieces of direct mail every week.

Market Context

The current UK market for eyecare products and services is estimated at more than £2 billion, with less than 40% still being provided by small independent opticians (Source: Mintel). In the UK optical market, Specsavers currently has a 30% share of transaction – three times that of its nearest competitor, Dollond & Aitchison (Source: GfK December 2005).

While most opticians suffered a decline in turnover as the number of eye examinations dropped and consumers deferred buying their glasses (Source: Mintel February 2006), this didn't affect Specsavers, which continued to expand, opening 40 new stores in the UK and Republic of Ireland and increasing its Hearcare outlets.

Expansion in Europe, where Specsavers is one of the few British retail success stories, has also been brisk with the acquisition of the 32-store Louis Nielsen chain in Denmark and a move into Norway, where there are now 23 Specsavers Optikk stores. The company also opened new stores in

Achievements and Future Prospects

Specsavers has already achieved record sales of almost £15.8 million in one week in 2006, while annual turnover for the group reached a record £758 million for the financial year 2005/06, with sales for 2006/07 predicted to reach £830 million.

The future looks bright for Specsavers, with a new store opening somewhere in the UK or Europe every week. Its Hearcare service is also set to double so that a Specsavers hearing service will be available in more than 200 locations by the end of 2006.

www.stanleyworks.com

The Stanley brand is positioned to meet tomorrow's competitive challenges and is committed to being a leading worldwide manufacturer and marketer. Its vision is to be the world's biggest and best branded tools supplier and to develop its high-growth security systems business. Stanley has moved effectively to expand its products into market areas such as the Far East and Eastern Europe. Today, the Stanley name is known around the world as a reliable guarantee of quality and value.

Offerings and Values

As a world leader in the design, development and delivery of tools, Stanley aims to bring to market the strongest and most innovative tools available. With thousands of products on the market and hundreds introduced each year, Stanley develops the tools consumers need to get the job done. Since 1857, Stanley has produced some of the most innovative and useful tools ever made. Among these tools are the PowerLock® tape rule, the Stanley Knife and the Stanley Magnum Screwdriver.

With its professional tools, Stanley's Industrial Tools Group delivers big tools for big jobs, such as industrial hand tools, professional and industrial mechanics' tools, electronic diagnostic tools, pneumatic fastening tools and fasteners, hydraulic tools, shearers, breakers and crushers. Recognised as leaders in industrial tools, its family of brands builds everything from cars and trucks to roofs and floors.

Stanley is committed to effecting positive change. It supports an array of local and global causes and pledges to continue its legacy of charitable responsibility. Every year, Stanley and its employees partner to support thousands of worthwhile organisations across the globe.

Innovations and Promotions

Today Stanley continues to be an industry leader in tool innovation: in 2006, Stanley plans to launch more than 350 new products, including the new Quickslide knife and the brand new range of consumer fastenings. The Quickslide knife has an all metal construction, no tools are required to change the blade and it also boasts a one-handed operation blade slider. In consumer fastenings, Stanley is launching a complete range for DIY and trade users. This is the

Feel
the STANLEY **difference**

From the timeless Classic 199 "Stanley Knife", a design icon of the 20th century, to the new range of FatMax™ hand tools, innovation and quality are synonymous with the Stanley name. Stanley is the number one brand for tools – demanded for their performance by professionals, enthusiasts and DIYers alike.

Stanley in the 21st century is much more than just knives. In addition to the world famous hand tools the Stanley range now includes paint brushes and rollers, sliding doors, pneumatic fastening solutions and mechanics tools.

Stanley UK Sales Ltd, Beighton Road East,
Drakehouse, Sheffield S20 7JZ
Tel: 0114 276 8888   Fax: 0114 276 4078

first major innovation to hit this category for years, both in terms of product design and packaging. The Stanley new product development teams start by researching the product in use in order to develop products that solve problems or address changing materials or applications. New products are then tested and only launched if they pass rigorous criteria. These elements are key to developing the quality products that will continue to build the Stanley brand in the future.

Stanley is the only tool brand to have developed a major campaign around the 2006 World Cup; the Limited Edition range of products include Toolboxes, Screwdrivers, Chisels, Levels and Tapes all produced with a St George Cross design. In addition, each product has a World Cup cash giveaway game on the pack.

Market Context

The UK DIY market grew to reach a value of £9 billion in the four years from 2000 to 2004, however it fell 2% in 2005 and is predicted to fall again in 2006 (Source: Mintel). The hand tools market was worth £129 million in 2005, 5% down on 2004 (Source: GfK). The tools market is now at saturation point in the UK. Households have invested in tools over the last two decades, but these tools are built to last a lifetime, so overall consumption of tools has directly

slowed down as DIY in general has slowed down (Source: Mintel). Stanley is the number one brand in hand tools with a 27% market share (Source: GfK). Other major brands in the sector include Black & Decker, Bahco, Draper and Spear & Jackson whose market share combined is 7.5% (Source: GfK). 45% of the hand tools market is own label products (Source: GfK). In this increasingly competitive market Stanley's new product development programme will ensure that the brand maintains its position at the top by constantly innovating and offering new products to consumers.

Achievements and Future Prospects

Today, 160 years after the company was founded, Stanley is a worldwide manufacturer and marketer of tools, hardware and specialty hardware products for home improvement, consumer, industrial and professional use. The company stills bears not only founder Frederick Stanley's name but also the spirit and passion that drove him to succeed where others have failed.

In 2005, Stanley's Professional Mobile Tool Chest and its Multi Purpose Tool Bag both won silver awards at the DIY Week industry awards. Stanley is dedicated to continually testing, designing and improving its products to ensure quality and maximum functionality. In January 2006 The Stanley Works announced that it had completed the

acquisition of Facom Tools from Fimalac for 410 million euros. The acquisition brings together two leading European suppliers of tools with complementary brands and products; Facom will strengthen Stanley's offerings of high-end industrial and automotive tools.

1902
Stanley makes its first exports.

1926
The first overseas location is established in Germany for Stanley.

1937
Stanley enters the UK market via the acquisition of J A Chapman.

1966
Stanley is first listed on the NYSE.

1980
Stanley acquires MAC Tools, Proto and Bostitch.

1990
Stanley acquires Goldblatt and ZAG Industries.

2000
Stanley acquires Blick and CST Berger.

2006
Stanley acquires Facom.

Starbucks is the leading retailer, roaster and brand of speciality coffee, with more than 11,000 retail locations around the world. The company is committed to offering the highest quality coffee and the 'Starbucks Experience', while conducting its business in ways that produce social, environmental and economic benefits for communities in which it does business. Starbucks entered the UK market in 1998 and now employs more than 7,000 'partners' in approximately 490 wholly owned stores.

Offerings and Values

Starbucks Coffee Company was created and is run on what has been described as 'a new way of doing business'. Starbucks' mission is to establish itself as the premier purveyor of the finest coffee in the world, while maintaining its uncompromising principles as it grows. While applying the highest standards of excellence to the purchasing, roasting and fresh delivery of its coffee and recognising that profitability is essential to its future success, Starbucks aims to make a positive contribution to the global and local communities in which it

works, through working with a number of partners with expertise in areas such as social development, employability and literacy.

For example, in the UK, Starbucks has worked in close partnership with the National Literacy Trust (NLT) for the past six years to develop All Books for Children (ABC), which aims to introduce pre-school children and their families to the benefits of libraries and reading. Since its inception in January 2001, ABC has reached 7,445 pre-school children and their families, who have chosen over 22,300 free books to take home

and keep. Born out of the success of All Books for Children, The Starbucks Christmas Bookdrive is designed to encourage Starbucks customers and partners to collect books for primary school children. A total of 93,000 books have been collected since the Bookdrive was launched. Workwise, a third key component in the Starbucks community engagement programme, uses the skills and experiences of Starbucks' partners to provide advice and coaching for 14-15 year-olds on the world of work, including the skills and behaviours potential future employers require.

Innovations and Promotions

Starbucks continues to innovate whilst staying true to its mission and guiding principles. The company has an innovative beverage and food offering with favourites such as the Gingerbread Latte at Christmas, Frappuccino™ Light Blended Beverages, premium muffins, panini and wheat and gluten free products. Starbucks coined the phrase, the 'third place' – a relaxing environment between home and work, where you can enjoy your favourite cup of coffee on a comfy sofa. Partnerships with T-Mobile, to provide Wi-Fi hotspots and The Times in store, further enhance the in store experience. More recently Starbucks is innovating around entertainment with the introduction of Hear Music CDs enabling customers to discover, experience and enjoy all genres of music in store.

Market Context

The world coffee market has historically been susceptible to price fluctuations, which are linked to global supply and demand. In 2001, green, unroasted coffee prices hit a 30-year low, adversely affecting many coffee farmers. Regardless of market fluctuations, Starbucks has always been committed to purchasing high-quality coffee in a socially responsible manner but decided it could do more. Starbucks adopted a more integrated and sustainable model that is based on six fundamental principles, called Coffee And Farmer Equity (C.A.F.E.) Practices. These include: paying premium prices to help farmers make profits and support their families; purchasing conservation, certified, organic and Fairtrade Certified™ coffees; and investing in social development projects in coffee-producing countries.

In the UK in 2005, the branded coffee chain market continued to expand rapidly, with nearly 9,000 coffee shops exceeding £1.1 billion in turnover for the first time. The market is expected to grow by a compound annual rate of 8.9% in terms of numbers of outlets over the next three years to reach £1.4 billion in turnover. Branded coffee chains account for just over 30% of the market, and Starbucks leads with approximately 24% share of the market (Source: Allegra Strategies, Café6).

Achievements and Future Prospects

In 2005, the World Environment Centre awarded Starbucks Coffee Company the 21st annual Gold Medal for International Corporate Achievement in Sustainable Development. The award was presented to Starbucks for C.A.F.E. Practices. In 2005 and 2006 Starbucks' work in the community in the UK was recognised by Business in the Community with the award of a Big Tick for excellence in CSR. Going forward, Starbucks will stay true to its values, while innovating and exceeding customers' expectations. It aims to continue to embrace its local and global communities, deliver daily inspiration and a great cup of coffee.

1971
Starbucks is founded in Seattle by three friends who met at the University of San Francisco in the 1960s.

1982
The first store is a success and catches the attention of Howard Schultz, who joins the company.

1987
With the backing of local investors Schultz purchases Starbucks.

1991
'Bean Stock' is introduced – a stock option scheme for all employees to make them 'partners'.

1998
Starbucks enters the UK market through the acquisition of 60 stores from Seattle Coffee Company.

2000
The now-annual Starbucks Christmas Bookdrive is launched with the National Literacy Trust.

2003
The Starbucks Coffee Master Programme is launched.

2004
The Coffeehouse Challenge with the Royal Society of Arts is launched.

2005
Starbucks collects 50,000 books through Bookdrive.

2006
For the second consecutive year, Starbucks is awarded the Big Tick by Business in the Community for Excellence in CSR.

Stella Artois is admired by discerning consumers for its individuality in the beer category, its uncompromising quality, distinctive and sophisticated packaging, and highly esteemed positioning. Its differentiated position has enabled the brand to become the world's fifth-largest international brand (Source: ACNielsen), and one of the fastest-growing brands in the world.

Offerings and Values

Stella Artois is one of the world's best-selling beers and in the UK outsells all other premium lagers. Brewed with traditionally malted barley and the finest hops, it is renowned for its quality and flavour.

With origins that can be traced back to 1366, Stella Artois represents both the contemporary and the traditional. First produced as a Christmas beer, the recipe was never intended to be a regular inclusion in the Artois portfolio but was kept due to its popularity.

Only the very best barley and the finest hops are selected for Stella Artois. The care and attention at every step in the brewing process enable Stella Artois to mature into a full-bodied, well-balanced and thirst-quenching lager.

Innovations and Promotions

In 2006 Stella Artois established Brasserie Artois, a family of premium brands that share the Artois brewing heritage, spearheaded by the UK's number one premium lager. Stella Artois' parent

company, InBev, has invested £50 million in Brasserie Artois, which includes Artois Bock and a new refreshing and easy-to-drink beer, Peeterman Artois, launched in July 2006.

Brasserie Artois has been launched to bring impetus to the beer category and to offer consumers a better quality experience. The brands will be sold together through a new, technically innovative font that guarantees a perfect pint every time. The font incorporates a variable tap control, enabling bar staff to create the perfect head while reducing

wastage. Around 8,000 fonts are being converted in 2006 and over time will gradually replace the existing Stella Artois and Artois Bock fonts.

Inspiration for the brand developments, such as Artois Bock, is drawn from the Artois brewery archives in Leuven. The brand has an illustrious history – for example, Peeterman Artois was named after St Peter and was brewed from 1794 until the 1950s and became one of the most popular brews of the time.

Stella Artois has been instrumental in developing a range of events during 2006. Most notably, the Stella Artois Tennis Championships, which celebrated its 26th year. The Stella Artois film events continue to evolve, seeing the UK's first outdoor film festival: Studio Artois Live.

Stella Artois' advertising has always been a key influencer in the continued success of the brand. With its cinematic style, tone and subject matter, Stella Artois has developed a distinctive filmography of more than 15 years of advertising that aims to demonstrate the sacrifice required to obtain a product of such quality and worth. These campaigns, like the brand itself, have proven their success by appealing to consumers regardless of wide distribution and mainstream popularity.

Market Context

Consumption of alcoholic drinks continues to increasingly take place away from 'on-trade' establishments. This is particularly the case with the largest selling alcoholic drink, beer. The move to 'off-trade' consumption has been driven by a combination of consumers finding other ways to spend their leisure time and heavy retailer price discounting.

Volume sales of alcoholic drinks are predicted to fall slightly, driven by a decline in the largest-selling beverage, beer, with sales marginally down during 2005 (Source: Euromonitor).

Achievements and Future Prospects

Following rapid growth in the 1980s, the early 1990s saw Stella Artois lose market share and volume, but by persisting with its product and advertising strategy, Stella Artois returned to volume growth. It has since become the most widely-drunk

beer brand in Britain, and is today the only beer brand with growing penetration (Source: Alcovision). By volume, Stella Artois is now the largest premium lager brand, and the third largest lager brand, selling over 3,495 million barrels per year (Source: ACNielsen).

In the 'on-trade' Stella Artois is now the fourth largest lager brand by volume, behind the more widely-distributed standard lagers. In the 'off-trade', where consumers have a free choice of all brands, it is the largest lager brand (Source: ACNielsen). This success is attributable to the strength of consumers' sense of affinity with, and desire for, the brand. Consumers believe Stella Artois to be a 'quality' brand, which is 'worth paying more for'.

1894
Stella Artois wins Grand Prix La Plus Haute Distinction medal in Antwerp – the highest distinction.

1970s
The brand establishes the beginnings of a new beer category.

1978
The annual Stella Artois Tennis Championships, an invitation-only event held at the Queen's Club in the run-up to Wimbledon, begins.

1980s
Stella Artois helps define the 'greed is good' sensibility of the decade in its infamous 'Reassuringly Expensive' tagline.

1997
Stella Artois begins its sponsorship of films on Channel 4, making it one of the longest-running TV sponsorships.

2006
Stella Artois is now marketed in more than 80 countries.

TESCO
Every little helps

'Every Little Helps', a simple phrase, but one that underpins everything that Tesco, the UK's leading supermarket, stands for. Those three little words are embedded in the company culture, from shop floor to boardroom, and this ethos is what sets the company apart from its peers in a highly competitive industry.

Offering and Values

Customers have different needs at different times and the variety of Tesco pillar brands gives them a real choice. Finest*, Value, Healthy Living, Free From, Fairtrade and Organics offer variety and choice for customers on every trip to their local store.

But it's not just food that provides great choice and value at Tesco. The company's commitment to be as strong in non-food as food, is growing year-on-year.

Tesco knows its success depends on people, both customers and employees. Its core purpose is 'to create value for customers to earn their lifetime loyalty' and this is backed by two values – 'No one tries harder for customers' and 'Treat people how we like to be treated'. These Tesco values run through every part of the business and staff are recognised and rewarded for 'living' them in their everyday jobs.

Tesco's core values drive everything the company does, including its Community Programme, where the company takes a leading role in making a positive contribution to society by acting fairly, honestly and responsibly and by being a good neighbour.

Like its customers, Tesco cares about the environment and last year the company opened its first 'energy efficient store' in Diss, Norfolk, and a second opened in Swansea in April 2006.

It recently announced a £100 million fund to develop innovative and sustainable environmental technology, such as wind and solar power and to boost recycling.

A further positive contribution is Tesco's popular Computer for Schools campaign and

Granny Smiths.
What's the difference between ours and our competitors'?
Not much really.
They're the same quality as Waitrose.
And the same price as Asda.

Comparison based on loose Granny Smith Apples.
Asda price checked at Clapham Store 07.10.05.
Price comparison excludes Express, Metro and IOM.

TESCO | *Every little helps*

Chicken.
Comes with Clubcard points.
It's just our way of saying thanks.
Because without you, we're stuffed.

TESCO | *Every little helps*

the more recently introduced Sports for Schools and Clubs, which encourage children to try new sports and get fit.

Innovations and Promotions

Customers are more focused than ever before on health and Tesco is striving to make its existing range of products healthier by reducing fat, salt and sugar and introducing a new labelling system showing the levels of each, per serving, in its own-brand products, a first in the UK.

Last year Tesco also became the first supermarket to deliver a 'Kitchen Cupboard guarantee' on ready meals, meaning that only ingredients found in your kitchen cupboard are used in them. Further commitments to healthy eating include a new range of products for children and a Wholefoods brand focusing on pulses, nuts, brown rice and dried fruit.

Tesco's popular advertising campaign featuring Dotty – the mother of all shoppers – took Tesco directly into millions of homes, highlighting the company's commitment to customers and service through a series of comic situations.

As the business grew from selling just groceries to everything from mobile phones to loans, a campaign was needed that represented the changing face of the brand. The new 'Every Little Helps' campaign currently features 32 celebrity voiceovers highlighting every aspect of the Tesco offering. The voice has become more conversational and the business more transparent, hence: 'Bags. We'll pack yours, so you don't tell us to pack ours – Tesco, Every Little Helps.'

Market Context

One of Tesco's key strengths is its ability to adapt and innovate and keep ahead of the game in one of the most competitive markets in the world. In recent years

Tesco has expanded into non-food and retailing services.

The Tesco Express convenience store links local convenience with world class distribution and supply chain management. By providing cheaper prices and great product ranges, customers are being drawn back to their local neighbourhoods and car journeys are being reduced.

Achievements and Future Prospects

In 1997 Tesco announced its 10 year growth plan to develop a strong core business; to be as big in non-food as in food; to develop a profitable retailing services business and to be as strong internationally as domestically. The strategy delivered clear results and Tesco now has a well-established non-food offering, which is popular with customers.

Tesco.com, Telecoms and Tesco Personal Finance are established brands that offer customers simplicity and value in markets that can often be complicated.

Tesco Telecoms has grown rapidly to encompass 1.5 million customers, while Tesco.com handles 200,000 orders a week

and has just opened its first store exclusively for online deliveries. There are no customers, just staff assembling orders and relieving the strain on busy stores.

Overseas, Tesco focuses on being number one in a country rather than building sales across several countries and letting local markets dictate what they offer. This has proved successful for Tesco internationally and it is now planning a move into the US with a new convenience format, launching on the West Coast in 2007.

Tesco's recent accolades include being voted 'Britain's Most Admired Company' by Management Today magazine, as well as the 'Most Parent Friendly' store for the third year running by Tommy's The Baby Charity, and being ranked first for Social Responsibility by Fortune Magazine.

1919
Tesco is born as Jack Cohen invests his serviceman's gratuity of just £30 in a grocery stall.

1929
Cohen opens the first Tesco store in London.

1947
Cohen opens the first self-serve Tesco and the company goes public.

1993
The Tesco Value brand is launched.

1995
The Tesco Clubcard is launched.

1997
Terry Leahy takes over as Chief Executive from Lord MacLaurin.

Tesco Personal Finance is launched.

1999
Tesco.com is born out of an idea to make it easier to shop for people who find it hard to get to a supermarket. It is now the world's largest online grocer.

2003
Tesco launches Tesco Telecoms, a joint venture with O_2.

2006
Tesco operates in 12 markets in Europe and Asia.

THOMSON Local™

www.thomsonlocal.com

Thomson Local helps millions of buyers and sellers get in touch with each other every day. More than 22 million copies are distributed every year across 173 different editions, and referred to 25 times a second (Source: BMRB 2005). Thomson Local seeks to innovate while remaining a dependable, helpful brand that people can rely on for their information needs.

Offerings and Values

Thomson Local is designed with the user in mind to enable them to find information, quickly, easily and directly. The company prides itself on providing information for people regardless of where they are, or where they want to look – whether in print or online.

Thomson Local has always sought to give people more than they would expect from a local directory and has been first to market with many innovations. Its A-Z of businesses, consumer tips and information sections have pioneered new types of content within the directories market.

Innovations and Promotions

The most recent innovation has been the introduction of Localplus, which is a 'lifestyle' section full of community, home, leisure, health, travel and shopping listings and websites. This section contains information for businesses within the directory area, as well as outside, because 'local' may be different depending on what someone is looking for.

For example, there will possibly be several shopping centres within the traditional area of the directory, but probably not a theme park. Even if the nearest theme park is 50 miles away, it will be included, as people are generally willing to travel for this sort of attraction.

In 2002, the Thomson Local became available online as ThomsonLocal.com, which enabled people to search for businesses throughout the UK. Today, users can access more than two million business listings free of charge.

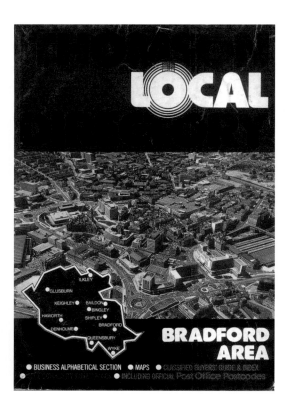

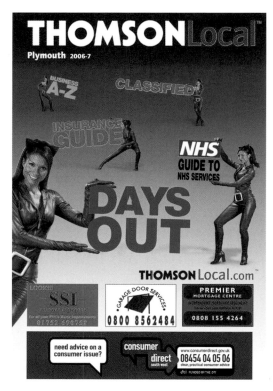

The brand's TV advertising helps drive usage of both Thomson Local and ThomsonLocal.com, which helps support its advertisers' investment. Since the early 1980s, Thomson has advertised on television using cats as a brand icon. Thomson the ginger cat was a familiar face and had a string of on-screen celebrity friends. The tagline 'For the Local answer, ask Thomson' is still remembered by many users.

However, in 1997, the blue cat was introduced with 'The Answer Comes out of the Blue' as the strapline. The latest Thomson Local TV campaign uses a cat lady character to promote the brand's 'Goes further than you think' message. Thomson Local supports its TV advertising with local activity such as radio, taxis and posters.

Market Context
Thomson Local is defined as a classified directory. In 2005 the total directory

market was worth just over £1 billion, with £972 million for printed directories and £90 million for online directories (Source: WARC 2005). As one of the top three directories brands in the UK, more than 15 million referrals per week are made using Thomson Local, with more than one in ten people using a Thomson Local directory in the past seven days (Source: NRS 2005).

Achievements and Future Prospects
In 2002 the Directory Publishers Association Champion Directory was Thomson Local, but as well as having won awards for its products, the brand has won awards for its advertising: in October 2004

the brand won the IAB monthly award for 'Best Online Campaign'.

In 2004 the Thomson Directories' database achieved the ISO 9001:2000 standard, which is testament to its quality control system and processes that ensure the maintenance and delivery of accurate, up-to-date business information.

As a business, Thomson Directories, the company behind the Thomson Local, is an 'Investors in People Champion', only a handful of companies out of 37,000 IIP accredited organisations are exemplars of this standard.

1980
Thomson Directories begins operating in and quickly establishes itself as the leading local directory publisher in the UK.

1981
Thomson Local undergoes a national roll out.

1994
A5-size directories are introduced in selected areas.

1999
Full-colour classified advertising is introduced to 39 Thomson Local directories.

2002
ThomsonLocal.com and WebFinder.com both go online.

2003
The Localplus section is introduced and full colour is rolled out to the majority of Thomson Local directories.

2004
A pioneering agreement with the Department of Health and NHS Direct sees the inclusion of the NHS Direct Self Help guide in 18 million Thomson Local directories throughout England. The Thomson Directories' database achieves the ISO 9001:2000 standard.

2006
Thomson Directories retains its status as a 'The Sunday Times Best Company to Work For'. It first achieved this in 2005, at the first attempt to qualify.

virgin atlantic *Virgin*

www.virgin.com/atlantic

Since 1984 when a young entrepreneur from the music business decided to start an airline in just three months, Virgin Atlantic has been challenging the norms of the airline industry. Today the airline is Britain's second largest flying to the world's major cities. It is the quintessential Virgin story: the small newcomer taking on the giant and complacent establishment, the people's champion with a reputation for quality and innovation.

Offerings and Values

From the start, Virgin Atlantic took a different approach to other airlines. Though it has grown significantly, its service still remains customer driven with the emphasis on value for money, quality, innovation and of course fun.

Many of the things air travellers take for granted today were pioneered by Virgin Atlantic. It broke the mould of the traditional cabin class hierarchy – first class, business class and economy. Its Upper Class service offered a 'first class service for a business class fare', its economy service offered value and, spotting a gap in the market, it invented Premium Economy for those happy to pay extra to upgrade their experience.

The business travel market is the most fiercely competitive sector in the airline industry and when Virgin Atlantic launched its Upper Class it was a revolution, changing

the face of business travel by offering limousine pick-up and collection, Drive-Thru check-in, an on-board bar area, in-flight treatments such as neck and shoulder massage and Clubhouses, which are designed to challenge the conventions of the airline industry and to create a different travelling environment.

In 2003 Virgin Atlantic launched its revolutionary Upper Class Suite, which consists of a reclining leather seat for take off, a place to sit and eat a proper meal opposite your partner, the longest fully flat bed in the world with a proper mattress for sleeping on, a private on-board bar to drink at with your friends, a treatment area where you can enjoy a relaxing massage and four limousines per return trip – all at a price thousands of pounds less than other airlines' First Class.

Innovations and Promotions

Virgin Atlantic has pioneered a range of innovations setting new standards of service, which its competitors have subsequently sought to follow. Yet the greatest and most well known advertisement for Virgin is Richard Branson himself. Branson is often perceived as the consumer's hero, an entrepreneur operating in a style all of his own, and Virgin's brand values emanate from his personality. At the same time as being one of Britain's most admired businessmen, Richard Branson's daredevil antics, such as ballooning across the Atlantic, have given the Virgin brand additional publicity. Branson also keeps a shrewd eye on promotional opportunities: when he heard of British Airways' decision to remove the Union Jack from their plane exteriors, for example, he capitalised on the

124 Superbrands

change by introducing the Union Jack onto Virgin planes.

Virgin Atlantic has proved an astute advertiser over the years. Its logo is highlighted on all its goods and services and is a highly protected property. Virgin Atlantic has implemented an integrated media strategy to promote its brands, including television, newspapers, posters, promotions, direct mail and the internet, often to wide acclaim.

Market Context
The airline industry was affected more than most by the tragic events of September 11th 2001. There was an immediate and significant reduction in passenger demand, particularly across the North Atlantic, and a number of airlines became bankrupt. 9/11 was quickly followed by further challenges of SARS and the effects of the Gulf War. The industry is slowly rebuilding passenger confidence and recent traffic figures show signs of a recovery from 9/11. However, it is clear that in order to survive and compete in this challenging environment it is vital for airline companies to adapt and evolve, focusing on capturing the market with an ever-improving range of services. Airlines with strong brand leadership, such as Virgin Atlantic, should be most likely to emerge from the challenge strengthened.

Achievements and Future Prospects
Virgin Atlantic's achievements have been recognised by a number of prestigious award schemes. In recent years the airline has won a huge number of well respected awards including the Best Long Haul Business Airline at the Business Travel Awards and FX and Design Week awards for its Upper Class Suite.

The airline has collected an array of awards including Best Business airline at Condé Nast Traveller Awards and The Guardian and Observer Awards and Best Transatlantic Airline at the Travel Weekly Awards.

1984
Virgin Atlantic is set up when an Anglo-US lawyer Randolph Fields approaches Richard Branson – the young and unorthodox chairman of the Virgin Group – with an idea for a new airline that would fly between the UK and the US. Within three months the airline begins to lease its planes and June 22nd marks Virgin's inaugural flight from London to Newark.

1990s
Virgin Atlantic buys new planes, expands its route network and innovates in passenger service, both on the ground and in the air.

1992
The revolutionary Premium Economy class is introduced, marking another first for the brand.

1999
Richard Branson signs an agreement to sell a 49% stake of Virgin Atlantic to Singapore Airlines to form a global partnership.

2006
Virgin Atlantic adds Montego Bay and Dubai to its list of destinations, which now stands at 30.

VISA

www.visaeurope.com

With more than 1.3 billion cards in circulation – one for every five people on the planet (Source: Visa International Y/E September 2005 results) – Visa is the world's largest electronic payment system. Globally, Visa is used in almost 50 billion transactions a year, taking place in 24 million locations. In Europe alone, up to 700 transactions per second have led to annual sales exceeding a trillion euros. Visa is determined to make electronic payments the preferred alternative to cash and cheques.

Offerings and Values

Visa began as a consumer credit card company. Today, the world of fast, safe, convenient electronic payments has become complex and diverse. Visa covers credit as well as debit, encompassing ATM, charge and prepaid cards and embracing consumer, commercial and government use. It can involve a physical piece of plastic, or a payment via the phone or internet.

In the UK, spend on Visa cards is 50% higher than its nearest competitor (Source: Visa Europe/MasterCard International). The brand has by far the highest awareness, recognition and reputation in its field.

Visa protects this reputation by ensuring that buyers, sellers and their respective banks all gain real value. Visa systems enjoy 99.999% availability, (Source: Visa Europe Annual Report 2005) providing fast, secure service in any currency.

Positive reputation is also fostered through openness and transparency, community activities and high-profile sponsorships. Visa's global association with the Olympic Games is now in its 20th year, but equal emphasis is given to supporting the Paralympic Games and Visa Paralympic World Cup. Visa also provides support to a number of young aspiring athletes in its pan-European sponsorship programme – Team Visa. Indeed, at the 2006 Winter Olympics, held in Turin, two brothers from the Team Visa programme – Andreas and Wolfgang Linger from Austria, pictured – won gold in the luge doubles event. Visa sponsorship activity is also complemented by sponsorship of the Rugby World Cup.

Innovations and Promotions

Visa has grown dramatically in recent years. It is now unifying around the strategic goal

of increasing its share of consumer spending. To get there it is focusing its activities around three words: 'Love Every Day'.

Historically, cards have been used for high-value, one-off purchases. Love Every Day invites people to see Visa as a safe, convenient alternative to cash or cheques when paying for everyday items.

Banks in 25 countries are collaborating in the most substantial integrated campaign ever run by Visa in Europe. From January 2006 the Love Every Day campaign rolled out a 65 million euro programme of TV, press and poster advertising, public relations, point-of-sale promotions, online, direct mail and more. The Love Every Day philosophy is also at the heart of preparations for the Beijing 2008 and London 2012 Olympics.

The Visa brand mark was refreshed in 2005, bringing its look and feel up to date.

Market Context

Visa Europe co-owns Visa International but is a separately incorporated organisation, controlled by its 5,000 European member banks. Visa Europe gives each competing bank access to the same powerful brand, a range of products and services, high service standards, marketing and other support, plus

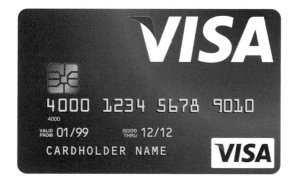

advanced technological systems to authorise, secure and process Visa transactions. The banks then provide a commercial service, issuing cards, setting prices, recruiting retailers and dealing with customers.

Visa Europe operates in 34 European countries, promoting Visa via its members to some 450 million potential users. Visa's competitors' products are found in the field of electronic payments, yet its true rivals are cash and cheques.

Each European market is at a different evolutionary stage. In Iceland, 80% of all consumer purchases use Visa, while the figure is in single digits in Germany, Austria and the Netherlands. In the UK, Visa Europe's largest market, £2.32 in every £10 is spent on a Visa card (Source: Visa Europe Y/E September 2005 results).

Achievements and Future Prospects

Visa has brought swift, convenient, safe payment options to consumers, boosted retail sales, provided profits for its members and made a positive contribution to Europe's economic development and market integration. Across Europe, card numbers are growing at 10.5% per year (Source: Visa Europe Y/E September 2005 results). Yet there is a huge untapped market still to be explored.

Visa is leading the response to an increasing debit opportunity in Europe through its V PAY product. Based on chip and PIN technology, V PAY builds on current domestic debit infrastructures to deliver a borderless European debit card.

Visa is a pioneer in 'contactless' technology, meaning that payment instructions are securely exchanged between a contactless chip card and acceptance terminal, using wireless communication technologies, for low-value transactions. This represents an ideal solution for merchants such as fast-food restaurants, convenience stores and transport terminals, which need to process a large number of low-value transactions.

Visa believes it is well-placed to pursue its ambition to become Europe's favourite form of payment, supplanting cash and cheques.

1958
Bank of America launches BankAmericard.

1969
Most US regional banks convert to BankAmericard or Master Charge.

1976
BankAmericard changes its name to Visa.

1979
Visa introduces the first point of sale electronic terminal.

1983
Visa launches the world's first 24-hour ATM network.

1986
Visa becomes the first card payment system to offer multiple currency-clearing and settlement.

1993
Visa issues the first smart card to allow loyalty points, plus corporate business and purchasing cards.

1999
Visa conducts the world's first euro transaction using a payment card.

2004
Visa is incorporated in Europe.

2005
Visa revitalises its brand architecture globally.

With annual grocery sales of £505 million (Source: TNS Superpanel) Walkers Crisps is the UK's biggest consumer goods brand – a pole position it has held since 2003. Backed by some of the most memorable and effective advertising of any UK brand, Walkers has consistently been a leader in its field, with a 45% volume share of the £2 billion UK bagged snacks market. It has also taken a leading role in the healthy eating debate, significantly reducing the saturated fat and salt content in its range.

Offerings and Values

Walkers positions itself as 'Britain's best tasting everyday crisp', offering consumers good quality and freshness. However the brand doesn't believe in taking itself too seriously and aims to make crisps 'fun', viewing them as one of life's simple pleasures, which everyone can enjoy.

A key pillar of the Walkers brand is its responsible approach to health. This is reflected in its moves to significantly reduce the saturated fat and salt content in its core range.

Innovations and Promotions

Walkers has continually innovated to improve its products and move with changing consumer needs, by making its products healthier, providing choice and delivering the best quality, best tasting crisps.

In February 2006 Walkers announced the most significant change ever made to its core range, cutting the amount of saturated fat by 70% compared to 2005. A packet of Walkers crisps now contains less than one gram of saturated fat, which is less saturated fat than in half a chocolate digestive and 5% of the guideline daily amount. This is because Walkers crisps are now being cooked in Sunseed™ oil, which is naturally high in mono-unsaturates and even lower in saturates than olive oil.

The salt content of the crisps has also been reduced, so that a standard bag now contains less than half a gram of salt. That's the same amount of salt as a slice of bread.

Walkers communicated this change to its products via a heavyweight TV advertising, press and outdoor campaign, starring Gary Lineker. Gary was seen communicating the messages in a straightforward 'just thought you'd like to know' tone of voice.

This was rapidly followed by a heavyweight TV and outdoor campaign to communicate the biggest flavour innovation in the brand's history with the launch of three new permanent flavours; Spicy Chilli, Lamb and Mint and Cheddar Cheese.

The Match of the Day presenter and former England striker has been the face of Walker's advertising since 1993, when he returned from playing in

Japan and starred in the 'Welcome Home' commercial.

Lineker has played a key role in the brand's promotion ever since. In May 2006, he and Charlotte Church starred in a campaign to re-launch the Sensations brand, featuring new and improved seasonings with real authentic food flavours, and stylish packaging.

Walkers is also famous for its innovative in-bag promotions, such as Moneybags, which offered consumers the chance to win real money in packets of crisps. In 2004 Walkers gave consumers the chance to win a Ford Street Ka or Ford Focus and in September 2005, it linked with Apple, giving consumers the chance to win an iPod every five minutes.

Market Context
Over the last two years, the increased profile of health and wellness has focused attention on the food and drinks industry, with government and pressure groups demanding that manufacturers play a proactive role by creating products that are less fattening and better for you. While Walkers has led the industry in the way it has addressed the issue, there is evidence that consumers are changing their behaviour. Although Walkers continued to lead the 2005 Biggest Brands Survey, compiled by Marketing Magazine, its sales fell 2% compared to the 2004 survey. According to IRI Infoscan, the £2 billion savoury bagged snacks sector is relatively flat, only growing by 0.5% between 2005 and 2004. However, new launches of healthier crisps by Walkers, such as Potato Heads, have helped Walkers grow its share.

Within its first year, Potato Heads was a £33 million brand, in line with the company's other established favourites, such as Monster Munch, French Fries and Squares.

Achievements and Future Prospects
As well as leading the savoury snack market and becoming Britain's biggest grocery brand overall, Walkers has also garnered a plethora of awards from the marketing and retail sector. The brand has twice been honoured with an IPA Advertising Effectiveness Award, in 1996 and 2001, and in 2003 it gained a Top Product Award from The Grocer magazine.

The brand's excellence in marketing has also been reflected by Neil Campbell, general manager of Walkers, being recently nominated as Marketing Professional of the Year by Marketing Magazine, while departing president and chief executive Martin Glenn was included in the magazine's top 100 poll of the top marketers in the country.

Walkers is also justifiably proud of its cause-related marketing record. In 1999 the brand launched Free Books for Schools. Under the scheme tokens were collected from special packs of Walkers Crisps in exchange for free books. Over its four-year duration the scheme donated nearly seven million books worth more than £35 million to the 36,000 schools taking part. In 2003 Walkers linked with Comic Relief and donated £1 million to the charity, working with them again in 2005.

The brand is also committed to encouraging physical activity. In 2004 Walkers gave away over two million free pedometers, or 'walk-o-meters'. Walkers also sponsors The Walkers Stadium and the Youth Academy at Leicester City FC.

1880s
Henry Walker opens a pork butchery in Leicester. Henry did well and expanded until his shops were dotted throughout the city.

1948
Post-war meat rationing leads Walkers to diversify the business. The company considers moving into ice cream but eventually hit on potato crisps,

which were becoming enormously popular with the public, and weren't subject to rationing.

1954
When meat rationing ends, the company continues making its popular crisps, introducing its best-selling cheese and onion-flavored variety the same year.

1970s
By the late 1970s Walkers Snack Foods aren't limited to Leicester but have spread across the Midlands.

1989
PepsiCo, Inc. acquires Walkers Crisps and Smith Foods for £900 million.

1993
Walkers and Smiths merge in March.

1995
The company is renamed Walkers Snack Foods.

Walkers launches north of the border into Scotland and following the success of this launch moves into Northern Ireland in 1997 and the Republic of Ireland three years later.

2006
Walkers announces the most significant change ever made to its crisps. Walkers crisps are now cooked in Sunseed oil, cutting the saturated fat by 70% compared to 2005. Walkers also reduces the salt content so that a standard bag now contains less than half a gram of salt.

When Richard Wall started making sausages in 1786 he could never have guessed that 220 years later, 44 million packs of Wall's products would be sold every year (Source: ACNielsen 2006). Consumed in eight million households (Source: ACNielsen 2006), Wall's sausages and bacon are eaten with eggs, on the BBQ, in pasta, hearty casseroles or on their own. The Wall's brand, worth £68 million, is recognised by 89% of the British public (Source: ACNielsen & Millward Brown 2006).

Offerings and Values

At Wall's the experience of good quality food is paramount, so the uncompromising standards first adopted by Richard Wall more than 220 years ago are still maintained. Wall's offers the consumer a wide range of both fresh and frozen products: Wall's Standard Fresh Sausages, available in thick, thin and skinless variants; Wall's Lean Recipe Sausages with less than 5% fat; Wall's Favourite Recipe Sausages available in Cumberland, Lincolnshire and Succulent Pork premium variants; Wall's Micro Sausages and Mini Bangers, which cook in 60 seconds and Wall's Brilliant Bacon, available in smoked and unsmoked varieties.

The brand aims to evoke a warm, fun personality and due to its unique heritage, is trusted by the consumer to provide tasty, good quality food for the whole family.

Innovation and Promotions

Wall's' advertising has for many years featured a border terrier who took a well-earned rest in 1999 from his TV appearances. In 2004 the brand reintroduced the much loved British icon for Wall's Favourite Recipe Sausages.

In 2006 the Wall's dog is back, to star in a revamped version of a £1.5 million TV campaign for Wall's Favourite Recipe sausages and Wall's Micro Sausages. The familiar Border terrier has several comical tussles with members of his family in a bid to get his paws on Wall's sausages.

This TV creative runs alongside a new press campaign for Favourite Recipe Sausages and Brilliant Bacon, showcasing Wall's' products through mouth-watering food photography.

During 2006, Wall's will also be stepping up its marketing and PR activity in a bid to

FIELD *fresh*

FARM *fresh*

FOIL *fresh*

Favourite Recipe SUCCULENT SAUSAGES
FOIL WRAPPED *for* FRESHNESS

strengthen its association with good quality family food. Specific products to be targeted include the Wall's Favourite Recipe range, plus Wall's Brilliant Bacon.

Tony Tobin, restaurateur and 'Ready Steady Cook' regular will be working with Wall's to endorse both the Brilliant Bacon and the Favourite Recipe sausages range. His involvement will include recipe development and an integrated PR campaign.

Market Context
Sausages are a quintessential British dish and have been a much loved staple in the nation's diet for many years. Almost 350 million packs of sausages are sold every year, with 19.8 million British households (79% of the total population) purchasing sausages at least eight times a year, spending £14.52 per household per year (Source: ACNielsen 2006).

The sausage market is now worth over £466 million and is growing at more than 6% year-on-year (Source: ACNielsen 2006). One factor driving this growth is the premium sausage category, which has seen the highest level of development using better quality meat and a wider range of recipes and ingredients. Consumers have been willing to switch to these products, pushing up market values as a result.

The bacon market is now worth more than £749 million and is static year-on-year. Between 2005 and 2010 the market is expected to grow by 16% and is set to reach an estimated worth of just under £1.3 billion in 2010 (Source: Mintel Report 2005). There has been a shift in usage from day-to-day to weekend as recent years have seen the cooked breakfast shift to a more lavish affair for the weekend only.

Achievements and Future Prospects
There is now so much variety in the British sausage market that Wall's' future range will cater for many different tastes and will offer a wider variety than ever.

The Wall's range is already one of the largest and most comprehensive on the market, catering for the needs and demands of all types of sausage consumer. But tastes change over time and so too do Wall's' offerings. Wall's Favourite Recipe Sausages are designed to meet demand for sausages that are meatier, tastier and more succulent than ever before. This premium sausage comes in three flavours – Lincolnshire, Cumberland and Pork.

Equally, with hectic lifestyles people want a good tasting Wall's sausage, but ready in an instant with no mess and no fuss. Wall's Micro Sausages are the result – and can be served hot or cold. The latest addition to the Wall's family is Mini Bangers – bite-size sausages packed in a microwave-ready tray with half the fat and 25% less salt than standard Wall's sausages.

2006 will also see the launch of a brand new Wall's website www.wewantwalls.co.uk, which has been revamped to incorporate recipes to inspire consumers. The site also includes relevant nutritional information as well as historical facts and frequently asked questions on the Wall's product range.

1786
Richard Wall opens a sausage and pie business in St James' Market, London.

1812
Richard Wall receives his first Royal appointment as pork butcher to the Prince of Wales.

1880
The business thrives under Richard's son, Thomas, gaining a Royal warrant from Queen Victoria.

1930
Wall's Bacon is introduced.

1939-1945
Wall's continues to thrive during World War II as sausages escape rationing.

1994
Kerry Foods buys the brand.

2003
Wall's introduces a new look for its sausage and bacon range.

2006
Wall's Mini Bangers are introduced.

Whirlpool has been in Europe for 16 years, and in that time it has gone from an unknown name to become the leading white goods brand across Europe. The strategic investments it has made in innovation, manufacturing, and the community are at the heart of its commitment to maintaining the loyalty of its customers and its leadership position within the industry.

Offerings and Values

Whirlpool Europe is a wholly owned subsidiary of Whirlpool Corporation, which is the world's leading manufacturer and marketer of major home appliances such as ovens, dishwashers, tumble dryers, freezers, microwave ovens, refrigerators and washing machines.

Whirlpool pursues its business objectives while contributing to improve the lives of people in the communities where it operates. The most important corporate social responsibility project supported by Whirlpool is its partnership with Habitat for Humanity which is committed to providing simple, decent, affordable houses for families in need, in more than a hundred countries. By the end of 2005, more than one million people were living in Habitat homes.

Whirlpool has supported this global, non-profit organisation, dedicated to eliminating poverty housing worldwide, in many ways over a number of years. It provides products and to date more than 3,500 employees have volunteered to build homes.

In 2001, the charity recognised Whirlpool Corporation for its commitment as the largest corporate donor to the project. Since the beginning of the programme, Whirlpool has supported Habitat for Humanity with an investment of more than US$25 million and donated 62,000 appliances.

Three years later, Whirlpool announced the extension of its collaboration with Habitat for Humanity in Europe, and created a three-way partnership, whereby tennis player Amélie Mauresmo represents the Whirlpool-sponsored Women's Tennis Association (WTA) as official ambassador for Habitat for Humanity in Europe.

In 2005, Whirlpool launched a series of initiatives including 'Aces for homes', the Whirlpool 'Love food' cookbook and the Whirlpool 'Players Painting' to raise further funds and awareness of the work done by Habitat for Humanity.

Innovations and Promotions

Whirlpool's success is born out of relentless innovation. It is consistently producing industry leading design and technological solutions to better meet consumer needs. New designs, advances in technology, evolutions in society and domestic behaviour have all informed the need for change.

The turn of the century saw Whirlpool launch a series of design innovation concept projects: 'Macrowave – new frontiers for the modern microwave' featured at the Milan Triennale and The Louvre; Project F, a concept design project looking at the future of laundry; and in 2004, In.Kitchen, a visionary design project on the future of kitchen space and appliances, became the third installment of the biennial research and design initiative by Whirlpool's global product design studio.

In.Kitchen is Whirlpool's vision for highly integrated built-in kitchens. Although not available to buy, these are not-too-distant product hopes; glimpses of product experiences that could be achieved in the very near future.

Its ability to look ahead is a cornerstone of the Whirlpool brand. Among Whirlpool's most recent innovations is Pret-a-Porter, a fabric freshener that revitalises clothes using steam; and Origami, the first cooking hob with a complete set of accessories.

Market Context

Whirlpool Europe became the wholly owned subsidiary of Whirlpool Corporation in July 1991. This followed Whirlpool's purchase of the remaining share of its 1989 joint venture with Philips of the Netherlands.

Today, Whirlpool has a presence throughout the Middle East, Africa and the Pacific. It is also a leading brand across Europe.

Achievements and Future Prospects

Whirlpool markets its products in 170 countries and manufactures in 13 countries across four continents, employing 68,000 people worldwide and its 2005 revenues topped US$14 billion.

In the annual UK Independent Market Awards, Whirlpool UK won the 'Ultimate

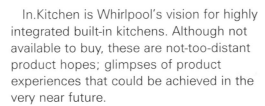

Things you didn't know

Whirlpool operates three of Europe's seven largest factories.

Whirlpool manufactures 60 million products per year.

Whirlpool products can be found in more than 200 million households worldwide.

Whirlpool has been a specialist in home appliances for 95 years.

Supplier of the Year' Grand Prix for the seventh consecutive year, 'Best Training' for the second year and 'Most Impactful Product' for the first time with its Sixth Sense laundry products.

In 2006 Whirlpool is launching 24 major product innovations and also presents In.Home, the fourth biennial conceptual research and design project. The project focuses on the product-user interface and interprets the domestic environment as constantly evolving and adapting to different situations and moods throughout the day.

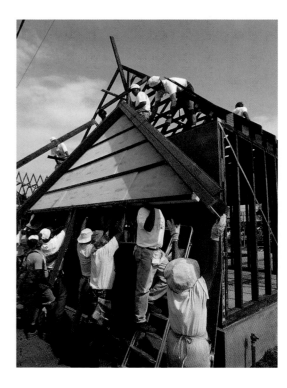

1911
Upton Machine Corporation is founded in St. Joseph, Michigan, to produce electric motor-driven wringer washers. It subsequently merges with the Nineteen Hundred Washer Co. in 1929.

1919
Gottlob Bauknecht starts a small electric workshop in Taillfingen, Germany, eventually establishing his first factory in 1933. Philips acquires the Bauknecht business in 1982.

1950
Nineteen Hundred Corporation changes its name to the Whirlpool Corporation.

1986
Whirlpool Corporation purchases KitchenAid.

1989
Whirlpool Corporation and Philips form a European joint venture. Whirlpool Corporation becomes the sole owner in 1991.

2003
Whirlpool is named as one of the most socially responsible companies in the world by Global Finance magazine.

Whiskas understands what it means to own a cat. In recognising that cats make people happy, they put their knowledge, passion and expertise into making the most enjoyable cat food. And why? Because they understand that the more enjoyable the food, the happier the cat and the happier the cat, the happier the owner.

Offerings and Values

The brand's guiding principle of creating the most enjoyable food for cats is reflected in the ranges that have been created and in the frequent developments and improvements.

Whiskas is constantly looking for new products that will deliver superior enjoyment. To demonstrate this commitment to enjoyable food, 2006 saw the launch of Whiskas' 'Oh So…Meaty & Fishy' variants. A product rooted in the idea that cats enjoy things that are more natural. The product captures the essence of this, containing visible pieces of meat or fish, which cats can really enjoy.

Whiskas has recognised that enjoyment for cats is not only confined to mealtimes – there are other occasions too. 2005 saw the launch of a different kind of cat product, Whiskas Temptations, which are designed as treats for cats. This product gives owners the opportunity to treat their cat beyond the traditional mealtime and find other occasions in the day when they may be able to spend time together.

Innovations and Promotions

Using the insight that some cats can be fussy eaters, Whiskas developed the claim that even the fussiest of cats would love

Whiskas – best captured in the statement '8 out of 10 cats prefer Whiskas'.

Whiskas advertising has consistently brought to life real owners and their cats espousing the enjoyment of Whiskas. The original campaign was effective, helping to position Whiskas as a leading cat food. This was further supported in 1998 with the launch of pouches, which converted many consumers (and their cats) from tins.

In reality, other brands caught up as increasingly their product performed just as well, and for consumers the Whiskas brand lost its relevance. So, in 2005 it was decided that the brand needed to refocus

As well as being the most popular brand of cat food in the UK (Source: IRI 52 w/e Feb 25th 2006), Whiskas is one of the broadest with a wide portfolio of products.

Since its launch, Whiskas has continued to evolve. It was the first to launch every day single serve portions in 1998, which for the first time meant that cats could have freshly opened food every meal. Since then this has become the most popular format in the UK (Source: IRI 52 w/e Feb 25th 2006), delivering both tasty enjoyment and convenience for the owner.

and create a modern interpretation of cat ownership. The brand needed to demonstrate that it not only understood what making good cat food was about but that it got the importance of a cat-cat lover relationship.

The new campaign has seen Whiskas underline the recognition that cat lovers choose to have a cat for the unique cat-cat lover relationship, and the executions have aimed to capture this individuality – first through 'Fred' in the UK.

Market Context
The British love cats, with nearly 25% of Britons owning one (Source: Pet Ownership Survey 2004). Between 1994 and 2004, the number of pet cats in Britain increased by 33% to a figure of 9.5 million (Source: Pet Ownership Surveys 1994 and 2004). Whiskas aims to understand what

cats mean to cat lovers; that they are members of families, who are cared for and loved in the same way.

At its most simple level, the cat food market is split into wet and dry food. However, the market has developed beyond this to now include snacks, treats and milk.

Increasingly, consumers are faced with a growing choice of brands, from mainstream brands through to more indulgent brands such as Sheba and Gourmet, as well as premium dry brands such as Iams and Hills.

Achievements and Future Prospects
Whiskas is present in more than 40 markets worldwide, can be found in five and a half million cupboards in the UK (Source: TNS Worldpanel 52 w/e Jan 29th 2006), and was voted Europe's Most Trusted Pet Food Brand in 2006 by Readers Digest.

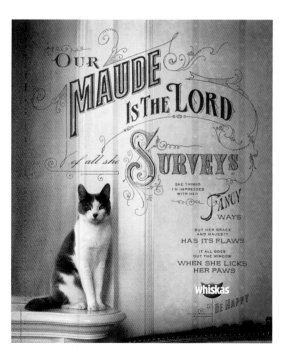

1958
Whiskas launches in the UK.

1965
Whiskas begins its testimonial campaign, which ran until 1996, using real cat owners to talk about their cats' enjoyment of the product.

1970
The claim '8 out of 10 cats prefer it' is first used, making the ad campaign possibly one of the best-remembered in the UK.

1998
The Whiskas pouch is launched. This has since become the most popular format for the product.

YELLOW PAGES ™

www.yellgroup.com

Yellow Pages is published by Yell, the leading international directories business whose brands include Yellow Pages 118 24 7 and Yell.com. Yell's overall business proposition is to put buyers in touch with sellers through a range of simple-to-use, cost-effective advertising solutions. More than 28 million copies of Yellow Pages are delivered annually to UK homes and businesses, ensuring that Yellow Pages is the UK's most used classified directory (Source: Saville Rossiter-Base 2005).

Offerings and Values

Yellow Pages has 2,200 classifications. By classifying businesses under the most relevant and up-to-date headings, Yellow Pages makes life simple for users wanting to find businesses and services. The Yellow Pages brand is built on its reputation for accessibility, trustworthiness, reliability and warmth.

Yellow Pages is ubiquitous, with huge reach. More than 95% of UK homes have a Yellow Pages directory and it is used by 80% of UK adults (Source: Saville Rossiter-Base 2005).

Yellow Pages directories offer advertisers sophisticated targeting geographically, socio-demographically and attitudinally. More than 100 area editions are published annually in the UK, and detailed demographic background information is available on the highest profile classifications.

Research shows that Yellow Pages is ahead of the classified advertising competition on value, with the vast majority of advertisers saying they feel it offers good value for money (Source: Saville Rossiter-Base 2005). On average, Yellow Pages helped advertisers generate £25 worth of new business for every pound spent on advertising (Source: Saville Rossiter-Base 2005).

In keeping with the brand's friendly and helpful personality, Yellow Pages' involvement with charity and environmental projects reflects its concern with issues that affect

individuals and communities throughout the UK. For instance, Yellow Pages has worked with Marie Curie Cancer Care since 1999, supporting the annual 'Great Daffodil Appeal', which has raised more than £15 million for the charity to date.

Yell is very aware of environmental and social issues and its impact on the wider community and is now working with 96% of local councils to encourage the recycling of old directories. The Yellow Woods Challenge – Yell's flagship schools environmental campaign run together with the Woodland Trust – was launched in September 2002 with Kirk, a woodland creature, as its mascot.

Innovations and Promotions

Yell is constantly looking at new and innovative ways to improve and enhance Yellow Pages, as well as extending into new areas to stay at the top of the increasingly competitive classified advertising market.

Classification headings in Yellow Pages directories are reviewed regularly to ensure Yellow Pages users find what they need easily. Alongside traditional classifications such as

Builders and Plumbers, recent additions include Talent Agencies & Management and Colonic Hydrotherapy, reflecting current social and market trends.

2001 saw the launch of the brand new Insurance Guide within Yellow Pages. The new section is designed as an easy-to-use way for Yellow Pages users to source all their insurance needs in one place. This was revamped in 2003 to include headings by product type.

In 2005 the Restaurant Guide was rolled out nationally and has recently been enhanced to include 48 headings ranging from Bistros & Bars to Nepalese.

Yellow Pages is also working in partnership with a number of organisations to ensure the preface has comprehensive information relevant to consumers. From July 2006, a new travel guide from Transport for London will be rolled out across London directories. The London Central directory will also be the first to feature a striking re-design of the Yellow Pages front cover which clearly signposts the new and relevant information inside.

Yellow Pages is well known for its award winning and memorable advertising and PR campaigns. Spring 2006 saw Yell make a major investment to drive Yellow Pages usage with the launch of an exciting new integrated campaign focusing on the Insurance sector. It included a humorous new TV ad which highlighted James Nesbitt's character's new needs in life following the discovery that his girlfriend is pregnant. The campaign also included radio advertising, directory inserts, door drops and public relations activity.

Things you didn't know

New classifications include Dog Walking (2006) and Colonic Hydrotherapy (2005).

The most popular classifications for users are Restaurants, Insurance (all), Garage Services, Plumbers, Builders and Car Dealers (new), (Source: Saville Rossiter-Base 2005).

On VH1's Storytellers programme, Chris Martin revealed that his inspiration for the title of the Coldplay song 'Yellow' came from Yellow Pages.

Yellow Pages can be recycled into animal bedding, stuffing for jiffy bags, egg boxes, newsprint and cardboard.

Market Context

Yellow Pages is part of Yell, a leading international directories business which is the biggest player in the £4.4 billion UK classified advertising market (Source: The Advertising Association 2004). The highly competitive market consists of a range of media, including other printed directories, local and national newspapers and internet search engines.

Achievements and Future Prospects

Since Yellow Pages was first published 40 years ago, the directory has become a part of everyday life and both consumers and advertisers trust Yellow Pages to deliver the results they require year after year.

Yellow Pages is a powerful medium, which is used more than one billion times a year, with seven out of every 10 'look-ups' resulting in a company being contacted and two-thirds of contacts resulting in a purchase (Source: Saville Rossiter-Base 2005).

Product innovation, value for money, advertising packages that deliver leads, and memorable marketing campaigns, all contribute to ensuring that Yellow Pages stays ahead of its game in today's competitive market place.

1966
The UK's first Yellow Pages directory appears, bound into the standard Brighton telephone directory.

1973
Yellow Pages is rolled out across the UK.

1979
Yellow Pages becomes a registered trademark.

1993
Talking Pages is launched.

1996
Yell.co.uk is launched.

2000
Yell.com is launched, replacing Yell.co.uk.

2001
Full colour advertising is launched nationally in Yellow Pages. In addition, Yellow Pages Insurance Guide is launched.

2003
Yellow Pages 118 24 7 is launched. Yellow Pages Insurance Guide is revamped to include headings by product type.

 YELLOW PAGES™

 YELLOW PAGES 118 24 7™

 **YELL.COM**™

Brands to watch

On the pages that follow you will find brands that the Superbrands Council have rated as:

"Brands that have, through exceptional marketing and communication strategies, positioned themselves as significant challengers to established rivals. These brands are expected to grow market share and have the potential to develop into Superbrands of the future. They are either new or rejuvenated brands, whose reputation and brand strength make them an emerging force in the market. These brands have been tipped as the 'ones to watch'."

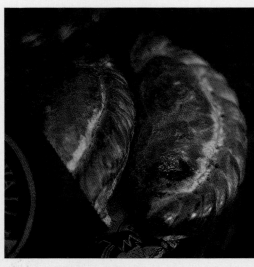

"Purity and harmony are qualities that have been associated with Asahi breweries throughout its 116 years. It is a brand that always aims to deliver the highest levels of quality and integrity to its customers. As it becomes more widely available this heritage and quality, coupled with its deep rooted values make it a strong contender to grow and become a Superbrand in the near future."

The Superbrands Council

Brand Overview

Since it was established in Japan, Asahi Beer has built up an enviable reputation for producing clean, crisp, contemporary products.

Asahi, pronounced 'Ah-sah-hee', is not only Japan's best selling lager; it is currently the most popular brand in Asia (Source: Plat logic 2005). Furthermore, its core brand, Asahi Super Dry – launched in Japan in 1987 and the rest of the world shortly after – now rates as the world's seventh biggest beer brand (Source: Impact 2004).

Since its launch, Asahi has exported its individual flavour and high standards to Europe, where it is now sold in more than 25 countries. Asahi's sale in the on-trade market has increased every year since its UK launch in 1998 and it now has a 60% share of the Japanese premium lager market in Europe.

Asahi Super Dry has been available in Japan on draught since 1987. Asahi has been test-marketing its draught beer in the UK at several venues since 2003, and has received positive responses from customers with regard to taste, serving temperature and overall brand. Asahi Draught Beer was officially launched in the UK in 2006.

Marketing and Communication

The Asahi brand continues to go from strength to strength. Its simple, strong visuals, which draw on the brand's Japanese heritage, emphasise the premium nature of the product and the uncompromising quality of its ingredients.

Asahi's belief that 'quality is more important than quantity' is evident through its marketing. By selecting venues that fit the brand concept Asahi ensures current stockists ooze contemporary style with an eye for modern design, like the newly opened Riverbank Plaza Hotel, situated on the Thames opposite London's iconic landmark, Big Ben.

Asahi's 'cool' credibility has contributed to its success. As a major supporter of many art and design-led events, such as London Fashion Week, it enhances its fashionable profile in trend-setting surroundings. Asahi has also sponsored some of the UK's leading young artists, the likes of Sarah Lucas, Tracy Emin and Damien Hirst – whose White Cube Gallery show in London's East End saw over 1,000 people drinking Asahi.

Asahi's marketing success owes much to its focus on a target audience of hip, urban consumers. Selective ads in style magazines and branded rickshaws through central London highlight its uber-cool appeal. Asahi

can be found in many top Japanese restaurants, such as Nobu, Roka and Wagamama, and is also served in trendy celebrity nightspots, including Eclipse, Boujis, China White, Alphabet and Lab.

An ability to constantly evolve and adapt to market forces has kept Asahi at the forefront of imported premium beers. It is hoped that this market dominance will continue to grow with the UK launch of Asahi Draught this year.

Future Plans

Asahi aims to be the best selling Asian lager in the UK in the next five years. In 10 years time, Asahi would like to be one of the top 15 selling premium lagers in the UK.

Asahi also plans to launch and market its draught beer in Europe.

By March 2006, Asahi draught could be found in nearly 100 bars and restaurants. This is expected to more than double by the end of the year.

In February 2006, Asahi's Sudoku Championship was such a success that a similar kind of promotion will be run next year.

Through focusing on the consumer's perspective and seeking to enhance trust and satisfaction, Asahi aims to grow and prosper in the next decade.

www.brahma.co.uk

"Brewed in Brazil since 1888, Brahma Beer fuses authentic Brazilian heritage with contemporary style. It is inspired by the ethos of 'Ginga' – a creative and optimistic Brazilian attitude, evident in everything they do and how they approach their lives. Brahma has consistently champions the rich, creative talent of its homeland, to communicate brand identity; from its curved bottle to distinctive advertising, Brahma stands out in a crowded market." The Superbrands Council

Brand Overview

The Brahma brand name was registered in 1888 by Joseph Villiger, a master brewer with a passionate interest in the spiritual essence he found embodied in Brazil. It is one of the oldest, and most well-known beer brands on the Brazilian market, as well as one of the biggest beer brands across South and Latin America, including Argentina, Venezuela and Paraguay.

Brahma's Brazil is a world away from the clichéd stereotypes of carnival, beaches and football. It is a more sophisticated, dynamic and sensual world with a rich culture and artists that are making an impression on the global stage. Yet, it retains the passion and playfulness that Brazilians are known for.

All stories need a storyteller and the story of Brahma (and the real Brazil) is told through Brahma Ambassadors, a collective of Brazilian cultural artists (brought together by Brahma) who represent music, fashion and art. Together they are the living embodiment of 'effortless flair' – the Ginga attitude. To date Brahma has worked with Trama Records, Brazil's largest independent record label, and Speto (Paulo Cesar Silva), an established urban artist who stands as a credible expert on the current Brazilian art scene.

Brahma was launched by InBev into several worldwide markets in spring 2005 including the UK, the US, Canada, Belgium, France, the Netherlands, Russia and the Ukraine.

Marketing and Communication

Brahma's initial route to its consumer market came via a digital, PR and sampling campaign that utilised the Brahma ambassadors (Speto and Trama Records) to target core audiences.

Brahma UK launched with a media partnership in 2005, with Dazed & Confused. It included editorial coverage of the Brahma ambassadors and an exhibition of the Speto/Brahma artwork. This was further developed by associations with Brazilian activities based in the UK, including the London Brazilian Film Festival, initiating a Brazilian season of films at cinemas across the UK and strategic partnerships with style magazines as well as fashion and music events.

Brahma's first UK advertising campaign occurred in November 2005. True to the essence of the brand, it was different; unmistakably Brazilian in tone, the adverts aimed to intrigue audiences, luring them to seek out and savour Brazil's best-loved beer. Intelligent use of 'cross track' and outdoor media ensured that Brahma's largely urban audience was made aware of the brand.

2006 has seen Brahma continue to champion its Brazilian heritage, using the musical and creative heartbeat of Brazil to tell its story. It continues to develop, and expand upon, relationships with new and emerging artists, alongside larger activities such as the sponsorship of the Barbican's Tropicalia exhibition and a creative relationship with Brazil aficionado and DJ, Gilles Peterson.

Future Plans

Champion UK talent – UK musicians will have the opportunity to develop their skills with the launch of TrocaBrahma, an original music concept, supporting the collaboration of UK and Brazilian musicians.

Bring flavour, colour and culture to the streets of the UK, throughout 2006, with a series of live billboards and art exhibitions.

Target cinema advertising – first release is scheduled for the summer of 2006.

Remain true to its Brazilian heritage, whilst growing and building the brand with experiences and events throughout the UK.

"Bugaboo revolutionised the pushchair industry with an innovative and functional design that increased the freedom of movement of modern parents. No other stroller on the market took account of the needs of both parents, as well as the welfare of the child. Bugaboo was the first, representing mobility in its purest form and functionality at its best, with transparent design at its core."

The Superbrands Council

Brand Overview

Bugaboo was founded in 1999, by designer Max Barenbrug and physician Eduard Zanen. The aim was to design a stroller that could be used both in and outside of the city, with the focus on the parents – specifically appealing to fathers. After trying unsuccessfully for several years to sell the design, the duo – with a strong belief in their concept – decided to manufacture it themselves. The design was an instant success.

Parents who buy a Bugaboo stroller discover over time the benefits of its innovation and functional characteristics. What becomes apparent is that Bugaboo designers have come to grips with the realities of dynamic, curious parents, who want to continue living their lives to the full, even after having a baby. Mothers – and fathers – feel comfortable with the sturdy, rough and clear design of Bugaboo strollers, a practical product for modern-day parents.

What started off as a small ambitious Dutch company, with just one model, has grown into a design company with over 250 dedicated staff, a presence in 26 countries worldwide and four unique models.

Marketing and Communication

Bugaboo currently advertises in a select number of lifestyle, fashion and parent magazines, as well as on the internet, choosing to focus on the multi-functionality of its products. The company has also introduced two unique creative marketing initiatives, Bugaboo daytrips and Bugaboo By.

Bugaboo Daytrips is an inspirational web-based service for parents. The arrival of a baby inevitably has a major impact on both parents, giving them a new way of looking at the world. But many retain the curiosity and sense of adventure they had pre-child. Bugaboo Daytrips offer these parents an opportunity to experience the rhythm of a city in a personal and active way: a funny museum, the place for the best chocolate, a special clothes shop or a spot with stunning views. Bugaboo Daytrips can be downloaded for free from the bugaboodaytrips.com website. In 2006 there are about 20 Daytrips available in cities like New York, London, Copenhagen, Berlin, Paris, Milan, Barcelona and Amsterdam.

Bugaboo By is a striking series of limited edition strollers; white yet colourful, with digitally printed fabric and hand stitched white leather on the frame and handlebar. It is designed for parents who want to make a statement – a celebration in modern mobile parenting. Only 1,000 Limited Edition Bugaboo By strollers are available worldwide, designed by the Dutch fashion designer and artist Bas Kosters, the first designer to give a new identity to a Bugaboo stroller.

Perhaps the strongest marketing tool that Bugaboo has is recommendation by word-of-mouth. Friends, relatives and parents, who already have experienced life with a Bugaboo stroller, become the true Bugaboo ambassadors.

Future Plans

Design new models to complement existing models, the Bugaboo Cameleon and the Bugaboo Gecko.

Extend the range of products it offers, outside the pushchair and parent-focused sector.

Invite other designers and creative people to try their hand at designing future Bugaboo By models.

Create new, functional and appealing accessories for its existing Bugaboo range.

www.lioneggs.co.uk

"The Lion Quality mark is a world-leading initiative by an agricultural sector, which has succeeded in turning the industry's fortunes around. Based on in-depth consumer research, the British Lion has restored confidence in eggs and enabled the industry to return the market to growth after decades of decline."

The Superbrands Council

Brand Overview

While the Lion Quality mark is not a traditional brand, it has become the defining quality mark for the food industry.

Launched by the British Egg Industry Council in 1998, the Lion Quality mark now represents more than 90% of eggs on retail sale, appearing on more than 3.6 billion eggs, on supermarket shelves, every year.

During its relatively short history, the Lion Quality mark has transformed the UK egg market. From a position of an annual volume decline of around 6% during the 1990s, the category now regularly delivers both volume and value growth.

Developing the Lion into the powerful mark it has become has been the result of a stringent product quality programme, supported by mainstream advertising and marketing, delivering the British Lion's

Soldiering on

SO VERY
BRITISH

prominence as the foremost quality mark in the food and drink industry.

Such has been the success of the Lion mark, that a procession of parliamentarians, Government organisations and other bodies have praised the scheme for the success it has achieved in changing consumer opinion of eggs.

Marketing and Communication

The Lion Quality eggs' marketing campaign has been developed to restore consumer confidence in British eggs and reverse the long-term market decline. In 1999, the British egg industry returned to television advertising after a 20 year absence, using the theme, 'Fast Food. And Good For You', which reinforced the core values of eggs as quick, healthy and convenient, as well as highlighting the specific benefits of Lion Quality eggs. Following the initial launch, visibility of the Lion mark as a food safety reassurance was increased through advertising on bus sides, magazine advertisements and further television advertising.

Key to the success of Lion Quality eggs has been the support of the major retailers, who, in recognising the benefits of the Lion, almost unanimously carry the Lion mark on their egg packs.

The Lion mark received a huge boost in 2000, when then Agriculture Minister, Nick Brown, supported the return of the Lion on egg shells. Consumer reaction was very positive and since then Lion Quality eggs have continued to deliver impressive sales growth in a mature, mass market.

Having established its food safety credentials, the industry turned to developing the market for Lion Quality

eggs and focussed on advertising eggs as a contemporary meal solution. The 'Eggs make a meal out of anything' campaign led to a sustained period of market growth.

In 2006, the industry developed the 'So very British' campaign highlighting the Britishness of the Lion mark.

Consistent advertising has been reinforced with proactive PR campaigns, concentrating both on the Lion and positioning eggs as a modern, convenient, healthy food. In 2004, the egg industry's return to favour was completed by a PR campaign fronted by Edwina Currie, whose remarks in 1988 first questioned the safety of UK eggs.

All this has been achieved in a relatively short period of time and the Lion Quality mark has reversed the long-term decline in the market. It is consistently delivering strong sales growth in a retail sector which is now worth almost half a billion pounds.

Future Plans

Reinforce consumer awareness of the specific characteristics of British Lion Quality eggs.

Continue to develop other opportunities for retail market growth.

Support retail partners.

Develop market for Lion Quality eggs in the food service sector.

"Putting taste at the heart of everything it does has helped Onken to secure a premium position in the UK chilled pots market. As a family-run business, it has pioneered and developed products, gaining a reputation for quality and building up a loyal customer base. The brand's acquisition, by German food group Dr. Oetker, promises further growth aided by its additional resources and expertise."

The Superbrands Council

Brand Overview

Onken was founded in 1940 by Mr Hermann Onken and subsequently run by his son, Enno Onken, until its sale in 2004 to Dr. Oetker – another family-run business. In 1989 Onken entered the UK market as an importer, and has since built up the brand (now worth an estimated £50 million) through innovative products: Onken BioPot, launched in 1989 and Onken Mousse which followed in 1998.

Onken BioPot – made with three live bio-cultures – was one of the first products in the chilled pots sector to contain live bio-cultures. It is sold in the distinct 'big pot' (480g-500g) format. Two of the three types available in the range, Natural and Wholegrain, are the UK's number one sellers within their respective sectors. As a stand-alone sub-brand Onken BioPot is worth over £30 million.

Onken Mousse was the brand's first venture into desserts and is also available in three ranges: fruit, confectionery and a selection of 'lite' varieties. It is now the UK's number one selling mousse, worth approximately £18 million.

Onken BioPot and Mousse have enabled it to operate across the yogurt and the dessert sectors of the chilled pots market, allowing the brand to be purchased both for health reasons and as treats.

All Onken products are made in a state-of-the-art manufacturing complex, Moers, in West Germany; built in 1990 at a cost of £60 million.

Marketing and Communication

Onken has focused on maximising its premium position, with activity centred on solid product innovation, continuous product improvement and communication that highlights the brand quality.

Product quality is never compromised and only high quality ingredients are used. Recipes are continuously developed and improved. Onken offers a wide range of flavours within its sub-brands to increase consumer choice, with some rotated on a seasonal basis to keep the brand feeling fresh. For instance, Onken BioPot Summer started out as just a summer line but consumer demand led to it becoming a permanent part of the range.

On-shelf display is crucial in such a competitive chiller cabinet; packaging design needs to be distinctive for the brand to stand out amongst competitors. The 2002 Onken BioPot re-design won plaudits for having a different bright colour for each pot, providing on-shelf impact and instant brand recognition. Onken Mousse was also re-launched, in 2005, with new packaging that emphasised the quality of the ingredients used.

In 2001 Onken moved away from using just PR, sampling and consumer exhibitions, as a way of marketing its products, and diversified into the mainstream media with its BioPot TV campaign, featuring the memorable 'dancing man'. Further TV campaigns and consumer advertising followed. In all cases the Onken product is the hero, prominently featured to illustrate the brand's self-effacing, humorous personality. More recently (in 2006) the brand's website was re-launched with Onken adopting an email and an electronic CRM strategy to keep customers informed about latest brand development.

If you want to be even more natural eat it in the nude

Onken Natural BIOPOT SET YOGURT

Mild, creamy yogurt made with wholemilk, bio cultures and nothing else · feel good · Onken

Dr.Oetker

Future Plans

An expansion into other sectors of the chilled pots market.

Add more value to the mousse sector with the launch of Onken Luxury Mousse in 2006.

The launch of BioPot Wholegrain Lite multi-packs, to appeal to a younger audience.

The re-launch of the 'dancing man' campaign, aimed at encouraging a new generation of BioPot consumers.

"SUBWAY® has come a long way since Fred DeLuca opened his first store in Connecticut in 1965. What began as one teenager's bid to put himself through medical college has since become a multi-million pound global business, ranking top of Entrepreneur Magazine's Franchise 500 for the past five consecutive years."

The Superbrands Council

Brand Overview

It was in the summer of 1965 that 17 year-old Fred DeLuca (helped by a US$1,000 cheque from family friend, Dr Pete Buck) opened his first submarine roll sandwich store in Bridgeport, Connecticut USA.

Despite having no business plan (other than to raise funds for his college education) the venture proved a success. As the number of stores grew so too did the brand's vision, and within nine years they had turned to franchising as a way to expand the business further.

SUBWAY® now operates 25,767 franchises across 83 countries, making it the largest single brand restaurant chain, in terms of actual numbers. Of these, the US market is the most dominant,

accounting for some 20,080 stores – a higher number than McDonald's.

Going forward, the aim is to emulate this stateside success in the UK and Ireland; a market that now accounts for 680 SUBWAY® stores, 10,200 staff and serves over six million customers a month. The vision? To have 2,010 stores, up and running within this sector, by the year 2010.

Marketing and Communication

SUBWAY® may be a global player, but it still recognises the importance of presenting the brand in a way that is relevant to its local markets. During 2005/06 SUBWAY®'s US Head Office sanctioned a new wave of planning and insight into the UK and Ireland market; work that highlighted a number of differences between the competitor landscape and consumer in the UK and Ireland and those in America. The outcome saw local creative work targeted to local marketplaces, and new product innovation driven by local demand.

For example, the new national promotion 'SUB® of the Day', which offers a different six-inch SUB® every day of the week at the same value price of £1.99. Integrated from store to TV screens, the promotion has not only helped embed the word 'SUB®' into the everyday vernacular of the UK (and in doing so, strengthened SUBWAY®'s ownership of the submarine roll sandwich market), but it also gives SUBWAY® 'virgins' an easy first point of order.

The recent launch of a new brand campaign – the first time the UK and Ireland market has had its own dedicated TV campaign – promotes the very thing that SUBWAY® customers say appeals

most about the brand; that SUBS are made in-house from freshly-baked bread and filled with fresh produce, to the customer's own specification, in front of them. 'Eat fresh' in every sense of the expression. Launched across both TV and radio, the campaign features the proposition 'There are some things you don't want to see… and some that you do' – positioning SUBWAY® as 'champions of freshness'.

Future Plans

Maximise penetration and market share.

Continue to build brand equity and day part.

Innovate to meet the demand of local markets.

Carry out recruitment campaigns to drive new users.

Loyalty scheme to increase frequency amongst existing customers.

"While many mainstream brands offer healthier options to consumers, few manage to successfully combine a quality taste and appealing brand personality with a healthy product. Feel Good Drinks does; by offering superior products and packaging that are competitive in terms of both taste and price. Brand growth is driven by a range of still and gently sparkling natural juice drinks that provides a strong platform for its future expansion." *The Superbrands Council*

Brand Overview

In 2002, three friends, Dave Wallwork, Chris Wright and Steve Cooper, left jobs at Coca-Cola to set up an independent soft drinks business. Recognising that adults were increasingly looking for healthier soft drinks (but that many 'healthy drinks' tasted bland and looked staid), they had a simple aim: to create a range of natural, healthy drinks that tasted and looked great. The name, 'The Feel Good Drinks Company' quickly followed.

Feel Good Drinks contain no added sugar or artificial flavours. Currently, there are two ranges: Feel Good Juice Drinks, available in six flavours including top sellers, Orange & Mango and Apple & Blueberry; the second range, Feel Good Spritz, launched in 2004, was developed as a healthy alternative to

fizzy drinks. Made from fruit juice and gently sparkling spring water, it is available in four flavours in 375ml and 750ml bottles. All Feel Good Drinks are packaged in stylish recyclable glass bottles and embossed with the brand mascot, Felix, and the brand name in Braille.

Feel Good Drinks now sell over one million bottles a month, doubling volume every year. In the UK the brand is stocked in 15,000 outlets, ranging from major supermarkets, cafés and pubs to garage forecourts and high street shops. The brand is also growing internationally, with around 15% of all business now happening outside the UK.

Growth has come at a time of increased competition, with the quality of the drinks and the broad appeal of the Feel Good brand contributing to its success. With an impressive track record and an ambitious and innovative growth plan, Feel Good Drinks are a company to watch.

Marketing and Communication

Much of the brand's marketing focuses on sampling. Targeting parks and beaches on hot days, the Feel Good Team help people to celebrate 'Feel Good Moments' with a cold Juice or Spritz drink. Other marketing activities include welcome packs for new home-owners and a selection of wedding themed activities.

On-pack promotions have also been effective for the brand, helping to drive awareness and sales. Most recently, Feel Good Drinks has teamed up with the 'feel good' movie of the year, Confetti. The promotion follows the Confetti theme with Feel Good offering a range of prizes that includes a weekend trip to a nudist camp – the movie features a naturist wedding.

The Feel Good Drinks website sums up the personality of the brand: fun, friendly and optimistic. It is full of quirky features that include a Drinks Stall, a Park to chill out and meet friends, an Ideas Orchard and the Beach.

Feel Good Drinks has also promoted the brand with posters and radio advertisements, where instead of using professional voice-over artists, it held auditions amongst the staff. The youngest member of the team, Anita, recorded the advert after being voted best performer.

Future Plans

Further brand extension into other healthy drinks categories.

Reach the target of selling two million bottles per month by the end of 2006.

Extension of international business to 20% of business by 2007.

For staff to keep enjoying what they do and to continue to employ more 'feel good people' to work for the brand.

"Established in 1998, West Cornwall Pasty Co. has taken the Cornish pasty out of its traditional heartland, repackaged it in a contemporary way, and positioned it at the upper end of the bakery market. In direct competition with style conscious coffee shops and premium sandwich bars, the company has helped to transform the humble Cornish pasty into a modern day designer food."

The Superbrands Council

Brand Overview

West Cornwall Pasty Co. (WCPCo.) was established with the aim of selling top quality handmade Cornish Pasties beyond Cornwall. Founding Cornish directors – brothers, Arron and Gavin Cocking, father Ken, sisters Victoria and Sarah Barber as well as school friend Mark Christophers – opened the company doors in Chippenham, Wiltshire in 1998, with just £40,000 start-up capital. Today the company has 47 outlets, two mobile units, 450 staff and sells over six million pasties a year, amounting to an annual turnover in excess of £20 million.

With all the directors originating from Cornwall a strong Cornish brand image was integral for the concept to be

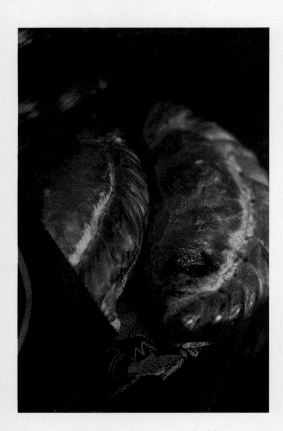

successfully exported to the rest of the UK. The pasties are handmade in Cornwall (with ingredients sourced locally wherever possible) and many of the shop features, such as reclaimed wood and memorabilia, are sourced from the county, giving an authentic feel and atmosphere. All signage and packaging has a strong visual Cornish identity, making use of the county colours of black and gold, and WCPCo.'s distinctive pirate logo, creating an instantly identifiable brand image that gives the customer a clear, visual association with Cornwall.

WCPCo. recognised the opportunity to position this niche business in prime London locations and railway stations, in direct competition to coffee shops and premium sandwich bars. The company has also developed a Cornish theme bar/shop concept and mobile catering, based around the 1960s camper van, an iconic symbol of the Cornish 'surfing' scene.

Marketing and Communication

As one of the first Cornish pasty chains outside the West Country, WCPCo. kept a low profile until 2004, to maximise first mover advantage. Since then it has raised its visibility by concentrating on strong branding and a company culture that focuses on communicating its key themes: an independently run business with an informal feel; a business that has grown rapidly from its own cash generation rather than outside funding; and a team of directors with individual personalities and business responsibilities.

By concentrating on the brand's entrepreneurial prowess, it has achieved over 15 national profiles and featured in over 120 publications. This widespread media

exposure has reached a circulation of over 50 million and an estimated readership of over 130 million, delivering in excess of 10 times the WCPCo.'s initial PR investment.

WCPCo. has been listed in The Sunday Times Fast Track 100 for the past two years and won numerous business awards, including The Sunday Times Fast Track 100 'Best Emerging Brand' award last year, positioning the company as a successful brand with both the public and within The City.

The company is responsive to new ideas; an approach by three Cornish marathon runners led to it developing giant branded Cornish pasties, whose first outing was the London Marathon. The runners got national coverage including a high-profile 30 second BBC interview with Sally Gunnell. The company also recently rolled out an 'all about us' booklet across its network of UK outlets to provide customers with an insight into the company.

Future Plans

Continue geographic expansion across the UK.

Increase presence across the UK events and hospitality sectors.

Target new locations, such as motorway services and airports and develop overseas expansion opportunities.

Brand extension – apply the brand to a range of retail products.

"With a history dating back as far as 1856, Zywiec is renowned for the calibre and flavour of its beer. Brewed from the crystal clear waters of the Polish Skrzyczne Mountains, its commitment to producing quality beer and a respect for tradition has secured it a place in the hearts of beer lovers, the world over. Brand loyalty is built around consistency and distinction – which Zywiec aims to deliver every time."

The Superbrands Council

Brand overview

Brewed in southern Poland (in the city of the same name) Zywiec's heritage goes back to the Middle Ages, when the Prince of Oswiecim granted beer-producing privileges.

The Zywiec logo – a Cracow dancing couple over a branded red banner – despite recent modifications, has stood the test of time and is instantly recognisable; no other Polish beer has been produced under the same label for as long as Zywiec.

A commitment to exceptional quality and taste, coupled with an ethos that respects tradition and the environment, has ensured the growing success of the brand, both at home and internationally.

Zywiec is currently the best-known Polish beer abroad, spanning a diverse global market that extends from the US to Russia and Israel to the Bahamas.

One of the brand's most enigmatic products, Zywiec Porter, is a favourite amongst beer connoisseurs. This strong, dark brew (produced only once or twice a year) has been made to the same traditional recipe since 1881, using a combination of special malts and high quality aromatic hops. Its unique flavour has earned it (and the brand) a host of Gold Medal awards.

It is not only beer that Zywiec excels at; the brand's internet site was honoured with a distinction in the new 'interactive' category at one of advertising's most prestigious events, Eurobest 2005 – the first distinction to be given in the contest's history.

Marketing and Communication

Zywiec expanded considerably during the 1990s by increasing production to the domestic market. This contributed to an overall expansion strategy that saw the brand invest more in its sales and distribution network. Particular emphasis was placed on extending the availability of Zywiec beer within retail outlets: shops, restaurants and pubs. The strategy paid off by strengthening the company's market position. Zywiec is now the largest selling Polish beer in the premium segment, employing over 6,000 people and brewing almost two million hectoliters of beer, every year.

In 2002, BDD took over the entire distribution of Zywiec in the UK. At that time the brand was sold mainly to Polish outlets, giving it a limited

market distribution. However, switching to a wholesale distribution strategy has secured Zywiec a wider profile, with a listing now at one of the UK's best known pub estates, JD Wetherspoons, and retail outlets including Tesco in Eire and major UK wholesalers such as Booker and the Todays Group.

Sophisticated and witty advertising campaigns make Zywiec stand out from its main competitors. Its marketing strategy has ensured that the brand is so well known in its home nation that its straplines are not only incorporated into Polish advertising, they have also become part of the country's everyday language – a testament to the brand's popularity.

BDD

Future Plans

Launch Zywiec draught beer – imported directly from Poland – in the UK.

Introduce more of the Zywiec product range to UK consumers, including its flavoured beer Freeq.

Be the first choice in every segment of the Imported Polish Beer market.

Continue supporting innovative sports and leisure projects, such as its sponsorship of GOPR, the Volunteer Mountain Rescue Team.

Drayton Bird
Chairman
Drayton Bird Associates
www.draytonbird.com

Drayton Bird has been a council member of
Superbrands since its inception. In 2004 the Chartered
Institute of Marketing named Drayton one of the 50
living individuals, worldwide, who have shaped today's
marketing. His firm, Drayton Bird Associates, helps
clients achieve measurably better ROI online and off in
three ways: better strategy, creative and training. They
work with a number of famous brands in the financial
services, home improvement, automobile and IT
sectors. Drayton has been involved with many of the
world's leading brands, including American Express,
British Airways, Ford, Microsoft®, Nestlé, Procter &
Gamble, Philips, Royal Mail, Unilever and Visa.
He has spoken in 39 countries on various marketing
matters and written three best-selling business books
which have been published in 14 languages.

A Tale of Two Books

And why they should matter if you want to build a brand

By Drayton Bird

Consider these names.
Dell. Amazon. Ryanair. eBay. Direct Line. Churchill. MBNA. Expedia.

All either are brand leaders or close to it. Not one invests in classic brand advertising. All, as it happens, sell directly. They want people to buy now.

Here are some others: Manolo Blahnik, Jimmy Choo and Christian Laboutin in shoes; Dr. Hauschka, Aveda, La Prairie, MAC and Bobby Brown in cosmetics; Lulu Guinness in handbags.

Some advertise a little, but that's not how they built their brands.

The plain fact is, the model most followed in the past often doesn't apply now. The spiralling cost of conventional media – always rising faster than inflation; proliferating online, SMS and other media: they're killing it off.

So smart people have found new ways to build a brand. They had no choice. They just couldn't afford to do it the old way.

My Australian partner tells me the hottest thing there now is Experiential Marketing – wonderful, as I have an interest in that area. Others talk of Guerrilla Marketing, Advocacy Marketing and Ambient Marketing.

Two books shed a revealing light on the difference between what I would call the 'traditional' way of building a brand and the way many are building them now.

Shocking – but they were right

Nineteen years ago the late David Ogilvy sent me the proofs of a book. Its authors had solicited his opinion: he asked for mine.

Generously he wrote: "The authors are my competitors, but this does not blind me to its merits." That appeared on the book jacket.

David Ogilvy was one of the best at building and understanding brands. Today brands like Dove still benefit from his thinking half a century ago.

But this book's authors suggested something almost shocking: that many were building brands in an outdated, inefficient way. And Ogilvy agreed.

The book was 'Maxi-Marketing' by Stan Rapp and Tom Collins, direct marketers who founded a big international agency. I gravely doubt whether more than a fraction of those who are brand custodians at any level today have read the book – or even heard of it.

That's a shame, because what has happened since demonstrates that their thesis was absolutely on the money.

Right idea – but not always the right tool

That lugubrious philosopher Nietzsche remarked: "To a man with a hammer, everything looks like a nail."

To many, if not most, who wish to build or maintain brands, the hammer that comes easiest to hand is advertising: 'brand-building' advertising.

It is hugely effective if you wish to convey a simple message to large numbers of people very fast. What is more, besides promotions it is the tool most marketers know best; the one they are used to wielding.

You don't ask people to buy immediately. You hammer away at a simple message repeatedly so that it sticks in the mind firmly enough to motivate an eventual purchase. You start by building awareness, then go down the well trodden path to the happy moment when you actually ask people for money.

Messrs. Rapp and Collins suggested that you should not wait. That if possible you should build a brand and get sales at the same time. That you should be as direct and

quick as possible. They used the phrase 'double duty advertising'.

No advertising in the old sense

Here's a different way of building a brand, where virtually nothing was spent on promotion and advertising to the consumer. Design, price and good distribution base were the advertising. The success came from clever thinking.

That brand is Britvic's J₂O.

In little more than three years, in a bitterly competitive market, even though that the name behind the brand was not doing that well, J₂O became not just a new brand, but pretty much a category on its own.

Bold decisions were taken, not least that of ignoring its parentage: there was no overt mention of Britvic.

J₂O satisfied an unmet need: for a modern adult soft drink brand to appeal to both sexes. Something people would buy when they didn't want alcohol.

I knew just how well the strategy had succeeded when in a bar a while ago I heard someone ask "Do you have any of those J₂Os?" – not "Do you have any long fruity drinks?"

(How long did it take for champagne to become synonymous with sparkling wine? Or cheddar and camembert to signify a type of cheese? Centuries, I imagine.)

What breaks through clutter best? Advertising – or better design?

How well did J$_2$O do? The figures are startling. In less than four years it became the fastest growing adult soft drink in take-home and Britvic's third biggest money maker.

You could define J$_2$O as a drink you have when you can't have a drink – so its size, bottle shape and crown cork (not screw cap) remind you of a beer bottle. The name is simple – easily heard when shouted in a noisy bar. The design is highly visible and recognisable. You can spot it at a glance eight feet away through a crowd. For much the same reason, it's easily recognised in crowded chiller cabinets.

The single-minded design makes it hard to copy – it took three years to develop Schweppes Deuce, the rival.

Little to do with the traditional advertising route to building a brand.

The invisible line: a menace

There has long been a murky cellar 'below-the-line' to which marketers consign so many activities. There is no line in customers' minds; it's just a convenient catch-all for anything except advertising.

It's a menace, for years encouraging a fatal division of marketing focus. So much so that a few years ago the phrase was formally banished from the pages of 'Advertising Age', which is, I guess, the world's premier marketing publication.

There would never be so much costly talk and effort devoted to integration now if communications had not been disintegrated, as it were, in the 1960s and 1970s.

Every message affects how people see your brand, from the logo to the in-store displays to (sometimes the most important) staff training and motivation. In fact its what you do rather than what you say that makes the difference.

Indeed, I would suggest that in any service organisation, how fast or politely your staff answer the phone will do more to help (or hinder) your brand than anything else. This is how things are in the real world, as opposed to the make-believe one many marketers occupy.

The good people in our business are anchored in reality. They remember that in the end what we do comes down to the simple objective defined by Sergio Zyman: "To sell more stuff more often to more people at higher prices."

He was pretty good at it, too. During his six years at Coca-Cola sales rose 50% – and the share price quadrupled.

So what actually makes people buy things?

Three years ago Cap Gemini did research into why people buy new cars. Was it the TV ads most marketers lavish so much on? 17% of buyers said that was what motivated them. 26% said they saw something on the internet. 48% said it was direct mail from the dealer.

But 71% said it was a recommendation from someone they knew. It was advocacy. That person probably thought the car was better than alternatives.

Don't be different: be better

My other book is 'Simply better', by Patrick Barwise of London Business School and Sean Meehan of IMD in Lausanne.

Their thesis is simple. That instead of concentrating so much on differentiation by means, for instance, of finding and promoting a USP, firms should just do what they do better. That they should pay more attention to service, prompt delivery and better products.

The book has been praised by such varied luminaries as the Chairman of Sony, the honorary chairman of Nestlé and Philip Kotler.

What they say will, I hope, change your ideas about what makes good marketing. For they suggest that many things we spend much of our time and energy on are plain wrong – or far less important than others that we take for granted.

The book gives many revealing examples from firms like Orange, Toyota, Ryanair – that name again – and Tesco, whose prodigious success owes much to being the first supermarket chain not just to build a database but use it intelligently.

Some stories in the book are funny – rare and admirable in any business book. One that made me chuckle was about the boss of Eurostar, illustrating how so many big corporate bananas talk about service – but do far too little to ensure it is delivered.

Another name I have already mentioned is quoted at the end of the book. Michael Dell says, "Everything can be done better. There is nothing that cannot be improved."

I believe one major improvement should be thinking and acting far more imaginatively about how to build and sustain brands today – rather than settling for how it was done yesterday.

Cheryl Giovannoni
Managing Director
Landor Associates, London
www.landor.com

Landor Associates is currently Marketing magazine's Design Agency of the Year and is the world's leading branding and design consultancy. Founded by industry pioneer Walter Landor in 1941, Landor has a rich heritage of brand strategy and design leadership. Partnering with clients, Landor drives brand-led business transformation.

Landor's holistic approach to branding builds upon the combined rigour of disciplined thinking and process and exceptional creativity. Landor's work spans the full breadth of branding services, including brand positioning, brand engagement, brand asset management, brand architecture, brand research, packaging and structural design, branded experiences, corporate identity design and naming.

With 22 offices in 17 countries, Landor's current and past clients include some of the world's most powerful brands, such as BP, Cathay Pacific, Delta, Emaar Properties, FedEx, Frito-Lay, Hong Kong, LG Group, Microsoft©, Numico, Procter & Gamble, PepsiCo and Telefónica.

Landor is part of WPP Group plc, one of the world's largest global communications services companies.

Don't 'live the brand', make the brand live

Thinking differently about brand engagement

By Cheryl Giovannoni

If you've ever gone through a brand launch, you're probably aware that for all the excitement surrounding the new brand, all the fanfare and giveaways and special events, it's hard to know what to do after the dust settles. The brand idea might sound terrific – visionary, distinctive, irresistible – but what are you supposed to do with it? How do you actually take what you stand for and make it real? How do 'innovative', 'partner', or 'supersonic' apply to your day-to-day job?

Many start by asking the question "How can I ensure my people live the brand?" This is fundamentally the wrong question – not only does it beget an introspective process with little tangible output, but it also misses a big opportunity. Instead, you should ask "How can the brand transform the way our customers experience us?" Taking this somewhat different perspective will provide focus, tangibility and substance to an otherwise airy topic that can become easily dismissible by cynics. No one can argue with the requirement to provide a better experience for customers.

We all know a powerful brand can help generate not only a better customer experience, but one which is both memorable and differentiated – one that creates stories and engenders reconsideration. Just look at the Virgin Upper Class head massages as a powerful example of this. It is no longer enough for a brand to distinguish itself through an ad campaign or logo. Brands such as Apple, Google, IKEA and Starbucks are considered global leaders not because of their sleek logos but because of the relevant and unique experiences they offer to customers – be it online, in the retail shop, or through the products and services themselves.

Of course it's your people who deliver your brand's promise to customers, so any serious branding initiative must engage employees as a priority. Ultimately, this is about putting the brand at the centre of your business then making sure everything you do and say delivers on it, always keeping your customers firmly at the forefront of your decisions.

To do this, your employees must understand how to use the brand promise as a filter for all their decision-making. So if a brand is all about 'the friendly, personal touch,' a sponsorship manager may opt to align his brand with local village fetes rather than with a football team. Or the HR department may decide to review all job specs and the interview process to ensure that only friendly, personable individuals are considered as viable candidates.

Internal branding, brand assimilation, brand alignment, employer branding – call it what you will. The point is, brand engagement programs capture employees' hearts and minds so customers can get a brand-differentiated experience. All too often these types of programmes focus too much on internal navel gazing rather than delivery to customers.

Successful brand engagement programmes aim to inspire, educate and enable employees to deliver the brand in their day-to-day roles. They shift brand to the centre of the organisation, where it becomes the focus of everything the company and its employees think about and do. With this new mindset,

brand becomes not only a medium of communication with the outside world but also a driver of internal 'on brand' choices and decisions. The result is a transformation in the way business is conducted throughout an organisation – and more importantly, the delivery of a differentiated customer experience.

Easier said than done. Putting brand at the centre of a business is admittedly a long-term effort, not an overnight fix. Many systems may need to be revisited, such as operational processes, organisational structure, training, key performance indicators and employee rewards.

The trick to making your brand engagement programme work lies in providing an engaging and inspiring dimension as well as a practical component that grounds the brand in day-to-day activities.

If your aim is to deliver a differentiated customer experience then a brand engagement programme must achieve three things. First, it must help people understand their role in delivering the brand through the customer experience. Second, it must help people understand and be passionate about the brand so they are motivated to do what's required. And third, it must provide ways for people to immerse themselves in and experiment with the brand.

Connect to the customer
Each time your brand touches a customer, an opportunity is created for the company to build a relationship, elicit an emotional attachment, earn trust and engender loyalty. Employees are often busy with the operational aspects of the business and forget to think about their customers' perspective. They need to be reminded to do so.

A customer journey framework is a useful way to help employees understand the connections they build with people through their brands. By mapping each instance that a customer touches your brand, it helps employees visualise the way their specific roles within the firm influence brand delivery. For example, people in charge of a company's user interface or network services need to realise that they may have an even larger role to play in delivering the brand promise than do customer service representatives and sales associates.

The framework of the customer journey can be used by management and employees alike to focus on important touch points, identify on and off-brand delivery, benchmark areas for improvement, and find places where they can create a 'brand spike', a wow moment that delivers the brand story to customers in a memorable way. For management, the customer journey helps them define the strategic imperatives they must commit to in order to deliver on the brand promise. As noted, these imperatives often include organisational and process changes. For employees, it is a useful working tool for determining specific actions they can take to improve the customer experience and deliver the brand more powerfully.

Make it memorable

People remember the things that excite them, and you want your brand to be one of them. A new brand should stick in the minds of employees long after they leave the launch presentation. This is no easy task; it requires a certain familiarity with employees and a dose of ingenuity.

Painting a portrait of the future can be a powerful way to make a brand real and to generate excitement. Lacklustre attempts at this are sometimes made in brand films by using swelling sound effects and footage of soaring eagles. But a tangible illustration that captures the potential of a brand is much more effective. One accounting firm used a 30-minute play to gain buy-in of the new brand by 300 senior partners. The play began by depicting current life at the company and its difficulty functioning as a global entity, then fast forwarded three years to show what things might be like for employees and clients once the new brand becomes fully embedded in the company. The play made such an impact that participants ranked it highest among all events at the three-day conference. Not only this, but they unanimously endorsed the global internal roll-out of the new brand.

Symbols and stories also help make a brand memorable and keep it fresh. One seemingly small but effective touch that energy giant BP uses is placing potted Aloe Vera plants in the lobby of its headquarters. Of all the green plants, Aloe Vera converts the most carbon dioxide to oxygen. As such, it embodies a core value of the BP brand: to be 'green'. Every day as employees walk into the office, the plants remind them of their shared corporate vision – to go beyond petroleum – and the imperative to develop renewable energy.

Practice makes perfect

The best way to learn something is to be immersed and stimulated by it. You don't learn to speak Spanish by taking a class once a week. You do learn it by living in Spain for a while, surrounded by Spanish with every opportunity to practice it.

Similarly, to turn a brand concept into reality, it must be brought to life for employees. One of the ways to do this is to establish what we call a brand lab – a physical place where your employees can actively 'experiment' with the brand. Make it a place where people can experience the brand in much the same way it might be experienced by the customer. As an interactive environment full of brand and customer stimulus, this is a practical, hands-on way of letting people learn about the brand and its delivery to customers. To be effective, it should be a place where employees and outside partners can practice what they do day-to-day, be it marketing, product development, business planning, or customer service. Think of a brand lab as a learning-by-doing centre, an on-going brand-training experience for everyone who touches your brand.

Engage to transform

Brand engagement isn't about bombarding people with autocratic orders; instead, it gives them the vision, structure and confidence to turn brand into action. When people are engaged with your brand's promise, they become active participants in its delivery, in all aspects of your business.

By rallying your people around your brand promise, you don't just help them to 'live the brand', they can help you to transform your business. Your people become your most powerful asset for delivering the brand. And that's powerful change.

Brand Guardians

Ask.com
Rachel Johnson
VP Marketing Europe

Rachel is responsible for the strategic development of the European Marketing Plan, supporting the global brand strategy for Ask.com in the UK and Europe. She is accountable for managing the implementation of all TTL activity and is a member of the European Executive Committee for Ask.com. She joined Ask.com from Levi Strauss & Co. where she held the role of Marketing Director Northern Europe. Previous roles, which she held during her time at the company included, Acting UK Country Managing Director and Marketing Manager North Europe.

Rachel's extensive marketing experience has also included roles for Whitbread Beer Co. as Marketing Manager for the Heineken brand where she drove the strategic re-positioning of the brand in the UK and also with SmithKline Beecham as a Group Product Manager.

Barclays
Jess Ward
Cashier, High Wycombe Branch

Jess volunteered to become one of 1,000 'Brand Agents' in September 2005. Her first contribution was to help launch Barclays' new brand positioning, 'inventive spirit' to 30 colleagues. This involved brain storming sessions to devise ways in which the brand experience could be delivered to customers on a daily basis. Jess also helps bring the Barclays brand to life with her team by communicating key messages, including the latest advertising plans prior to their launch, sharing best practice and generating new ideas that emerge from her contact with customers and colleagues alike. Jess' advocate role is vital to the continuing success of the Barclays brand across the organisation.

BRITA®
Marketing Team

As part of a relatively small but growing organisation, the BRITA UK Marketing Team all play an important part in the continued success of the brand. Whether working on new product development, advertising strategy, consumer research or trade marketing activity, the team are committed to understanding and meeting the needs of consumers.

Voted recently as one of The Sunday Times Top 100 Best Small companies to work for, BRITA has a culture of teamwork and co-operation, which has been integral to its success as the UK's number one name in domestic water filtration.

Brylcreem
Julie Baker
Marketing Director

Julie is Marketing Director for Sara Lee H&BC,
and is responsible for brands such as
Brylcreem, Radox, Sanex, Ambi-Pur, and Kiwi.
Julie has been with Sara Lee for 11 years,
prior to this she worked for Unilever.

Cosmopolitan
Jan Adcock
Group Publishing Director

Jan started her career in media when she
joined Ulster TV as a Sales Executive.
Her first magazine appointment was with
Carlton Magazines on Options. She then
worked on the Murdoch magazine launch,
Mirabella, as Advertisement Manager.

Jan joined Hachette Magazines in 1991 as
the Advertising Director on British ELLE and
after two years moved to the National
Magazine Company. Within a year she had
been promoted to Publisher on Company,
before moving to the parenting titles,
M and Having A Baby as Group Publisher
in April 1999.

In 1998 Jan was short-listed for PPA
Publisher of the Year, and Company magazine
was short-listed for Magazine of the Year.
Jan was made Publishing Director of the
Cosmopolitan group in September 2000.

She joined the National Magazine Company
Executive Committee in June 2002 and
became a company director in April 2003.

Dr Martens
David Suddens
Chief Executive

Born in the UK in 1947 and educated at
Cambridge University (MA) and INSEAD
(MBA), David has spent 27 years in CEO
positions across Europe, mostly in the textile
and clothing industries; in manufacturing and
retail. He has managed both private and
quoted companies. David was brought into
Dr Martens in 2002 as a turnaround executive
to bring the company back to sound
production, management and profitability.

Dr Martens has closed its UK manufacturing
plants and moved production to Asia. It has
repaid most of its bank debt and is now
trading profitably.

Under the leadership of David, Dr Martens
has undergone a dramatic shift from a
manufacturing company to one now focused
on brand and product.

George

All 150,000 ASDA employees, from the head office in Leicestershire, to colleagues in ASDA stores, George stand alone stores, George department stores worldwide and distribution centres are all responsible for the continuing success and growth of George at ASDA.

Glenfiddich
David Stewart
Master Blender and Malt Master
William Grant & Sons Ltd

David started as an apprentice with William Grant & Sons in 1962. Twelve years later he was appointed Master Blender of William Grant & Sons, a position he has held ever since, making him the longest serving malt master in the industry.

One of his key achievements during his 43 years with Glenfiddich, was the introduction of Glenfiddich Solera Reserve 15 Year Old, the first single malt to use the innovative Solera maturation process.

In 2005 David was awarded The IWSC Outstanding Achievement in the Scotch Whisky Industry Award, recognising David's long career and praising his exceptional work.

IBM
Brendan Dineen
Director of Marketing

Brendan was appointed Director of Marketing for IBM UK Ireland and South Africa in January 2003 and leads a team responsible for IBM's marketing activities in these countries. Prior to this appointment, Brendan was EMEA Director of Direct Marketing, a position he took up on return from an international assignment to the US, where he worked in the Distribution Channels Management team, on the development and implementation of lead management for the corporation.

NIVEA
Andrew Frost
Marketing Director

Andrew's involvement with the NIVEA brand dates back to 1990 when the brand was owned by Smith and Nephew. Since the NIVEA trademark was re-acquired by Beiersdorf in 1992, he has been instrumental in the significant development of NIVEA in the UK, entering new categories such as body, hand, deodorant, lip and men's care. He describes having UK responsibility for the world's largest skincare brand as a privilege and a continuing challenge.

O₂
Russ Shaw
Marketing Director

Russ joined O₂ as Marketing Director in January 2005 and is responsible for the main customer P&L's, content, products, brand communications, CRM, and marketing strategy.

Prior to joining O₂, Russ was CEO of Mobileway (now Mobile365), a global mobile messaging business backed by venture capital firms including 3i, Mayfield, Investcorp as well as Citigroup, Intel, and Visa. Russ successfully merged Mobileway with US-based Inphomatch in 2004.

Previous roles that Russ has held include a Managing Director role with NTL, SVP of Commercial Operations for Charles Schwab across Europe, and various international advertising and marketing roles with American Express.

RAC
Shaun Meadows
Marketing Director

Shaun has been with Norwich Union for 15 years, during which time he has led a number of groundbreaking projects, including wealth management, off-shoring and IT build. As Marketing Director he has responsibility for both RAC and Norwich Union Insurance.

Alastair Pegg
Director of RAC Marketing

Alastair has overall responsibility for marketing across RAC businesses, and for building RAC as an innovative Superbrand, following its successful acquisition by Aviva in 2005. Formerly with Virgin Money, Norwich Union Insurance and Centrica, Alastair's current role enables him to bring his extensive commercial experience to the RAC leadership team. Alastair is married with two children.

Imodium™
Karen Heather
Marketing Director

Karen joined the Johnson & Johnson group of companies in 1995 and has been Marketing Director at McNeil Ltd for six years. As a Chemistry graduate from Imperial College, London, Karen blends the science behind Imodium with consumer marketing skills gained in the fashion accessories world. As a fully fledged Brand Guardian, Karen ensures that toilet humour is only allowed in internal company meetings and never in any consumer communication.

Silvia Rocchetto
Marketing Manager

Silvia brought her Italian flair to the Johnson & Johnson group of companies, when she joined in 2003 with a background in the hair care, spice and pasta worlds. She is a champion for the consumer in everything she does and has been instrumental in developing the European Brand Footprint and bringing other European markets up to the UK Superbrands standard. She is also developing a new breed of enthusiastic junior Brand Guardians in the marketing department.

Miss Selfridge
Sim Scavazza
Brand Director

Sim's professional career spans 17 years, working in buying for some of the UK's most successful young womens' fashion retailers, including River Island, Next, and French Connection. In 2000, she joined Miss Selfridge as Head of Buying, and was subsequently promoted to Buying Director and then to Brand/Managing Director in 2003.

As Brand Director, Sim's role encompasses the building of the Miss Selfridge brand in the UK and internationally, recruiting and developing new talent both in head office and across the 190 stores as well as managing the global sourcing strategy.

Nationwide
Peter Gandolfi
Head of Brand Marketing

Peter is Head of Brand Marketing for Nationwide Building Society. Nationwide is the world's largest building society and a major UK financial services provider.

Peter is responsible for driving forward the Nationwide brand. He is personally responsible for the design, development and implementation of Nationwide's overall brand strategy, comprising all above and below-the-line communications.

He has been instrumental in the development of Nationwide's successful television advertising and sponsorship activation, as well as all communications through-the-line to the point of sale. This has led to the development of 'proud to be different,' as the tone of voice for all advertising.

Royal Doulton
Keith Appleby
Director of Group Brands

Key marketing champion, Keith Appleby joined Royal Doulton in 2005 following a career in design and home furnishings. He has been a key figure since his arrival, helping to develop Royal Doulton. His main task centres upon developing the three main brands within the company, Royal Doulton, Royal Albert and Minton.

Wayne Nutbeen
Chief Operating Officer

Chief Operating Officer since January 2000, Wayne joined Royal Doulton in 1996, as Managing Director Australia. In 1999, he became President of Royal Doultan's North American business, and shortly afterwards was appointed to the Board as Director of Sales and International Markets. In his earlier career, he worked with leading brand names including Lladro, Lalique, Baccarat and Waterford Wedgwood.

Royal Mail
Alex Batchelor
Marketing Director

Alex joined as Marketing Director in 2005, and is responsible for £7 billion of mail-related revenues and delivering three key strands of Royal Mail's strategic programme: revitalising the product portfolio; rebalancing prices and making Royal Mail 'easy to do business with'. He was previously VP Worldwide Brand at Orange and joint Managing Director at Interbrand.

Tom Hings
Director, Brand Marketing

Tom joined Royal Mail in 2002, and is responsible for all external communications and maintaining the integrity of the brand. After stints in advertising at Cogent and Lintas he became a client at Allied Breweries. There he re-launched Castlemaine XXXX and then at Carlsberg-Tetley, as Marketing Controller for Lagers, he successfully re-launched the Carlsberg portfolio.

Shell
Venetia Howes
General Manager SIPC-SBI
Marketing Services, Brand
Strategy Project Manager

Venetia has responsibility for the strategic development of the Shell brand. Her experience includes business-to-business marketing in chemicals, shipping, and lubricants, and she was previously the Marketing Manager for Shell's global aviation business. She took the CIM post-graduate Diploma mid-career and is an active member of the Worshipful Company of Marketors.

Raoul Pinnell
Chairman, Shell Brands
International AG

Raoul developed an early interest in business whilst at school. He studied at Bradfield College, leaving to pursue Business Studies, subsequently followed by a postgraduate Diploma in Marketing. Following 17 years with Nestlé, five years at Prudential and three years at NatWest, Shell International appointed him to head its Global Brands and Communications division in 1997.

**Specsavers Opticians
Andrew Molle
Marketing Director**

**Doug and Mary Perkins
Founders**

Andrew has been instrumental in establishing the brand as a market leader in the UK and Ireland and was responsible for developing the logo, making it instantly recognisable. He also leads the in-house creative and marketing team that are behind the hugely successful award winning 'Should've Gone to Specsavers' campaign, which has become a much repeated catchphrase.

Doug and Mary founded Specsavers Optical Group in 1984 as a result of their passionate commitment to make fashionable eyewear affordable and accessible. The couple met at Cardiff University, where they both studied ophthalmics. Specsavers is the largest, privately owned opticians in the world and the Perkins take a hands-on approach to ensure the long-term security of the joint venture partnership.

Tesco

The heart of Tesco is its people, which makes the whole team Brand Guardians.

At Tesco everyone works together to create value for customers and to earn their lifetime loyalty. This underpins everything everyone does. No matter what their role or position, delivering 'Every little Helps' for customers is a key objective. Everyday Tesco people work hard to ensure that 'No one tries harder for Customers'.

Thomson Local™

The Thomson Local brand is strong and successful due to its employees – over 1,000 of them. Throughout the business, each individual employee is considered a Brand Guardian and embodies its brand values. The brand is focused on its customers, helping millions of buyers and sellers get in touch with each other every day.

The brand is also committed to growth and building an even stronger brand for the future.

Brands to Watch

**The Feel Good Drinks Company
Dave Wallwork, Managing Director
Chris Wright, Commercial Director
Steve Cooper, Marketing Director**

Before founding The Feel Good Drinks Company, Dave's career included running a pub, and lots of soft drinks marketing roles at both Britvic Soft Drinks and Coca-Cola Enterprises.

Chris spent the majority of his early career at Coca-Cola Enterprises and Warner Bros. in a variety of sales, trade marketing and operations management roles.

Steve's consumer marketing career has been mixed across beer and soft drinks, which includes working in Sydney for three years, followed by five years creating new products for Coca-Cola and Cadbury Schweppes plc.

**Zywiec
Laurence McCarthy
Chairman**

Laurence came to the drinks industry from the telecommunications sector, where he had held senior management positions with a number of the major European telecoms companies in Operations and Marketing roles. With a Masters degree in business and a background in product management and logistics he felt comfortable growing Zywiec from a special interest product to the market position it has attained today. Laurence feels confident that this is the year of Zywiec and looks forward to introducing the brand to a wider audience.

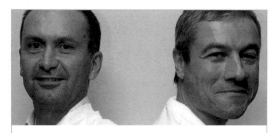

Visa
Joe Clift
Senior Vice President of
Brand Management

As Senior Vice President of Brand Strategy and Creative Development, Joe has overall responsibility for Visa Europe's brand management activities. Most recently this has included the pan-European marketing campaign 'Love Every Day' which is designed to support Visa Europe's long-term objective of encouraging consumers to use cards over cash and cheques to purchase every day items.

Mark Giffin
Vice President of Brand
Strategy and Creative
Development

Mark is Vice President of Brand Strategy and Creative Development, responsible for brand development and the implementation of advertising campaigns, sponsorship and promotions throughout Visa Europe. Visa's marketing in Europe aims to stimulate card usage to increase its current market share of 10% of all consumer payments. Visa's vision is to replace all cash and cheques in the future.

Walls
Tim Barkey
Marketing Manager

Tim joined Kerry Foods in October 2004 following his brand marketing role at PepsiCo on the Tropicana and Copella juice brands.
Tim is responsible for the full portfolio of sausage and meat brands at Kerry Foods including, Wall's, Richmond, Porkinson and Mr Brain's Faggots. He is currently heading up a marketing programme across the brands and is responsible for above and below-the-line strategy and execution.

Stéphanie Brillouet
Senior Brand Manager

Stéphanie joined Kerry Foods in 2000 following a marketing role at Bacofoil. Since then she has worked across the full sausage and meat portfolio including Richmond and Mattessons. Stéphanie is now the Senior Brand Manager on the Wall's brand and also has responsibility for Porkinson and Bowyers.

Yellow Pages
Ann Francke
Chief Marketing Officer

Ann joined Yell in May 2004 as Chief Marketing Officer in the UK. She was previously Director of Strategic Marketing at Boots. From 1999 to 2002, she was Vice President, European Petcare Portfolio, at Mars. Ann spent 13 years in various European roles within Procter & Gamble, ending as General Manager of Beauty Care. Ann received a BA from Stanford University, California and an MBA/MS in Business and Journalism from Columbia University, New York.

Charities supported by the Superbrands

On the pages that follow you will find details of some of the charities supported by the Superbrands featured in this publication.

Age Concern
www.ageconcern.org.uk
Tel: 020 8765 7200
Registered charity no: 261794
"Age Concern is the UK's largest organisation working for and with older people. In England, we are a federation of over 400 charities working together to promote the well-being of all older people, helping to make later life a fulfilling and enjoyable experience. Ageism is unacceptable: we are against all forms of unfair discrimination, and challenge unfair treatment on the grounds of age. All people have the right to make decisions about their lives. We help older people to discover and exercise these rights and seek to support older people to live their lives with dignity. It is only through working together that we can use our local, regional and national presence to the greatest effect."

Supported by: Tesco, Microsoft®

Amatuer Swimming Association
www.britishswimming.org
Tel: 0871 200 0928
"The Amatuer Swimming Association is the English National Governing Body for Swimming, Diving, Water Polo, Open Water, and Synchronised Swimming. It organises competition throughout England, establishes the Laws of the Sport and operates comprehensive certification and education programmes for teachers, coaches and officials. As well as providing learn-to-swim providers, with the industry preferred delivery framework, The National Plan for Teaching Swimming, the ASA runs the most successful sports award scheme in the world, the Kellogg's ASA Awards Scheme. The scheme presents nearly two million awards every year in recognition of the swimming achievements of children and adults. The ASA supports 1,600 affiliated swimming clubs through a national, regional and county structure. The ASA aims to ensure everybody has an opportunity to learn to swim."

Supported by: Kellogg's

BBC Children in Need
www.bbc.co.uk/pudsey
Tel: 020 8576 7788
Registered charity no: 802052
"BBC Children in Need helps disadvantaged children and young people in the UK.

Some have experienced domestic violence, neglect, homelessness or sexual abuse, and others have suffered from chronic illness, or have had to learn to deal with profound disabilities from a very young age.

Many organisations supported by the charity aim to create a lasting impact on children's lives. Some offer low achieving children from areas of deprivation a chance to develop their educational skills and ambitions and others create opportunities for young people who are homeless or socially excluded, to enable them to move forward and secure a fulfilling future.

The charity offers grants to voluntary groups, community groups and registered charities around the UK that focus on improving children's lives. Grants are targeted on the areas of greatest need and money is allocated geographically to ensure that children in all corners of the UK receive a fair share of what is raised."

Supported by: BT, Kellogg's

Breast Cancer Care
www.breastcancercare.org.uk
Tel: 0808 800 6000
Registered charity no: 1017658
"Every day 100 people discover they have breast cancer. Breast Cancer Care is there for every one of them, 24 hours a day, seven days a week. Through our helpline, website forums and face-to-face activities we offer the chance to talk to someone who has 'been there' and has experienced breast cancer themselves.

We respond to over two million requests for support and information about breast cancer or breast health concerns each year. In addition our highly specialised team provides all the latest knowledge and information through our website, helpline, booklets and fact sheets, helping people understand their diagnosis and the choices they have.

Breast Cancer Care is committed to campaigning for better treatment and support for people with breast cancer and their families."

Supported by: George, La Senza, Royal Doulton

British Red Cross
www.redcross.org.uk
Tel: 0870 170 7000
Registered charity no: 220949
"The British Red Cross helps people in crisis, whoever and wherever they are. We are part of a global voluntary network, responding to conflicts, natural disasters and individual emergencies.

We enable vulnerable people in the UK and abroad to prepare for and withstand emergencies in their own communities. And when the crisis is over, we help them to recover and move on with their lives."

Supported by: Tesco

Child Bereavement Trust
www.childbereavement.org.uk
Tel: 01494 446648
Registered charity no: 1040419
"The Child Bereavement Trust (CBT) is a national charity that works to help bereaved

families where a baby or child has died, or where children have lost someone important in their lives, through bereavement. Through its comprehensive training programme the charity trains and supports those who come into contact with child bereavement in the course of their work; within healthcare, education, social care, the emergency services and the voluntary sector. It also offers a confidential Information and Support service for both professionals and families to provide a 'listening ear' and, if appropriate, signpost to further local and national sources of support specific to the particular situation."

Supported by: BANG & OLUFSEN

CHILDREN with LEUKAEMIA
www.leukaemia.org
Tel: 020 7404 0808
Registered charity no: 298405
"Leukaemia is cancer of the blood. It is the most common childhood cancer and is a devastating disease, killing one in four children who are diagnosed with it. The number of new cases is rising every year and we don't know why.

CHILDREN with LEUKAEMIA is Britain's leading charity dedicated exclusively to the conquest of childhood leukaemia through pioneering research into the causes and new treatments, as well as providing support for leukaemic children and their families."

Supported by: BANG & OLUFSEN

CLIC Sargent
www.clicsargent.org.uk
Tel: 0845 301 0031
Helpline: 0800 197 0068
Registered charity no: 1107328
"CLIC Sargent is the UK's leading children's cancer charity – caring from birth, through adolescence to adulthood. Formerly CLIC and Sargent Cancer Care for Children, we have combined our strengths by merging in January 2005. We want to see a world where all children and young people with cancer live life to the full. Our promise is to be there for each family every step of the way, providing individual support to children and young people with cancer and leukaemia and their families.

Every 48 hours, 10 children or young people are diagnosed with cancer or leukaemia. CLIC Sargent offers a lifeline to those children and their families by providing services tailored to their needs. We give children, young people and their families a strong national voice, helping them to be heard and understood and are committed to improving survival rates further by helping to fund research into causes and treatments."

Supported by: Chelsea Football Club

COMIC RELIEF

Comic Relief
www.comicrelief.com
Tel: 020 7820 5555
Registered charity no: 326568
"Comic Relief was launched from the Safawa refugee camp in Sudan, on Christmas Day 1985, in response to crippling famine in Africa. The aim was to take a fresh and fun approach to fundraising and, through events like Red Nose Day, inspire those who hadn't previously been interested in charity, to get involved. Since then there have been 10 Red Nose Days and two Sport Reliefs, raising over £400 million. Red Nose

Day 2005 raised over £65 million.

Comic Relief has worked with some of the biggest names in entertainment, sport and business and tackles some of the biggest issues facing people across the world. Their work ranges from supporting projects that help children who are living rough in India to community programmes helping the elderly across the UK. A number of high profile partnerships have brought in millions of pounds to help reach these aims but the biggest group of supporters remains schools with over 60% taking part in Red Nose Day 2005."

Supported by: BT

ContinYou
www.continyou.org.uk
Tel: 020 8709 9900
Registered charity no: 1097596
"ContinYou is one of the UK's largest community learning charities that uses learning to tackle inequality and build social inclusion. We develop partnerships to link education with health and with economic community regeneration.

We work in two ways: we develop learning programmes and services that offer opportunities to people who have gained least from the formal education system and training; and we work with a range of organisations, including schools, to enhance what they do to change lives through learning."

Supported by: Kellogg's

Deafness Research UK
www.deafnessresearch.org.uk
Tel: 0808 808 2222
Registered charity no: 326915
"Deafness Research UK is the only national charity dedicated to improving life for deaf and hard of hearing people through medical

research and information. The charity has already helped bring more effective, digital hearing aids to the general public, improved cochlear implants to restore hearing to profoundly deaf people and developed a simple, painless test now used nationwide to identify deaf babies at birth. Ultimately, it aims to prevent and cure deafness and related problems such as tinnitus, transforming the lives of millions of people who suffer these invisible, isolating and neglected conditions."

Supported by: Specsavers Opticians

Donna Louise Trust
www.donnalouisetrust.org
Tel: 01782 654440
Registered charity no: 1075597
"The Donna Louise Trust cares for children, who, due to illness or accident, are not expected to reach adulthood.

We give physical and emotional support to both the child and their family. Respite and end of life care is provided at our hospice, Treetops, and in the family home. We also provide ongoing bereavement counselling for the whole family, including for siblings who are left behind.

Providing this service for Staffordshire and South Cheshire costs £1.5 million. The Trust does not receive any statutory funding, relying entirely on the generosity of donations from both the local community and companies."

Supported by: Royal Doulton

Douglas Macmillan Hospice
www.dmhospice.org.uk
Tel: 01782 344300
Registered charity no: 1071613
"Douglas Macmillan Hospice is the only specialist palliative care provider in north

Staffordshire and surrounding areas for adults facing cancer and other life-limiting illnesses.

Douglas Macmillan Hospice provides the following primary services: 28 bed In-Patient Unit, where patients are admitted for respite care, symptom control and pain relief. A Day Care Centre, serving up to 25 patients each day (Monday to Friday) in a comfortable and reassuring environment and specialist community nurses who visit patients in their own homes to provide specialist palliative care."

Supported by: Royal Doulton

EYE RESEARCH

Fight For Sight
www.fightforsight.org.uk
Tel: 020 7608 4000
Registered charity no: 1111438
"Fight for Sight has been at the forefront of research into the prevention of blindness and treatment of eye disease in the UK for 40 years.

In the next 24 hours 100 people will start to lose their sight. At least one child is born or becomes blind every day in the UK. Over half of all people over the age of 65 in the UK are visually impaired.

Fight for Sight funds research with the aim of helping to prevent this."

Supported by: Specsavers Opticians

Groundwork
www.groundwork.org.uk
Tel: 0121 236 8565
Registered charity no: 291558
"Groundwork works to improve the quality of the local environment, the lives of local people and the success of local businesses in areas in need of investment and support.

Our projects aim to bring benefits equally

for: People – creating opportunities for people to learn new skills and become more active citizens; Places – delivering environmental improvements that create cleaner, safer and greener neighbourhoods; and Prosperity – helping businesses and individuals achieve their potential.

Groundwork delivers over 6,000 local regeneration projects in partnership each year."

Supported by: Kellogg's

Guide Dogs

Guide Dogs for the Blind Association
www.guidedogs.org.uk
Tel: 0870 600 2323
Registered charity no: 209617
"Whatever one's age, whatever the condition, sight loss causes a huge adjustment to everyday routines and activities. Above all, it can mean a severe loss of mobility. The Guide Dogs for the Blind Association is here to help, with the extraordinary partnership between guide dog and visually impaired owner at the core.

In 2006, Guide Dogs is celebrating 75 years since the first working guide dog partnerships appeared on the country's streets. Three quarters of a century later, the charity's dedicated team of staff, volunteers and supporters continue to provide freedom, mobility and independence for blind and partially sighted people."

Supported by: Specsavers Opticians

Habitat for Humanity
Tel: 01295 264240
www.habitatforhumanity.org.uk
"Habitat for Humanity builds and renovates simple, decent and affordable homes with the help of volunteer labour and donations of money and materials.

We build a new home every 24 minutes.

Habitat homes are sold to low-income families at no profit and financed through affordable, no-interest loans. Future homeowners also help to build their own home and the homes of others.

Every day Habitat for Humanity turns hope into homes for families living in poverty housing. We work in partnership with Whirlpool, who help through supplying products and manpower and by raising both awareness and funds."

Supported by: Whirlpool

Help the Hospices
www.helpthehospices.org.uk
Tel: 020 7520 8200
Registered charity no: 1014851
"Help the Hospices is the national charity for the hospice movement, and supports over 220 local hospices across the UK. This support is provided through a wide range of services aimed at helping hospices provide the very best care for patients and their families. These include training and grants for hospice staff and volunteers, national programmes of advice, information and support, special award programmes to fund new services and the co-ordination of national fundraising initiatives. In all that we do we aim to make a real difference to the care given to patients and their loved ones."

Supported by: Royal Mail

Lavender Trust at Breast Cancer Care
www.lavendertrust.org.uk
Tel: 020 7384 2984
Registered charity no: 1017658
"The Lavender Trust at Breast Cancer Care raises money specifically to fund information and practical support for younger women with breast cancer. It is the only fund in the UK dedicated to addressing the particular needs of this age group.

80% of breast cancer cases in the UK are in women over 50, so being diagnosed with breast cancer as a younger woman can be a very isolating experience. An uncertain future, early menopause, and caring for children are just some of the issues which younger women may have to face.

The Lavender Trust at Breast Cancer Care is committed to campaigning for better treatment and support for younger women diagnosed with breast cancer."

Supported by: Miss Selfridge

Leonard Cheshire
www.leonard-cheshire.org
Tel: 020 7802 8200
"Leonard Cheshire exists to change attitudes to disability and to serve disabled people around the world. It has been supporting disabled people for almost 60 years and is active in 55 countries. The charity directly supports over 21,000 disabled people in the UK. It is also a 2006 'The Sunday Times 20 Best Big Companies to Work For' organisation.

For the last eight years Leonard Cheshire has worked in partnership with Microsoft® to provide opportunities for disabled people to access computer and IT training. Leonard Cheshire's Workability scheme provides clients with computer equipment, structured IT training and job seekers advice. Discover IT gives disabled people access to computers and the internet and provides instruction in 'soft skills' such as email, digital photography and shopping online. There are currently seven Discover IT centres across the UK, with plans for a further three in 2006.

Supported by: Microsoft®

Make-A-Wish
www.make-a-wish.org.uk
Tel: 01276 24127
Registered charity no: 295672
"Make-A-Wish Foundation grants wishes of children and young people aged 3-17 who are living with life-threatening illnesses.

Make-A-Wish Foundation® UK has no cures to offer and all too often some of our endings are sad, but during desperate times when there seems to be no hope, Make-A-Wish steps in to provide positive, and uplifting relief. Most of all, a wish granted brings a time of magic and joy, for the special children and the families that we serve.

Make-A-Wish Foundation® UK has granted over 4,000 special wishes since 1986. Originally formed in Phoenix, Arizona in 1980 there are now over 30 affiliates throughout the world."

Supported by: Fairy

Marie Curie Cancer Care
www.mariecurie.org.uk
Tel: 0800 716 146
Registered charity no: 207994
"Marie Curie Cancer Care provides free high quality nursing to give terminally ill people the choice of dying at home, supported by their families. Every day 410 people will die of cancer in the UK. Most want to be cared for in their own homes, close to the people and things they love. This year Marie Curie nurses will make this possible for more than 18,000 cancer patients. But for every family that we help there are always others that we can't. We want to reach all of these families – making choice a reality for them all."

Supported by: BUPA, Yellow Pages

National Literacy Trust
www.literacytrust.org.uk
Tel: 020 7828 2435
Registered charity no: 1015539
"The National Literacy Trust is an independent charity working to build a literate nation, and is the only organisation concerned with raising literacy standards for all age groups throughout the UK.

The charity's close relationship with Starbucks started in 2001. Starbucks supports fun events for early years children in over 20 libraries across the UK at which toddlers choose and keep three free books. Starbucks also encourages its customers to donate books to local children through its Book Drive, which in three years has raised over 100,000 books for local communities."

Supported by: Starbucks

the children's charity
NCH
www.nch.org.uk
Tel: 020 7704 7000
Registered charity no: 4764232
"NCH is the leading UK provider of; family and community centres, children's services in rural areas, services for disabled children and their families and services for young people leaving care.

NCH runs more than 500 projects, supporting over 140,000 of the UK's most vulnerable and excluded children, young people and families, many of whom face difficulties such as poverty, disability and abuse.

We believe that all children and young people have unique potential and that they should have the support and opportunities they need to reach it. We have been working to make this vision a reality for over 135 years."

Supported by: Tesco

FUNDING VITAL RESEARCH FOR
NEPHROTIC SYNDROME

Nephrotic Syndrome Trust (NeST)
www.brita.net/uk/brita_charity.html?&L=l
Tel: 01869 365813
Registered charity no: 1107601
"The Nephrotic Syndrome Trust (NeST) was launched by ambassador Jonah Lomu at Twickenham Stadium, in May 2005. Founded by Dave Yearsley, whose son James is a sufferer, its purpose is to raise funds for research into the kidney disorder Nephrotic Syndrome (NS). Specific projects include identifying rogue proteins in the blood that cause NS, investigating how steroids work on the kidney to treat NS, and also how diabetes can have an impact. There are around 10,000 sufferers of NS in the UK, mainly children. With NS, the kidney can fail at any time, gradually or suddenly. When this happens, the sufferer needs kidney dialysis and ultimately a transplant."

Supported by: BRITA®

Cruelty to children must stop. FULL STOP.

NSPCC
www.nspcc.org.uk
Helpline: 0808 800 5000
Registered charity no: 216401
"The National Society for the Prevention of Cruelty to Children (NSPCC) is the UK's leading charity specialising in child protection and the prevention of cruelty to children.

The society has been protecting children from cruelty since 1884, when it was founded by Benjamin Waugh. It is the only children's charity with statutory powers enabling it to act to safeguard children at risk. It has 177 teams and projects around the UK as well as five Divisional Offices, a National Centre (Weston House) in London and the NSPCC Training and Consultancy Centre in Leicester.

The NSPCC provides an independent campaigning voice for children. It works to influence government on legislation and policy that affect the lives of children and

families, and runs public education campaigns to raise awareness of, and encourage action to prevent, child abuse.

ChildLine and the NSPCC joined together on February 1st 2006."

Supported by: BT

RNIB
www.rnib.org.uk
Tel: 0845 766 9999
"Every day another 100 people in the UK will start to lose their sight.

There are around two million people in the UK with sight problems. RNIB is the leading charity working in the UK offering practical support, advice and information for anyone with sight difficulties. If you, or someone you know, has a sight problem RNIB can help.

Our pioneering work helps anyone with a sight problem – not just with braille, Talking Books and computer training, but with imaginative and practical solutions to everyday challenges.

We fight for equal rights for people with sight problems. We fund pioneering research into preventing and treating eye disease. Our projects such as Talk and Support and Parents' Place make a difference to people's lives."

Supported by: Rotary

Lifeboats

Royal National Lifeboat Institution
www.rnli.org.uk
Tel: 0800 543210
Registered charity no: 209603
"The Royal National Lifeboat Insitution is a registered charity that saves lives at sea. It provides the 24-hour on-call service to cover search and rescue requirements to 100 nautical miles out from the coast of the United Kingdom and Republic of Ireland with

over 230 lifeboat stations manned by 4,800 crew members. It also provides a lifeguard service at more than 60 beaches in the south of England.

The RNLI relies on voluntary contributions and legacies for its income that goes towards, training and equipping its volunteer crew members and its lifeguards."

Supported by: Tesco

RSA

RSA
www.rsa.org.uk
Tel: 020 7930 5115
Registered charity no: 212424
"The RSA is an independent, registered charity which encourages sustainable economic development and the release of human potential. Its work is framed by five manifesto challenges: encouraging enterprise; moving towards a zero-waste society; developing a capable population; fostering resilient communities; and advancing global citizenship.

The RSA's current projects include a new curriculum network for schools, exploring personal trading of carbon emissions and the UK's most prestigious award scheme for student designers. The RSA has been creating impact in cultural, social and economic life for over 250 years, and plays a unique part in inspiring the future."

Supported by: Starbucks

RSPCA
www.rspca.org.uk
Tel: 0870 33 35 999
Registered charity no: 219099
"The RSPCA is the world's oldest and best-known animal welfare charity. Funded entirely by donations, the Society works across England and Wales to prevent suffering and promote kindness to animals.

The Society's 323 inspectors and 146 animal collection officers are the RSPCA's frontline men and women who prevent cruelty, through vigilance, advice and education.

Together with the RSPCA's 174 branches, and the Society's network of animal centres, clinics and hospitals, staff and volunteers rescue and re-home thousands of animals every year."

Supported by: Tesco

SPARKS
www.sparks.org.uk
Tel: 020 7799 2111
Registered charity no: 1003825
"SPARKS funds pioneering medical research that has a practical, positive impact on the lives of babies and children.

Since 1991, SPARKS has funded over 160 medical projects in the UK, committing over £12 million to tackle conditions as diverse as cerebral palsy, meningitis, the dangers of premature birth, spina bifida, childhood arthritis and cancers.

In the UK, many important areas of paediatric research depend heavily on funding from charities like SPARKS rather than the public purse. It's this knowledge that motivates the dedicated SPARKS team and its corporate and individual sponsors."

Sponsored by: BANG & OLUFSEN

The Royal British Legion
www.britishlegion.org.uk
Tel: 08457 725 725
Registered charity no: 219279
"The Royal British Legion is the UK's leading charity providing financial, social and emotional support to millions who have served, and are currently serving, in the Armed Forces, and their dependents. Nearly 10.5 million people are eligible for support from the Legion, and we receive around 300,000 calls for help every year.

Every year the Legion spends nearly £60 million providing a wide range of welfare assistance to the ex-service community. From grant making to pensions and benefits advice; from counselling and job retraining to pilgrimages; and from home and hospital visits to the provision of full nursing care, the Legion is there to help."

Supported by: Tesco

The Wildlife Trusts
www.wildlifetrusts.org
Tel: 0870 036 7711
Registered charity no: 207238
"Founded in 1912 as The Society for the Promotion of Nature Reserves, the organisation has become the largest UK charity dedicated to conserving our habitats and species. Today The Wildlife Trusts are a partnership of 47 local Wildlife Trusts across the UK, the Isle of Man and Alderney, whose vision is 'an environment rich in wildlife for everyone'. With a membership of more than 600,000 people, the Trusts campaign for protection of the UK's natural heritage and wildlife. The Wildlife Trusts lobby local authorities and government agencies, for robust legislation and policies to safeguard habitats and species. We invest in the future by helping people gain a greater appreciation of the value of wildlife and we provide advice on a wide variety of wildlife topics and environmental issues such as wildlife gardening, recycling and using natural resources wisely. The Trusts manage more than 2,200 nature reserves covering 80,000+ hectares and each year over 25,000 volunteers help the Trusts in their work."

Supported by: Beechams, Ribena

TimeBank
www.timebank.org.uk
Tel: 0845 601 4008
"TimeBank is a national charity inspiring and connecting a new generation of people to volunteer in their communities, and enabling charitable organisations and businesses to develop innovative and effective volunteer recruitment programmes.

Locally, regionally, nationally and internationally, TimeBank is transforming the way that individuals, organisations and businesses give back to their communities and contribute to a better world. We appeal to people who know that their time and skills are in demand – but just don't know what to do about it or where to start."

Supported by: Starbucks

Trafford Community Leisure Trust
www.traffordleisure.co.uk
Tel: 0161 912 4802
"Trafford Community Leisure Trust was established for public benefit with the key aim of providing the provision of facilities for recreation or other leisure time occupation and promoting and preserving good health and well-being through community participation in healthy recreation.

The Trust is a totally independent organisation and whilst it receives a grant from the council, the majority of income the Trust generates comes from customers, i.e. those coming through the doors. A Board of 13 Trustees, made up of local people, are responsible for the strategic management of the Trust.

Currently the Trust operates six leisure centres, one sports centre, two golf courses and one all weather pitch. However, as well as managing a number of facilities the Trust works in partnership with a number of local voluntary, social and commercial organisations, to improve the health of the community of Trafford. Amongst the major partners are: Kellogg's, North & South Trafford PCT's, Manchester United, and Trafford Council. However, the Trust also works with small community groups or organisations to assist them in promoting good health."

Supported by: Kellogg's

Vision Aid Overseas

Vision Aid Overseas
www.vao.org.uk
Tel: 01293 535016
Registered charity no: 1081695
"Vision Aid Overseas is a charity dedicated to helping people in the developing world whose lives are blighted by poor eyesight, particularly those where spectacles can be of help. It works by sending abroad teams of volunteer optometrists and dispensing opticians who set up clinics, screen large number of patients and provide appropriate spectacles. Started in 1985, Vision Aid Overseas has provided 500,000 eye tests and given 250,000 people the ability to see with a pair of spectacles."

Supported by: Specsavers Opticians

Whizz Kids
www.whizz-kidz.org.uk
Tel: 020 7233 6600
Registered charity no: 802872
"Whizz-Kidz aim to ensure that every physically disabled child fulfils their potential and leads an active childhood. Like all children, disabled children need to move around independently and enjoy the freedom to live full and active lives with their families and friends.

The NHS is often unable to provide the mobility equipment, training and advice that they need. Looking after a disabled child can increase the emotional and physical strain on families. Having to spend time and effort in obtaining mobility equipment and support services is an additional stress.

This is where Whizz-Kidz comes in, changing disabled children's lives – literally overnight – by providing them with customised mobility equipment, training and advice.

But we also give them something much more important: the independence to live a life of freedom at home, at school and at play, the independence to be themselves."

Supported by: Tesco